You've Got The Job—Now Keep It!

T.I.P.S. For Tackling Your First Year of Teaching

By Maria Calamito-Proto and Rachel James

Editor: Ann James
Cartoons and Logo: Carlos Gelpi
Additional Graphics: Steve Thornhill and Rob Riggs
Additional Logo: Michael Griffin
Cover Design: Perri Poloni, Knockout Design
Concept and Creative Design: Maria Calamito-Proto and Rachel James
Graphic Design, Composition and Printing: FOCUS/Graphics
Published by TIPS Inc. © 2004

© 2004 by TIPS Inc.

All rights reserved. Reproduction of these materials by an individual teacher for use in a classroom is permissible. No part of this publication may be reproduced, stored in a retrieval system, or tansmitted, in any form or by any means, electronic, mechanical, recording, photocopying or otherwise, without prior agreement and written permission of the authors.

TIPS, Inc.
"Teacher Inspired Practical Stuff"
Weston, Florida 33327
www.tipsforteachers.net

ISBN 0-9755956-0-1

Library of Congress Control Number: 2004097287

ATTENTION SCHOOLS, UNIVERSITYIES, COLLEGES, AND PROFESSIONAL ORGANIZATIONS: Quantity discounts are available on bulk purchases of this book. Special books or book excerpts can also be created to fit special needs. For more information please contact Teacher Inspired Practical Stuff, Inc. at info@tipsforteachers.net.

We'd like to thank our husbands, our families, our fearless editor, and our coworkers at TIPS—without their time, effort, advice and support (and the occasional late night pizza) this book would have remained a topic of supper conversation.

—Rachel and Maria

Contributors

You've Got the Job—Now Keep It! has been written for first year teachers with the intent of sharing experiences and advice from veteran teachers and principals alike. Although it would be impossible to list everyone who has taken time to help with this endeavor, we'd like to especially thank the following teachers:

Donna Pelikan
Kindergarten Teacher
Coral Springs, Florida

Dianne Duga
Reading Specialist
Hollywood, Florida

Lyzeth Rojas
Teacher
Weston, Florida

Kara Clark
Teacher
Lauderhill, Florida

Rosemarie James
Teacher (retired)
St. John's, Newfoundland
Canada

Kathryn Kavanagh
Teacher
Surrey, British Columbia
Canada

Vicci Godbold
Teacher and Vice Principal
Cambridge, England

Wendi Walton
Third Grade Teacher/
    College Instructor
Pine City, NY

Carrie Chapa
Fifth Grade Teacher
Woodstock, GA

Inez Kelso
Fifth Grade Teacher
Bethany, CT

Monique Sluymers
University Professor
Fort Lauderdale, FL

Rob Riggs
University Professor
Weston, FL

Thank you to the following principals for their time and invaluable input:

E. James Cahill
Principal (retired)
St. John's, Newfoundland
Canada

Judy Gard Puddester
Principal
Bishop Feild Elementary
St. John's, Newfoundland
Canada

Dr. Susan Neimand
Principal and Professor
Miami, Florida

Kumari Rambhatla
Principal
Vizag, India

Patricia Hart
Principal
Kiel School
Kinnelon, NJ

Mary Draper
Assistant Principal
The Sagemont School
Weston, Florida

Anita Lonstein
Principal
Fort Lauderdale Preparatory
    School
Fort Lauderdale, Florida

Bill Carroll
Principal (retired)
St. John's, Newfoundland
Canada

William Arden Hall
Principal (retired)
St. John's, Newfoundland
Canada

Stephen Pollinger, P.D.
Principal
Beacon Hill School
Hollywood, Florida

A special thanks to the following schools for allowing us to speak with their teachers and for sharing their classrooms with us:

The Sagemont School
Weston, Florida

Fort Lauderdale Preparatory School
Fort Lauderdale, Florida

North Ridge Elementary School
Surrey, British Columbia

Thank you to our network of parents whose invaluable perspectives helped guide many chapters of this book.

Contents

Introduction ix

Section One **Starting Out—Everything You Need to Consider**
Before the Students Arrive 1
CHAPTER 1 What You Should Know 3
CHAPTER 2 Introducing Yourself Before the First Day 10
CHAPTER 3 Setting up Your Classroom 13
CHAPTER 4 Making Your Classroom Cozy 21
CHAPTER 5 Designing Bulletin Boards 23
CHAPTER 6 Creating a Classroom Library 27
CHAPTER 7 Designing a Reading Area 39
Summary Section One 42

Section Two **Sorting Out and Straightening Up—**
Organizing Yourself and Your Students 45
CHAPTER 8 Organizing for Survival 47
CHAPTER 9 Organizing Your Own Personal Space 50
CHAPTER 10 Organizing Your Paper Trail 56
CHAPTER 11 Organizing Your Students 70
CHAPTER 12 Organizing Your Time 81
CHAPTER 13 Organizing for the Sub 89
Summary Section Two 93
Reproducibles 96

Section Three **The Good, The Bad, and The Ugly—**
Behavior Management in the Classroom 103
CHAPTER 14 The ABCs of Behavior Management 105
CHAPTER 15 From the First Day of School 108
CHAPTER 16 Using Behavior Management in Your Class 113
CHAPTER 17 Serving the Time—Consequences for Negative Behaviors 124
CHAPTER 18 Dealing with Special Situations 129
Summary Section Three 132
Reproducibles 134

Section Four **The Students Arrive—Thriving During the First Weeks of School** 135
CHAPTER 19 Smooth Sailing from Day One 137
CHAPTER 20 Breaking the Ice 155
CHAPTER 21 Bringing the Parents Onboard 160
CHAPTER 22 Helping with Homework 175
Summary Section Four 186
Reproducibles 188

Section Five	**Staying on Top—The Importance of Grading**	195
CHAPTER 23	To Grade or Not to Grade—That is the Question	197
CHAPTER 24	What to do When the Grading is Done	208
CHAPTER 25	Writing Report Cards	212
	Summary Section Five	215
	Reproducibles	217
Section Six	**Say What You Mean and Mean What You Say—**	
	Effective Communication	219
CHAPTER 26	Faculty Communication	221
CHAPTER 27	Parent–Teacher Communication	226
CHAPTER 28	Levels of Parent Communication	231
CHAPTER 29	Including Students in Meetings & Conferences	243
	Summary Section Six	246
	Reproducibles	249
Section Seven	**Working in the Classroom—Surviving Groups**	253
CHAPTER 30	Grouping Students	255
CHAPTER 31	How to Group Students	258
CHAPTER 32	Getting Students to work Cooperatively	267
	Summary Section Seven	272
	Reproducibles	274
Section Eight	**Livening Things Up—Learning Centers in the Classroom**	277
CHAPTER 33	Starting out with Centers	279
CHAPTER 34	Scheduling and Managing Centers	286
CHAPTER 35	Do-it-Yourself Math Center Activities	298
CHAPTER 36	Setting up a Writing Center	329
	Summary Section Eight	341
	Reproducibles	343
Section Nine	**Unavoidable Interruptions—**	
	Vacations, Celebrations, and Other Distractions	351
CHAPTER 37	You Give and You Give and You Give . . .	353
CHAPTER 38	Happy Birthday, Merry Christmas and Mazel Tov—	
	Dealing with Field Trips, Parties and Holidays	358
CHAPTER 39	Tuning Out and Taking Off—When Your Students are No Longer There	365
	Summary Section Nine	369
Section Ten	**A View from the Top—Tips for New Teachers from the Principal**	371
	Your Principal—The Voice of Reason	373
	Index	381

Introduction

If you have purchased this book then you are most likely about to embark on your new teaching career, and want to better prepare yourself with teaching and organizational strategies that will help you succeed. You've been through the college courses, completed your student teaching, and now the time has come for you to have your own classroom. Even if you've been in the classroom before as a substitute or a student teacher, the thought of having your own classroom, with all the responsibilities it entails, can be quite overwhelming. Don't be surprised if you're feeling a mix of exhilaration and dread. Try to relax—it's quite normal and once you start the year, your anxiety will subside.

As authors of this book, we aren't claiming to be experts who hold lofty professorships at universities or have a multitude of degrees after our names. We are simply teachers who have been exactly where you are now. We've discovered that the best resources for helping teachers solve classroom problems are *other teachers*. Whether your question is what to put on your new bulletin board or how to deal with difficult parents, veteran teachers have the knowledge that can only be learned through experience. Believe us when we say that all the Bloom's Taxonomies and hierarchies of learning theories won't help you figure out how to squeeze 35 students into a classroom meant for 25, how to keep grading from piling up, or how to handle a confrontational parent.

Your first year in the classroom in some ways is the best year because you've finally reached your goal of being a teacher. It will be a year full of inspiration and motivation, as you experience for the first time the simple joy of teaching. This book was written to give advice that will help you understand what will be expected of you during that year. Obviously your job will be to teach, but *being* a teacher involves so much more. Most of the daily demands of this job aren't taught in college courses—you learn them yourself in the sort of "sink or swim" experience that is your first year. These extra demands often discourage teachers early in their career. Embrace your first year and immerse yourself in the fun of being a teacher, and don't get so caught up in the job that you forget to enjoy what you're doing.

In creating this book we surveyed teachers from several countries who have taught in a wide variety of school settings. Through their diverse backgrounds and experiences, they've supplied us with ideas and strategies that will help you maneuver through the mine fields of your first year teaching. In addition to the content provided by countless veteran teachers, each section of this book has been read by current teachers and administrators. We've compiled all of their information, and, along with our own observations and experiences, given you the best of the best in one easy-to-read, friendly book that takes a common sense approach to surviving (and enjoying) your first year as a teacher.

The book has been laid out in sections that follow the school calendar, starting with how to prepare yourself before the school year begins, what to do during the first weeks, and how to handle various demands that come up during the year. We take you through dealing with simple situations such as assigning classroom jobs to more complex issues such as parent conferences and behavior management. Each section gives you strategies and tools you can implement immediately. We've also included stories written by a variety of teachers to give you a look at real classroom experiences, as well as tips from veteran teachers.

With the help of our book you'll be able to spend less time worrying about unknown challenges that lie ahead and more time on the activities and lessons you've dreamed of implementing in the classroom.

We wish you the best of luck. Remember that although teaching is one of the hardest jobs there is, it's also one of the most fun. When things seem overwhelming, look around at your students. If you watch and listen to them you'll find something to smile about each and every day.

Maria Calamito-Proto and Rachel James
June 1, 2004

> *A teacher affects eternity; he can never tell where his influence stops.*
> —Henry B. Adams

Use our icons as flags for easy reference.

 Means you can refer to the section and chapter indicated for more information. (The section is on the left side and the chapter is on the right side.)

 Represents a tried-and-true TIP from a teacher.

 Represents a TIP from a principal.

 Represents one of our favorite suggestions.

 Means that you can refer to our website for more information.

 Means there is a blank copy included at the end of the section.

SECTION ONE

Starting Out—Everything You Need to Consider Before the Students Arrive

- ✦ Knowing the ropes
- ✦ Introducing yourself to students and parents
- ✦ Getting the classroom ready
- ✦ Creating a cozy classroom
- ✦ Using bulletin boards
- ✦ Drowning the students in books
- ✦ Setting up a reading area

IN THIS SECTION

Chapter 1

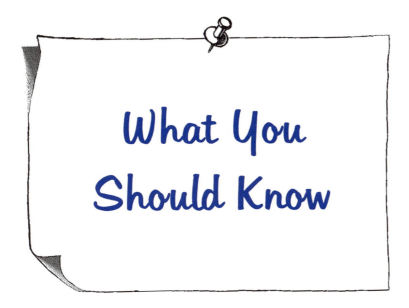

What You Should Know

Learning the Ropes

Knowing as much as you can about your student population before you meet your class is a smart move. Spend time learning about the culture and socioeconomic background of your students and your school. Understanding the background of your audience will help shape your approach with your students from the very first day of school, and will help you understand and appreciate some of your school's standard policies and procedures.

Before setting up your own procedures in the classroom, always check to see what overall standards, policies and procedures are in place for your school and district. Most likely you will receive an employee manual or a book that defines all relevant policies and procedures. You'll need to read this thoroughly and, before the school year begins, familiarize yourself with:

 Try to integrate into the culture of your new school.

- **Student arrival times**
  Know what time students are to arrive at school and if they are allowed in the classroom before the official start of the day. Most teachers prefer not to have students in the room early, since they normally use this time for teacher preparation. Make sure you know where students should be first thing in the morning—i.e. the school cafeteria or the gymnasium or the classroom—and how long they are expected to remain there. If students arrive late, do they require a note from home? From the doctor's office? Are late arrivals your responsibility to record or the office's?

- **Attendance**

  You will be expected to take attendance each day and send it to the office. Know how your school handles attendance. Some schools use student messengers to take attendance to the office, some have teachers phone in attendance each morning, while others send it via computer. Make taking attendance and getting it to the office on time part of your morning routine.

"You said we could bring in games from home . . ."

- **Recess break**

  Find out if your grade has a specific time for recess and what type of games students are allowed to play in the classroom or on the playground. Often students like to bring in hand-held video games or CD music players. Many schools don't allow these types of electronic devices at school. Find out if your school does.

- **Lunch period**

  Many schools, especially larger public schools, are extremely strict on their lunchroom procedures. Be punctual and follow the rules—if your class is scheduled for lunch at 11:25, make sure that's when your class is at the lunchroom. If you have lunch in your classroom, arrange a classroom helper to pick up supplies like milk, napkins, and other items from the cafeteria before lunch begins. Know what to do with both school issued lunch menus and lunch monies that will be returned to you by students.

- **Hallway travel**
  Know the procedures for having students travel through the hallways. Should there be a buddy with them or is a hallway pass enough? Ask about line-up procedures. Most schools require students to walk quietly in a line. Even if your school doesn't mandate this, you should make it part of your classroom discipline.

- **Early dismissal**
  What is the procedure for parents signing their child out for appointments? Does the parent come to the class? Do you send the student to the office or another designated waiting area? Will the school require a note from the doctor's office if the child is returning later that day?

- **End-of-day dismissal**
  The end of the day can be chaotic. Know how students will be getting home: are they walkers, will they be picked up or do they take the bus? Keep a chart on a classroom wall or door that quickly shows which students are going where.

- **Medical emergencies**
  If there is a medical emergency while a child is in your care, what are the steps to follow? Do you call a specific staff member, send another child to the office or to the school nurse, or call in another teacher to help? Knowing exactly what the procedures are can save valuable moments.

Never allow students to be in a classroom unattended.

- **Dispensing medication**
  Most schools require that a school nurse or an office staff member dispense daily medications. Often, schools do not allow students to self medicate even something as simple as a cough drop without a note from a parent. Most schools are required to keep all student medication safely locked in the office or nurses area. For liability reasons, at the beginning of the year inform parents that all medications (cough drops, aspirins, cold remedies) will not be administered by you and must be dealt with through the office. (Exceptions here might be an asthma inhaler or a shot for anaphylactic reactions, which may need to be kept in the classroom by an individual student or teacher). If a student requires daily prescription medication, you need to know exactly what time she must be in the office or at the nurse to receive it.

What You Should Know

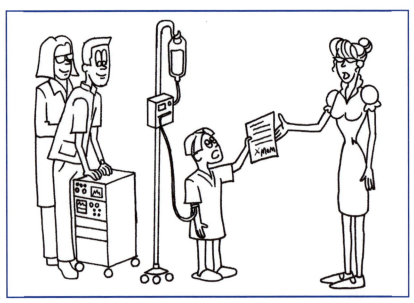

"Don't worry, I have a note from my mom . . ."

- **Fire drills or lock downs**
  Know exactly where to lead your class during a fire drill. Also, be aware of any additional procedures such as bringing your gradebook or a class list with you. Many schools have implemented lock down procedures. A lock down is when the school gets completely shut down and nobody gets in or out. Make sure you find out the procedures for this type of situation.

- **School supplies and reimbursements**
  Some schools reimburse you for purchasing supplies, others give you supplies such as staples, chalk, and paper for your classroom, or provide you with a limited budget to purchase what you'll need. Find out what your school does.

- **Unions and other school groups**
  Is there a teacher's union for your school district? If so, find out about dues, union responsibilities, and the part the union plays in your school district. Are there other clubs or organizations that you will be expected to be involved with during the year?

Finally, chat with other teachers to see if there are any "tried but true" school-wide practices not covered in the policy and procedures manual that you could incorporate into your class. Perhaps teachers clap their hands to silence students and gain the children's attention; or maybe they follow an unwritten homework policy in your grade. There's no use in reinventing the wheel if procedures are already in place and the children are expecting to follow them.

A Note about New Teacher Programs

Most schools have a program to track your performance as a first year teacher. What's required of you may vary slightly, depending on whether you're new to the teaching profession or just new to the school. In any case, it means that during the year, you, your lesson plans, and your teaching style will be constantly monitored and evaluated by a supervisor (usually your principal). Your evaluations will be frequent and the criticism, although usually constructive, may be harsh, but that's part of the program. Many principals judge the success of a first year teacher not only by how well she accepts advice and criticism, but also by whether or not she takes it (which will be obvious to the principal during future evaluations).

At the start of your new position, you will probably receive information about the new teacher program at your school. Even if you don't, it is your responsibility to make sure you are aware of and fully understand how your school's new teacher program operates and what is expected of you in order to meet its requirements.

In-class observations will make up a large part of your evaluations. Follow these guidelines to make sure that you are fully prepared:

Know your three P's: Population, Policies, and Procedures.

- At the start of the year, ask your principal for information about the evaluations, and request a copy of the evaluation sheet. This way you can familiarize yourself with what she will be looking for. Be aware, however, that she may not be able to provide you with a copy (possibly due to the program's rules).

- If given a choice, teach your strongest curriculum area.

- Don't try something new—save the inaugural run on the latest method of teaching a new math concept until *after* the evaluation has been completed. Although it's important that you teach the lesson as you normally do, your principal will most likely be looking for the common elements of a well-planned lesson: an introduction, a body, some independent practice, and a brief review.

- Don't put on a dog and pony show—your principal is bound to notice and you lose some of your credibility instantly. Instead, do what you would normally do for any lesson, but be sure to include the necessary elements on which your evaluation will be based.

- Don't prep the students with a "the principal is coming so you better be on your best behavior or else" speech. Again, your credibility will be questioned, especially if a student mentions the warning.

What You Should Know

If the whole class is perfect, the principal will know something is up. Chances are she will be looking to see how you handle any disruptions that occur. Look at any disruptions as a chance to show how you have control in the class.

- Don't be surprised if your principal doesn't stay for the full length of the lesson. Often a principal will step out as soon as the formal part of the lesson is over and students begin their independent practice. On the other hand, some principals will stay during independent practice and walk around to see how the students are doing with the assignment.

Remember, you might not be given any advance notice of an evaluation—the principal may just stop in at any moment. It is important that the lessons on which you are evaluated are a true reflection of the way you teach on a day-to-day basis.

Disagreeing with Policies and Procedures

As a teacher there will be many policies and procedures that you will need to know and follow. For the most part, these requirements are straightforward and rarely questioned. However, at some point during your career, you're bound to encounter policies that you just don't agree with, such as the school's homework policy, holiday policy, or administrative requirements. Many policies are not the choice of the school, but are handed down by the district, or determined by law, insurance policies, or outside bodies (i.e. school commissions or governor groups). Before you decide to challenge a policy, consider these points:

Although you might not be new to teaching, you may feel like a first year teacher if you're new to your current position.

- Don't jump on the bandwagon. As a new teacher you'll have a lot to be dealing with, and you might be biting off more than you can chew. For the first year, you'll want to stay neutral whenever possible. Unless the policy directly affects you or you have very strong feelings about it, try to stay quietly uninvolved. If you feel the matter is serious enough, consider bringing it up privately with your principal. If you choose to do this, then:

  ○ Learn everything you can about the policy in question. Why was it put in place? How long has it been in place? Has anyone ever addressed changing it?

  ○ Ask yourself why the policy is upsetting to you. Consider how the policy relates to the principal, the parents, the students and the teachers. Make sure you're not overreacting to a policy that makes sense but is inconvenient for you, i.e. getting grades in by a certain date when report cards don't go out for another two weeks.

- Listen to other teachers. Find out if others are upset about the same issue and, if so, why. Have they tried to do anything about the situation? Do they have solutions to offer?

- Come up with an alternative to the policy. As we discuss in the cooperative group work section of this book, if students don't like something, they need to help develop a solution. The same is true for you. It's not realistic to approach the principal and say, "I don't agree with this, it should be changed." A principal will expect your concerns to contain recommendations that reflect other teacher's points-of-view, not just your own.

- Finally, even if you disagree, try to maintain a positive and professional attitude when discussing policies, and any other school issues. It is better to be constructive and professional than destructive, especially in your workplace.

Keep in mind that not all school policies are decided by the principal.

What You Should Know

Chapter 2

Introducing Yourself Before the First Day

Sending Welcome Letters

Before the new school year begins, your school might give you the names and addresses of the students you will have. If this is the case, you can send out a letter over the summer to the students welcoming them to your class, telling them a little bit about yourself, and what to expect in the coming school year. This letter will help lessen their anxiety over starting a new grade with a new teacher.

Some teachers like to enclose a blank piece of paper along with a self-addressed stamped envelope so the children can write back and tell about themselves and their summer. Displaying these letters for the first day of school is a nice and welcoming touch.

You should also consider sending out a letter to parents with some information for the coming year. You don't need to go into great detail or bombard them with policies at this time. Keep the letter simple. Parents are often **as** if not **more** apprehensive than students during the first few days of school. A brief welcome letter can ease anxiety for all those involved.

Before the start of the new school year I send "Welcome Letters" to all of my students. I tell them about my summer, what they'll be learning about in the next year, and I enclose a picture of myself as well. That way, any new student will have at least one familiar face to look for on the first day—mine! I encourage the children to write me back before the year begins and include a self-addressed stamped envelope for them to use. I display all letters that I receive on a bulletin board, ready for the first day of school.

"Don't worry Mom, it's only the first day of school. It'll be okay, really!"

The following are samples of letters that can be sent home to students and parents.

Introducing Yourself Before the First Day

Dear Beth,

My name is Mrs. Carter and I will be your teacher this school year. I'm very excited that you will be in my class and can't wait until school begins. I have lots of fun activities planned for the year. We will be learning multiplication and division, writing stories, reading books and creating interesting science experiments.

I have enclosed a piece of paper and an envelope. Please write me a short letter and let me know something about yourself. You can tell me about your family or what you did over the summer.

I am looking forward to meeting you on the first day of school.

Sincerely,

Mrs. Carter

Dear Parents,

My name is Rose Carter and I will be your child's teacher this year. Along with the daily curriculum, the third grade has many exciting projects planned. I feel very passionate about reading, so many of the students' daily activities (as well as their homework assignments) will include reading assignments. I have a large selection of books and magazines in the classroom, but suggest that you send in a book with your child so he or she has something to read each day. As well, please consider donating any old books you have around the house to our classroom library.

If you do not yet have the supply list, I have enclosed a copy for your convenience. As soon as the school year begins, I will be sending home various papers including emergency medical forms, classroom schedules, and my homework policy packet. Please look over the forms and return any necessary paperwork.

I feel it is very important for teachers and parents to work together to ensure a successful school year for the children. Once the school year begins, please feel free to contact me by email, telephone or simply via a note with your child if you have any questions or concerns.

I am looking forward to meeting you and your child and to a wonderful year together.

Sincerely,

Rose Carter

Chapter 3

Setting up Your Classroom

Deciding on the Basics

Teachers never know when they might get their first teaching job, but hopefully you'll be hired by June for the following school year. This way you'll probably have the chance to peek into your classroom and be able to spend some time over the summer thinking about how you want to organize the space. Unfortunately, the reality is that many teachers are hired at the end of the summer or after the school year has already started. If this is the situation

"Welcome Ms. Jacobs! Your students will be here in five minutes . . ."

Setting up Your Classroom 13

you find yourself in, you'll have little time to decide on how to organize everything. You'll need to prioritize when deciding what you'll need in place immediately.

In any event, you should have your classroom ready for the first day of school. This includes organizing your room, yourself, and your students. Once the school year starts you don't want to worry about where students should store their lunchboxes. You'll always be able to change the layout of your room if you notice something isn't working, but it's better to be over than under-prepared.

Many of these topics will be dealt with in more detail throughout the book, but for the first day, make sure you:

- know your school policies
- have a behavioral plan established with rewards and consequences
- have a homework policy in place
- organize your desk and teacher work area
- know how and where your students will sit
- prepare basic center activities

If you only have a few days to get ready, don't spend the entire time on bulletin boards; focus on the items listed above. If necessary, you can do the bulletin boards and unpack your supplies during the first week of school.

Remember, you're the new teacher: students, parents and administrators will be watching to see if you know what you are doing. How you configure your classroom can say a lot about your teaching style. So let's get going and start with basic classroom setup.

Laying out Your Classroom

Classroom setup depends on a variety of factors. To help you determine what to put in your classroom, where to place the different components that will make up your room, and how to organize yourself and your students best, consider:

Where is your desk? Can you accommodate a teacher work area?

Unlike the movies where teachers sit in front of the classroom while students work, most good teachers rarely sit down. If they do, it will most likely be at a desk with a student or with a group of students working on a project. Here are some suggestions to keep in mind while planning your space in the classroom:

- Try to make your desk and a small area surrounding it just that—*your* area. Communicate this fact to the children and work hard to keep your space *your* space.

- Be creative when you organize your area. There are a variety of ways to do this that will be discussed in greater detail later; for now, however, just keep in mind that you will have a desk, hopefully some shelves and a filing cabinet.

- Ensure your area is not in a travel path for students—they shouldn't have to walk around or behind your desk to get supplies, use the centers, or move to another part of the classroom.

- Arrange your desk so that students can stand next to you when they talk instead of across from you.

- Be flexible. Many teacher desks cannot be moved for a variety of reasons: they are bolted to the floor, they have computer hook ups, or they need to be near a wall outlet. If your desk cannot be moved, you'll need to work that into your plan.

Your desk should be out of the way and include places for your teacher manuals, file folders, and important papers.

Your area should basically be like a pantry in your kitchen—it holds all your goodies while it stays out of your way.

Setting up Your Classroom

Find a spot near your desk to place a small table or student desk that will serve as a teacher work area. In this area you can keep work that needs to be corrected, your grading sheets, completed children's work that is to be displayed or any of the other piles that you need to keep organized over the upcoming few days.

> My mom was a fourth grade teacher. She always had a small round table in her classroom that was used for correcting, planning, and for working with students. She found it kept her from making piles on her desk, and that her students were more relaxed about being called to the table than being called to the teacher's desk. During conference week, she used it for sitting with parents and it gave her lots of room to spread out whatever work was needed. It allowed her to sit side-by-side with parents which she felt was less confrontational than sitting across from them.

How many students do you have?

- The number of students you start with will not necessarily be the number of students in the class at the end of the year. Throughout the year you may have students leave the school as well as have new students join your class.

- Find out from your school if there are a maximum number of students allotted for your class and prepare for that many students. It's not necessary to have the maximum number of desks ready, but make sure you'll be able to incorporate new students to your overall layout without much reorganizing.

Do you want students arranged in groups or rows?

- This may not be your decision because some schools have policies regarding how children are arranged when they are seated. Many schools today do not want children in rows because it doesn't allow for easy interaction between the students. Check with your school to find out if there is such a policy.

Be prepared to move students and desks during the first few weeks as you get to know the children.

For the first day of school I arrange the class desks into groups of four to six. As the students arrive, I tell them that they are sitting in their "Maybe" desk—maybe they will be sitting there tomorrow, maybe they won't.

New teachers may be too innovative when it comes to group seating . . .

- If your classroom is only equipped with tables, students will have to sit in groups. If you have desks, students can be seated in groups or individually. In either event, when planning your desk arrangements, place one or two desks slightly apart from the rest just in case someone may need to be separated from the class or a group temporarily.

- Whether you choose groups or rows, consider asking each student to list three people they think they would work well next to, and three students they think they wouldn't. This will help you understand friendships among the children and provide some insight about which students you may want to keep apart.

- If you've decided to seat students in groups, groups of four to six work best. There are two commonly used methods to define the groups: the children select their friends to sit with or the teacher randomly assigns students to their groups. A third method of grouping—grouping by ability—is not recommended for general classroom seating.

- When placing students in groups, be prepared to switch them around during the year, especially in the beginning. You haven't yet determined who should or shouldn't sit together and you will need to be able to make any changes quickly

- Find a spot in the classroom for students with behavioral issues. Instead of placing a disruptive student towards the center of the room, place the student closer to the front (when using the board) or closer to you when the student is working. This way you can reach the child quickly while keeping the disruption from becoming center stage.

Always keep a desk and set of books ready to go for a new student.

Where is the board, and will you utilize it for large parts of your lessons?

For many teachers, the board is an integral part of their lesson. If you plan on using the blackboard (or whiteboard) on a daily basis, use the following guidelines to help you arrange desks in the room:

- Position desks so all students can see the board comfortably.

- Rearrange desks regularly to avoid the same students from repeatedly turning in the same direction.

- Put students who have sight or hearing problems close to the board.

What space is left and how should you use it?

After you've decided how you want to arrange the classroom, the students' desks, your desk and your work area, you need to take a good look at how much space you have left. Ideally classrooms should have room for:

- a classroom library
- a reading area
- bulletin board displays
- activity centers
- a table and chairs for group work

- an area where the entire class can gather for story or discussion time

A long as you are creative, you will have lots of extra space in the room. Walls, doors, windows, tables, counters, ceilings (check the fire code in your school) and even the sides of filing cabinets and desks can all be used for something.

Decide what you want to leave in sight and what you want to keep stored away yet easily accessible. Items that are left out must be safe, pose no danger to the students and be sturdy enough to handle any student attention. Typically these items include learning center activities, folders, and games that can survive on counters, shelves, crates or boxes. Items you may want to put safely away in cabinets include art supplies, your teaching supplies, and any extra student supplies. Any items that are not used regularly or that could be hazardous to the children should also be stored safely away and made inaccessible to the students.

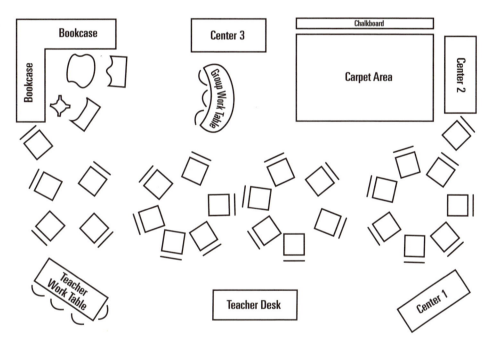

Samples of classroom layout. Each classroom contains

1. Student desks
2. Teacher desk
3. Bookcases & reading area
4. Table for group work
5. Class carpet area/ area to gather students
6. Teacher work table
7. Chalkboard
8. Area for Centers

Setting up Your Classroom

Samples of classroom layout. Each classroom contains

1. Student desks ▫
2. Teacher desk ▭
3. Bookcases & reading area ▭ ⌂ ⌨ ◇ ⌒
4. Table for group work ⌒
5. Class carpet area/ area to gather students ▭
6. Teacher work table ▭
7. Chalkboard ▬
8. Area for Centers ▭

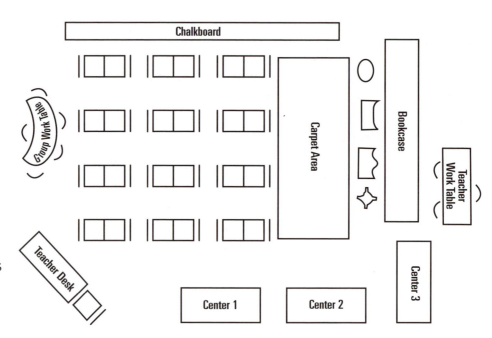

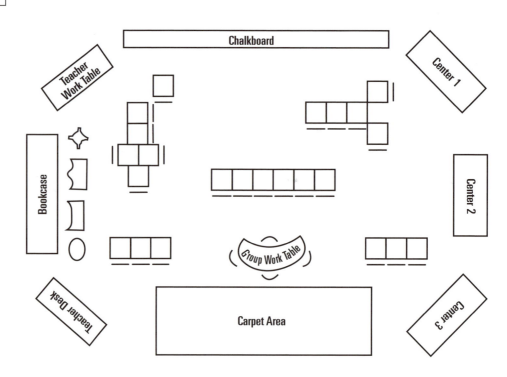

You've Got the Job—Now Keep It

Chapter 4

Making Your Classroom Cozy

Creating Atmosphere

So, you want to make your classroom a warm and inviting place for your students. You'll be there for a large part of the day too, so it should be comfortable for you also. To satisfy both sets of needs, why not turn your classroom into a "living room of learning"? There are many ways to achieve this feeling.

- Add comfy places to sit such as bean bag chairs and pillows.

- Create curtains by placing fabric along the tops or sides of windows. Depending on the size of the windows in your classroom, you can get inexpensive curtains that won't block the sunlight but will give your classroom a softer, more nurturing feeling.

- Add a table or floor lamp. Lighting makes a big difference. Most classrooms have that *loooovely* florescent lighting. Adding a lamp with a nice soft shade will add a warm glow to your room. Just make sure the cords are safely out of the way.

- Reduce overhead lighting. If you can't add a lamp, consider turning off one set of overhead lights—making sure sufficient light remains so the students can see what they are doing. This helps establish a quiet tone or mood in the classroom, which can help settle students and encourage them to be calmer and quieter.

A simple touch like curtains can help make your classroom more inviting to students.

- Place plants—either real or artificial—in different parts of the classroom. A touch of greenery brightens any room, especially a classroom.

Mrs. Noel took the "Make Your Classroom Cozy" idea a little too far . . .

Chapter 5

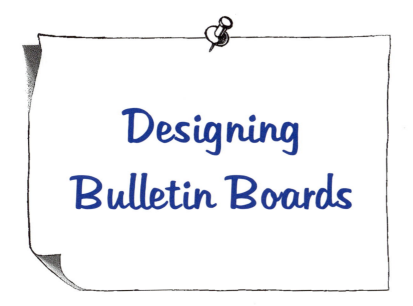

Designing Bulletin Boards

Types of Boards

Some teachers spend a lot of time on bulletin boards and change them often; others choose to put one up and leave it for the year. The appropriate approach falls somewhere in between—if you are spending hours each month redoing boards, you're devoting too much time to them and should consider enlisting a parent volunteer to help. Your time is better spent planning lessons or catching up on administrative work.

 Don't spend too much time preparing bulletin boards.

Most new teachers want their boards to look perfect from day one, and spend a lot of time and money putting up bought displays. You don't need to do this. There's nothing wrong with putting up the border and the paper and leaving the inside blank. You can use some of children's work from the first week to display on the board.

Bulletin boards can be used for a variety of purposes in the classroom, such as:

- **Display**
  There should be a large portion of your boards devoted strictly to showcasing the students' work. Hang up their art creations, or anything they've done related to music, media, or language classes. If you do decide to use your boards for graded work, remember not to display only the A students' work—include something from each child so no one feels left out. Also, don't feel pressured to change the board weekly; however, you don't want Halloween projects to still be on display in December.

- **Theme**
  If you teach using themes such as fairytales, the rain forest, or communities, you may want to make one board to display theme related ideas and completed activities.

- **Subject**
  Most teachers will have boards dedicated to specific subjects, like math or science. On these boards you can again display completed work or related items for that particular subject.

- **Routines**
  There should be one bulletin board in the classroom dedicated to school events. Include on this board: your class calendar, the school rules, a birthday chart, and any class policies or procedures such as fire drill rules or dismissal lists. This is one bulletin board that rarely needs to be changed.

- **Schedules**
  Many teachers will also utilize the wall behind their desk and make a bulletin board to tack up important announcements. Certain schedules and other important information that you, a substitute, or another teacher may need to access quickly can be maintained here including: lunchroom schedules, bus schedules, carpool duty, and teacher assistant schedules.

Materials for Boards

"I got the idea from this wonderful workshop about using 3-D bulletin boards in the classroom!"

Tired of the same old paper and border look on your bulletin boards? There are many different types of boards you can create and a variety of ways to make them unique. Involve the children as a class project and:

- **Opt for cloth**
  Many teachers use cloth to create their boards. It does not lose its color as quickly as paper.

- **Grow with felt**
  Felt also stands the test of time. If you use a felt bulletin board, cut letters and shapes out of felt instead of construction paper and apply them to the board. The felt shapes stick to the felt (or fabric) bulletin board. It may seem like more work, but you can probably use the felt shapes from year to year adding to your collection as you go.

- **Think 3-D**
  It's not difficult to make your bulletin boards stand out—literally. Crumpled tissue paper, boxes, paper towel rolls or anything that you can staple or tack to the board can be used. For example, if you are doing a math centered bulletin board and are working on measurements, stick some different sized milk cartons up on the board. For a rainforest theme place paper, boxes, and bags under fabric to create mountains or stones. Even board paper painted by the students will help make the display come alive.

- **Create a display table**
  Place a table underneath the bulletin board and display student projects or items brought from home relating to the board's theme.

- **Paint on paper**
  Instead of cutting out construction paper letters to use on your bulletin board, paint the letters on the paper. It will make your boards look different and will be much faster and easier. If you're teaching the older grades, like third, fourth, and fifth, and don't mind the odd imperfection, let the students help out. This is a great first day of school activity. If you are going to have the students help out, paint the paper on the ground before putting it on the wall, and never let students stand on desks, counters, or chairs.

- **Use the news**
  Newspapers are a fun way to do a variety of activities in your class. Why not create a small bulletin board out of newspapers? Students can bring in articles or pages from newspapers and you can pick and choose what to use on the board. You can even make this

Bulletin boards should be up-to-date and reflect what's going on in your classroom.

Designing Bulletin Boards

board a learning center. Put up interesting editorials as examples of letter writing, and display articles that are related to something you're teaching in the classroom. You can even include advertisements and link them with math activities. Students can highlight the board, looking for the *who, what, when, where,* and *how* in the stories. In younger grades, children can look for and highlight words they know, spelling words, or skill words (rhyming words, "ing" words, et cetera).

- **Reuse it**

    At the end of the year if your school doesn't make you take your boards down, cover the boards with newspaper to keep them in good shape until school reopens. Some teachers even redo their boards at the end of the year and cover them up so they are fresh and ready in the fall.

Being creative with your bulletin boards won't take more time, just a bit more imagination.

Chapter 6

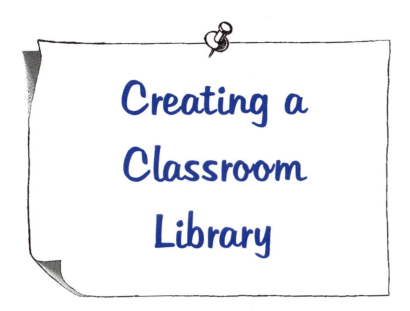

Drowning Students with Good Books

Having a classroom library for independent reading is an absolutely essential part of your room. Sure, students can go to the school library once a week and take out books, but if you plan to have independent reading each day and to immerse your students in all types of literature, then you will need to supply children with a large variety of easily accessible reading materials.

Drown the children in books by taking every opportunity to pop reading into their day. You can accomplish this by:

- Filling all "dead spaces" with books. Don't limit the children to finding a book in the classroom library, help them by sprinkling books liberally around the entire classroom—across the top of filing cabinets, stacked in the area under the chalkboard, throughout the various learning and activity centers, and on the windowsills. Wherever there's a space, fill it.

- Sticking a magazine rack or a shoebox filled with books inside the doorway of the bathroom. Some books might end up missing, but hopefully that means someone enjoyed the book enough to continue reading it upon leaving the bathroom.

- Leading by example. Let your students see you reading from time to time yourself—it sends a stronger message to your students about the importance of reading when they see you enjoying a book instead of correcting papers.

- Reading aloud to your students each day. Select a picture book, a poem and a selection from a novel to read to your students and try to set aside time each day to complete this task.

In order to do all this, you need to have plenty of books. There are many ways to get books, to organize your library, and to have students sign out materials. Let's begin with how to collect books.

Collecting Books for Your Classroom

If you haven't yet begun collecting books for your classroom, start now. There are some great sources where you can find inexpensive books. Even if you're not sure what grade you will be teaching, acquire all the books you can get and worry about sorting them later. Also keep in mind that you will undoubtedly have a mix of very low and very strong readers in your class. You may even have non-English speaking students, so you will want to keep a variety of reading levels and genres to satisfy everyone's interest and abilities. During your teaching career it is very unlikely that you will always teach the same grade, so don't limit your book collecting activities to the grade you are teaching.

Before the School Year

- **Donations**
  The first thing you should do is ask friends or family members if they have any suitable books they would like to donate to your classroom. Keep those that are slightly used and skip any books that have torn pages, ruined covers, or stains.

  In your introduction letter, let the parents know that you will accept both new and gently used donations of children's books for the classroom. Both parents and students seem to enjoy this idea, because it makes them feel as if they are doing something special for the classroom, which they are. As an added bonus, you may want to make up a thank you card for the donation or give a sticker to a student who donates a book. You'll be surprised at how many donations you'll receive.

- **Garage sales**
  Remember the saying, "One man's junk is another man's treasure?" Garage sales can be a reader's paradise. Here you can pick and

choose only what you want. Keep your eyes open for books that are more than just the current fad series. Along with novels, look for books of poetry, nursery rhymes, and jokes. Reference books such as dictionaries, thesauruses, atlases, magazines, and even cookbooks are great additions. Remember while you ideally want students reading good literature, above all else you want them *reading*. And, when it's independent reading time, they should be able to select from suitable material on their own.

- **Online auctions**
  Online auctions allow you to buy books quickly and inexpensively. Photos and detailed descriptions allow you to see the state of the books, and you can email the seller with any questions. You can purchase individual books, but look for lot sales (groups of books being sold together). Due to the nature of these auctions, the selection can vary daily so check the sites often for newly listed items.

- **Local libraries**
  Quite often libraries will have book sales. Give your local library a call and see if they have any children's books for sale or available as donations. They may even be able to refer you to other organizations that can donate books to your classroom.

- **Book fairs held by local universities**
  Frequently local universities will showcase authors and local writers. Watch for these book fairs because you can get great deals on books.

- **Bookstores**
  Obviously this is the most accessible place to find current books, but it can also be expensive, so head to second hand bookstores. These stores offer used books, out of print and hard to find titles at a fraction of the cost of regular bookstores. Most bookstores offer teacher discounts, so don't forget to ask.

> **TIP:** *Include books written in other languages to meet the needs of your ESOL students.*

During the School Year

- **Warehouse sales**
  Warehouse sales usually take place during the school year. During a warehouse sale a large publishing company, such as Scholastic, liquidates books for teachers. If you're lucky your school might give you some money for these sales, but even if they don't, the sales are definitely worth going to if you have a little extra cash and want to

buy some books. The low prices make it a great place to purchase duplicate sets of novels for use in reading groups.

- **Book clubs**

  Once you begin teaching you will be sending home book order forms from which students can purchase books. Popular book order clubs are Scholastic, Carnival, or Trumpet. Even though it can be somewhat time consuming, always send these book orders home. For each purchase a student makes, you will collect bonus points. You can use these bonus points to buy resource books for yourself and books for the classroom as well. These books then become yours and travel with you during your teaching career. Book orders are an excellent way to get quality books for little or no out-of-pocket expense.

As you can see, there are numerous ways to get your classroom library started with very little effort. At the end of the year, take the time to go through your library and gather up any books that are too damaged to use for the next year. Raffle these books off to your students at the end of the year.

There are few more thoughts to keep in mind when it comes to keeping books in your classroom.

- Make sure you write your name in ink in the front of every book that you bring to your classroom. Over time books can inadvertently disappear. Students may borrow books and leave them at home, or a teacher may borrow a resource book and leave it in another classroom. At the end of the year, send out a letter to parents asking them to check the inside covers of any books found under beds, in backpacks, or hanging around the house. If your name is there, the book can easily be returned to you.

- Teacher supply stores sell stamps that say, "This book belongs to _____." Stamp the inside of your books with your name or create personal labels and stick them inside your books.

- If you buy nice hardcover or chapter books with your own money, keep these books in an area with controlled access—a shelf by your desk works well. Have students ask permission to look at these books or have a sign out sheet for borrowing them. It will keep these books from getting worn out and makes them seem special. This added sense of mystique seems to make students want to read "the teacher's books" all the more.

Organizing a Classroom Library

Now that you've gotten your library started, what should you do next? The books you've collected won't get optimum use if they are not organized in some way.

There are a variety of ways to set up your library. You can organize by genre, theme, author, reading levels, or a mixed approach. Below is an explanation of how to organize by each of these categories.

- **Genre**

  A genre is the category of writing that the book falls into. Here are some guidelines for organizing your books by genre:

  > Picture book
  > Traditional literature (includes fairytales, folktales, myths and legends)
  > Modern fantasy
  > Poetry
  > Realistic fiction
  > Historical fiction and biographies
  > Information books
  > Reference books
  > Plays and scripts

- **Theme**

  You may choose to keep similar themes together. Organizing books by theme is commonly done by teachers. If you are studying dinosaurs in your class, you will most likely take all your dinosaur books and put them together.

- **Author**

  Creating an author collection means keeping many books by one author. Use bonus points from your book orders to buy books from authors you enjoy. In the same way that you may be drawn to specific adult authors, you will be drawn to certain children's authors. Although you should have a variety of books in your classroom library, there's nothing wrong with having several books by one author.

  If you are reluctant to organize your entire library by author, but like the idea of keeping books by the same author together, purchase small baskets from a dollar store, fill them with books by the same

Drowning Students with Good Books

author and place them throughout your reading center. These mini-collections can be changed or rotated throughout the year.

- **Reading levels**

    Another way to organize your library is to separate the books by reading level. There are advantages and disadvantages to this approach. One benefit to grouping books by level is that it makes it easier for students to find books appropriate for their reading ability. Students will often try to gage the difficulty of a book by the thickness of its spine, the size of its words, or the look of its cover. An obvious reason not to group books by level is that students may feel embarrassed to take the books from the "easy shelf." All too often students will pretend to read a hard book instead of taking an easier book and actually reading it. This is especially true if friends and classmates are choosing books from the more difficult levels.

    If you decide not to organize truly by reading level, devote a space for "more challenging" books to be kept among the regular books. Tell students that all the books are for the class, but the more challenging books, grouped together in one spot, are above grade level. Most students will look at these books and some will read them. However, because all the books are grouped together, students won't feel pressured to take a book that is beyond their ability.

- **Thrown together**

    This way of organizing your books is simple. Just place all your books on the shelves without any organization at all. For some teachers this is the easiest way because it requires little upkeep, yet for others it is too unorganized. Similarly while some children may enjoy browsing at such an eclectic shelf, others, perhaps searching for a particular title or genre, may find this approach frustrating.

- **Mixed**

    The final way to group books is by using a mixed approach. Most teachers choose this method because—with the exclusion of not organizing the books at all—this system is the easiest to maintain. Typically you'll want to create a section or two based on a particular genre, devote a space to more challenging titles, and establish a reference area for all dictionaries, thesauruses encyclopedias and information books. Magazines and non-fiction books can be grouped together and placed in different sections of the library while, throughout the entire space, your author collections are enticingly displayed in baskets.

Obviously, there are many ways to organize your classroom library. Think about what's most important to you and what will be the easiest for you and the children to maintain. Keeping the library organized should be a collaborative job among the students, so you'll have to explain the basic layout to the class. The younger grades—such as kindergarten and first—may need some assistance with this, but the older grades should be able to maintain an organized library on their own.

Storing Books

Often schools will provide book shelves or cubbies to use for classroom libraries. If they do not, or if what they give you is not enough, here are some inexpensive and easy-to-create solutions for your books.

"Don't you just LOVE it??? I picked it up at a church rummage sale!!"

- **Milk crates**

  Milk crates can work in many areas of the classroom because these versatile storage units are easy to stack and move around. To use in a library, turn them sideways to create instant book shelves. Affix crates together with plastic ties and don't stack more than two on top of one another. Milk crates can be purchased at major bargain stores and come in a variety of colors. Also, check your local grocery store, where you may be able to get them for free.

- **Shoeboxes**

  Shoeboxes are a great solution especially if you have limited space. Obviously, shoeboxes work best when kept flat, placing the books inside with the spines facing up. If you try standing them up you may encounter problems with the boxes tumbling over—especially if you stack them. Try to get a variety of sizes: men's shoeboxes are nice and big, as are the boxes for sneakers and boots. If you don't have enough you can always ask parents to donate some.

  Have students decorate and label the sides, so the books inside can be easily identified. Organize the boxes and label them according to how you are organizing your library, for example: Books by Judy Blume, Poetry or Biographies.

- **Shoe organizer**

  As long as you're in the shoe department consider purchasing a plastic shoe organizer that hangs from the door, although you'll hang this one from your ceiling. (Remember to check your school's fire policy before you hang anything from the ceiling of a classroom.) While it won't hold as many books as a bookcase, it's a unique way to show off favorite books or showcase a theme-for-the-month display.

A shoe organizer is a unique way to display books in your classroom library.

- **Bookcase**

  If you're a traditionalist, you may want to stick with a small, inexpensive bookcase. Before heading off to the store remember to ask friends and family to see if they have something they would like to donate. Also check out garage sales and online auctions. If you still haven't found anything try the bargain stores and look for sales! Bookcases made out of MDF (basically fake wood) are less expensive. Also try the Salvation Army, Habitat for Humanity, The Good Will, and consignment shops.

- **Plastic tubs**

  Small plastic tubs can be used to stand books up in, allowing students to see all the books at a glance.

Small plastic tubs to store books makes for an organized classroom library.

Lending Your Books

Once you have invested in your books, you don't want to lose them. Students will undoubtedly want to borrow your books, and you need to decide whether or not you want to permit students to remove your books from the room. Most teachers will let students take books home, but before you do make sure you have some type of a sign out system.

- **Sign-out sheets**

  One system that works well is a simple sign out sheet. The students can write their name, the title of the book, and the date it was borrowed on a piece of paper. When they return the book, they cross their name off the list. The list should be secured to a bulletin board,

Drowning Students with Good Books

countertop, or another permanent surface, and you should be the only one allowed to remove it.

- **Card holders**

    You can use the same system that the library uses. Glue library card holders to the back of each book. Write the name of the book on an index card and place it in the holder in the back of the book. Keep a small index box with dividers for each student's name. When students want to take a book, they simply remove the card from the back of the book and file it under their name. You can purchase library card holders at any teacher supply store.

- **Index cards**

    You can use a combination of the two methods above by keeping an index box with index cards containing each student's name. Instead of using a list on a single sheet of paper, have the students write down the name of the book they are borrowing on their index card. When the book is returned students put a line through or a checkmark next to the title.

"Says here that you've been late three times this month. You know what that means, don't you . . ."

- **A student librarian**

    You may want to choose a student to be the classroom librarian. At the end of each day, if students want to take books home, the librarian uses whichever system you've established to check the books out of the classroom library. Then, when they're finished, the students return the books to the classroom book drop—an empty cardboard box or milk crate works fine here—and the librarian returns the book to the proper shelf and records that the book has been returned.

- **Honor system**
  Of course there is always the honor system. Using this approach, you tell the students they may take home whatever books they want to, and that you trust them to bring the books back in good condition. You may want to limit this to one book at a time,

The easiest way to lend books is obviously the honor system, but it is also the easiest way to *lose* books. It is best to keep some type of record of where your books are going. Using the sign-out sheet or having a student librarian is the best way to go and can eliminate most problems quickly and objectively.

No matter what system you choose, be prepared to replace a few books through loss or general wear and tear.

Lending Special Books

As we mentioned earlier you may want to keep some higher quality books you buy, such as nice hardcover storybooks, behind your desk. Students will often want to take these books home. In addition you will find that if you borrow books from the local library for your classroom, students will want to take these books home too.

If you choose to let students borrow your personal, class or county library books, send home a letter stating your policy for lost or damaged books. Ensure parents and students sign the letter before any books go home. It may sound strict, but if one of your personal or library books becomes lost or damaged, **you** will incur the cost without a signed letter. Most parents respect this and will appreciate the fact that you are willing to lend your books at all.

"Mr. Clarke sent this note—he'd like his books back . . ."

Drowning Students with Good Books

Dear Parents,

I have a strong love of reading and encourage the students to read as much as possible. I have a large collection of books and magazines in my classroom that students are welcome to take home to read by themselves or to share with their families. In addition to the classroom library, I have a small selection of wonderful hardcover children's books. These books are part of my own personal collection, which I enjoy sharing with the class. Throughout the year I also have numerous books that I checkout from the local library and bring to the classroom for the students to read.

Many of the students have expressed an interest in taking books from my personal collection as well as my borrowed library books home to read. I'm thrilled that the students have taken such a strong interest in reading these books, but I am concerned over allowing these particular books to leave the classroom. If one of my personal books or a library book is lost or damaged, I will have to replace it.

I have decided to allow my personal books and the library books to go home; however, if any books are lost or damaged I will need to be reimbursed for the cost of the book. All students can continue to take home books from the general classroom library, but if you would like your child to be allowed to take either my personal or library books home, you must sign and return the bottom of this letter. Only students who return the signed letter will be allowed to check these books out. I will make sure to note any problems with the book before it leaves the classroom.

Thank you for your support,

Linda Brent

_____ Yes, I would like my child to be allowed to take the teacher's **personal books** home and will be responsible for its cost if the book is lost or damaged.

_____ Yes, I would like my child to be allowed to take the teacher's **personal library books** home and will be responsible for its cost if the book is lost or damaged.

Student's name: _____

_____   _____
Student's Signature   Parent's Signature/Date

Chapter 7

Designing a Reading Area

Making a Comfortable Area

Now that you have your books and have organized your library, it's time to set up a nice reading area for the students. Think about your favorite place to read. Is it a comfy chair, a sofa, or your bed? Chances are, it is not sitting on a hard chair at a desk. Some students don't mind sitting at their desks for free reading, but most students would like to sit somewhere more comfortable. This also gives the students the opportunity to move around the classroom and get out of their chairs.

If you want to engage students in reading, make books readily available and provide an inviting place to read.

So how should you create a comfortable, inviting area for reading? That all depends on how much room you have, how much effort you want to devote to it, and what supplies you have available.

- Very large pillows or small bean bag chairs can be used to make a great reading area. They are also light enough to move around easily. In the event that any of your students get lice, you should have pillows and beanbag chairs with removable cloth cases, and the pillows themselves should be machine washable. Children like to lay their heads on the pillows while they are reading, so washing the covers periodically is advisable even when there is no sign of infection. Better yet, use plastic coverings wherever possible. Plastic can be sprayed with disinfectant and washed down.

- Carpet remnants can be purchased at low cost from major home improvement stores or are available for free at many carpet stores. These small pieces of carpet can be stacked up and put away on a shelf, so they are great for a classroom where size and space are issues. Carpet can also be vacuumed and sanitized if an outbreak of lice occurs.

- New tires can be purchased at low cost from major automotive stores. One clever teacher we know washed and spray painted four new tires. She then took bright colored pillows and placed them inside the tires. These quickly became a favorite reading spot for all students. Just get your principal's permission first before bringing them into the classroom.

- Some other fun pieces you can add to your reading area are small couches or chairs made for smaller children. Director's chairs can be purchased also for a low cost. Again, it depends on the space you have available in your room and the amount of money you want to spend. Ask around to see if you can have some of these items donated.

- Think about adding a lamp to your reading area. If you have the space to do it safely, a shaded lamp adds a nice warm atmosphere to the classroom.

Ok, so you have the extra room in your classroom and the energy to do something really fun. What can you do that's different? Here are a few unique suggestions:

- Pop-up tents can be used to create a fun reading area. They can be put up and taken down quickly.

- A teepee—purchased from a toy store or made from PVC piping and fabric—can hold about six kids and will become an eagerly sought-after place for some quiet reading. Its novelty will position reading time as something the children look forward to each day.

- For good, clean fun bring in a bathtub!! Look for a free standing bathtub (the kind with feet) that you can paint a bright color and fill with pillows. Of course, you may need to get your principal's permission because old tubs are very heavy and—you never know—there may be some kind of weird bathtub policy in your school. Again, places to look for this type of item would be online auctions, local home improvement stores, or garage sales. You never know what people might want to get rid of.

Once you've created your reading corner, watch for those students who always hog the tires, bean bags, chairs, or pillows. If you have a really great place for reading, all of the students are going to want to use it. The easiest way to monitor the reading area is to just let the students know that the space belongs to the entire class. If someone uses the bean bags one day then another child should use them the next. Problems that arise can be quickly remedied when students know they will lose their "reading area privilege" for a few days. This way the students know arguing won't be tolerated and, in addition to learning how to share, they also learn how to solve problems on their own.

If this approach doesn't work in your class, create a system for signing students in and out of the reading area. A quick glance at the sign in list is all it takes to see if any students are not sharing the reading space. In the lower grades, however, you may have to set a schedule because such young children may find it more difficult to monitor themselves.

Summary Section One

- Remember the three P's—population, policies, and procedures. Know these areas before the year begins.

- Find out about your school's new teacher program and understand what is expected of you in order to meet its requirements.

- Before the year begins, send out welcome letters to both students and parents.

- Set up your classroom, planning areas for your desk, a teacher work area, centers, and a classroom library. Be prepared to accommodate new students throughout the year.

- Create a cozy feeling in your classroom by adding curtains, plants, lamps, pillows or other items that will make your classroom feel warm and inviting.

- When creating bulletin boards for your classroom, include boards that display students' work, keep track of upcoming events, and show thematic or subject areas being studied in class. Don't spend too much time creating bulletin boards, but do try to have one or two interesting boards that are 3-D, use felt, cloth, paint, or other unique ideas.

- Set up your classroom library. Decide on a bookcase, collect books, pick an organizational strategy, decide on a checkout system, and assign a student to maintain the library.

- Create a comfortable reading area for students. Use pillows, bean bag chairs, or carpet remnants. Be as creative as you'd like, but just make sure that all students are able to use the reading area for equal amounts of time.

Notes

SECTION TWO
Sorting Out and Straightening Up—Organizing Yourself and Your Students

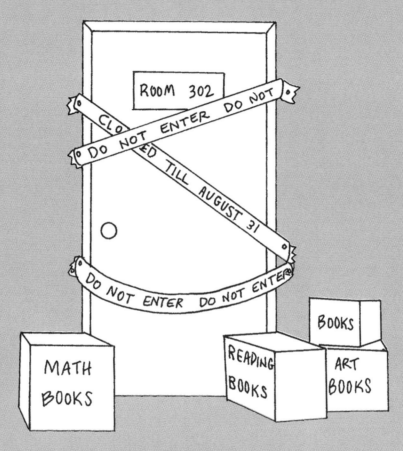

- ✦ The importance of having an organized classroom
- ✦ Organizing your desk and work area
- ✦ Tracking notes, papers, and more
- ✦ Getting and keeping your students organized
- ✦ Sharing responsibilities with other teachers
- ✦ Planning lessons
- ✦ Preparing for a substitute

IN THIS SECTION

Chapter 8

Organizing for Survival

In researching this book, parents were surveyed about what they deem to be key elements of their child's educational success. We asked them questions about teachers, administrators, policies, and schools in general.

Parents were asked to rate various components relating to teachers, the classroom, and classroom policies. These components were: classroom setup, teacher organization, homework and behavior policies, prompt communication, access to teachers and administration, volunteering in class, teacher appearance, and classroom structure. Parents rated teacher organization and classroom structure as very high indicators of effective classroom management.

Now that may seem a bit scary to you if organization is not one of your strengths, but don't despair. If you consider yourself organizationally challenged, read through this section carefully for helpful organizational strategies.

 Have all supplies ready to go when a parent volunteer or administrator is expected in the classroom.

Why Organizing is Important

There is more to being a classroom teacher than simply teaching your students. Keeping ahead of daily administrative tasks while sorting through the never ending paper trail are both time consuming parts of the job.

How important is it to be organized? VERY!! Aside from the teaching, let's look at the kinds of tasks you'll be responsible for as a typical classroom teacher:

- **Correspondence**

  Students will be bringing in papers and forms from home, and you'll be sending out newsletters, notes, and papers to parents.

- **Grading**

  You'll have papers to grade, marks to record, and report cards to write.

- **Scheduling**

  Among other things there'll be volunteers and fieldtrips to schedule, and faculty and grade level meetings to attend.

- **Communication**

  You'll need effective ways to communicate with the administration, the office, the lunchroom, the maintenance staff, other teachers, and parents.

Organize yourself carefully during the first weeks of school.

There are so many tasks to tend to that trying to remember them all in your head or making piles on your desk won't work, especially if organization is not your strong suit. You'll just end up creating more stress for yourself.

In order to make your job easier, you should enter the classroom with your organizational procedures established. You should assume that you will have minimal or no help from teaching assistants. If you're very lucky you'll have an assistant in your classroom to help you, but an assistant can only help once you've set up the policies and procedures for how you want things done. Once you've established your organizational system, a teaching assistant can then follow through on the procedures you've set in place.

Some teachers are naturally organized, so organizing a classroom comes as second nature. For those who could use some help, simple organizational procedures can mean the difference between a chaotic or a smoothly running day. The first year of teaching is a complete learning experience, where you often won't know exactly what you'll need until the moment arrives. However, a few tried and true organizational strategies that every teacher can use are covered in the upcoming chapters.

Wire racks are another practical way to store teacher materials.

Organizing for Survival

Chapter 9

Organizing Your Own Personal Space

Tackling the following areas will get you organized and off on the right foot.

- How to keep your desk from being the catch all for everything in the classroom.

- How to set up a user friendly teacher work area.

- How to set up files or notebooks containing pertinent school information.

- Different options for organizing all of the papers coming in to and going out from your classroom.

Your Desk

It is amazing how some teachers can keep their desks almost completely clean, while others only see the top of their desk in September and not again until mid-June. More and more schools are supplying their teachers with computers, printers, and telephones, all of which are landing on the teacher's desk, making it easier for "messy-desk-syndrome" to occur. You might think a constantly cluttered desk is no big deal, but think again:

- At the beginning of the year parents will make assumptions about you based on your appearance, the appearance of your classroom and the appearance of your work area. As the year goes on and as you gain a reputation for being a competent teacher, you may be

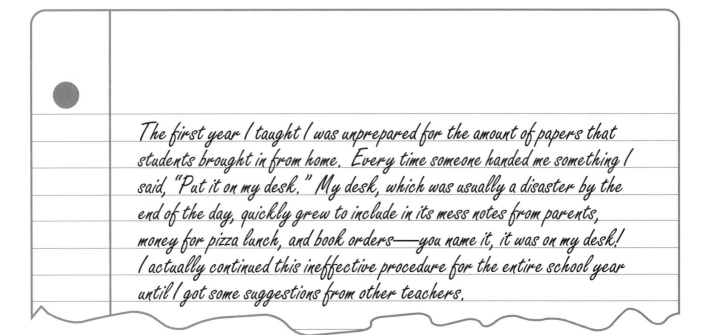

The first year I taught I was unprepared for the amount of papers that students brought in from home. Every time someone handed me something I said, "Put it on my desk." My desk, which was usually a disaster by the end of the day, quickly grew to include in its mess notes from parents, money for pizza lunch, and book orders—you name it, it was on my desk! I actually continued this ineffective procedure for the entire school year until I got some suggestions from other teachers.

able to overcome assumptions. However in the beginning, it is important to remember that parents and administrators don't know you, and if your area seems scattered and disorganized, that's how others may perceive you.

- You are a role model for the students. If you expect them to keep their areas neat, then you should expect the same of yourself. The old "Do as I Say Not as I Do" rule doesn't really work here. Give your students time at the end of the day to clean up, and use this time to organize your area.

- The most important reason for staying organized is to make your teaching life easier. Knowing where forms, lesson plans, copies, schedules, and papers are makes your day a bit less stressful.

Inevitably, there will be some things you'll need to keep close by, whether they're on your desk, stored in a drawer or in small baskets. These might include: a personal calendar, a notepad or sticky notes, some pens and pencils, a calculator, and a small dictionary, a thesaurus, and an English grammar reference book.

Set up a teacher work area near your desk.

Your Work Area

We strongly suggest that you have a teacher work area near your desk. Often teachers will ask "Why not just keep everything at my desk?" This strategy may work if you are an incredibly organized teacher; however here is why we recommend a separate work area:

- People who need to drop off "stuff" (photocopies, notes *from* parents, notes *for* parents, forgotten lunches, et cetera) drop it on your desk regardless of what it is, who it is from or if you're there to accept it. By the end of a day you can amass quite a pile, and if your desk is filled with your important supplies and papers, they can easily get mixed up with the other stuff or lost.

- If you have to leave in the middle of a task you have the freedom to leave it and come back because you know you won't need the space for anything else.

- The work area affords you a little privacy—unlike a desk, which is often the first thing people see when they enter your classroom. Therefore, it's a better area in which to keep papers and work that needs to be graded.

You don't need a huge amount of space—your teacher work area can be a small table or an empty student desk—and it's a great place to correct papers, write reports, sort files, create lesson plans, and handle paperwork. You should stock the area with stationary supplies. Drop trays for finished work can be located in this area so when it comes time to correct, the work is where you need it; try using crates and baskets underneath the table to store files and folders. It's also a good idea to ensure there are no grade sheets, graded papers, or future tests left lying around your work area.

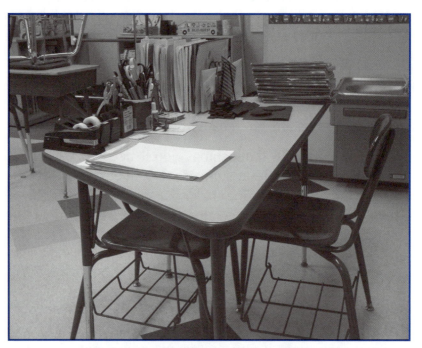

An organized teacher work area will save your sanity during the course of the year.

Using Daily Folders

Keep a folder for each day of the week in your teacher work area. Use these folders to help plan your week. Here are some helpful ways you can use daily folders.

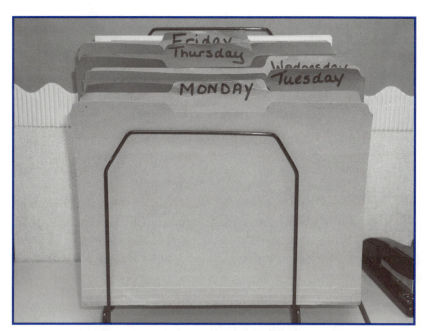

Use Monday–Friday folders to keep daily copies, schedules or other information at your fingertips.

- **Organize your copies**
  You can use Monday–Friday folders to organize the papers that you have copied. If you make copies for a lesson you're delivering on Tuesday, place them in the Tuesday folder; if you have materials to give out on Wednesday, place them in the Wednesday folder. **Just remember to check your folders before you begin in the morning and before you end in the afternoon.**

- **Notes to yourself**
  You may need an extra reminder to call someone or do something. By keeping a note in your daily folder as well as on your calendar you will be reminded the minute you start your day. (Those yellow sticky notes are used so often that many times they are overlooked.)

- **Notes for meetings**
  If you have a meeting during the week with a parent, teacher or other staff member and you want to remember to bring something along, place it in these folders.

Organizing Your Own Personal Space

Your Calendars

Teacher Calendars

Another important teacher strategy is to keep a well organized calendar. Items to include on your calendar are: school closings and holidays, faculty meetings, grade level meetings, due dates for administrative items, deadlines, assemblies and school events, and any school activity that involves your class. It is *not* advisable to keep specifics of parent-teacher conferences on a calendar that will be in public view. Parents may not want everyone who walks in the classroom to know that they have three meetings scheduled in one month. Either keep your calendar out of sight or use a code like "ptc" (parent-teacher conference) on the calendar and keep a more detailed schedule of conferences out of public view.

> **TIP:** *Post all long-term assignments on your classroom calendar.*

While there are a variety of calendars to choose from, calendars that show a month at a glance work best, such as:

- **Desk pad calendars**
  These large calendars are designed to lie flat on the top of your desk and are great for seeing the month at a glance. Office supply stores often give them to teachers for free at the beginning of the school.

- **Erasable wall calendars**
  Laminate these calendars (so they can be re-used each year) and use dry erase markers to keep track of upcoming events.

- **Standard desk calendars**
  Standard desk calendars are smaller than desk pad calendars and, consequently, often can display only a week or a day at a time.

- **Standard lesson plan books**
  Lesson plan books allow you to write your plans in calendar format and usually show a week at a glance.

Classroom Calendars

Somewhere in your classroom you should display a monthly classroom calendar for the students. Upcoming tests, due dates, school events, field trips, school closings, or anything that pertains specifically to your students should be marked on this calendar. Keep this calendar in plain view for students and parents.

Teacher Boards

Create a small teacher bulletin board, either behind your desk or next to the classroom door. If there isn't a bulletin board, purchase and

Displaying a class calendar keeps students and parents well informed about what's going on in your classroom.

A small teacher bulletin board will keep schedules and important notices at your fingertips.

mount a small cork board to use for putting up important papers. Certain schedules, such as lunchroom schedules, supervision duty, and bus schedules should be kept in plain sight so that you, a substitute, or another teacher can locate them easily.

Organizing Your Own Personal Space

Chapter 10

Organizing Your Paper Trail

Tricks of the Trade

If you are lucky, you will be provided with a filing cabinet to keep track of all your folders and papers. If not, invest in a cabinet that you can use throughout your teaching career. If you don't have the money for a cabinet, use milk crates instead. No matter what you use you need to have an organized system for organizing papers and folders first. The following inexpensive objects will become your best friends on the journey to organize your classroom:

Letter trays

Purchase these at your local office supply store and set them up as "drop spots" around your classroom to track loose papers.

Milk crates and Hanging files

Milk crates are often available for free from your local grocery store or they can be purchased cheaply at the dollar store. Because they are sturdy, stackable, and easy to move from one place to another, milk crates are an excellent place to store files or student folders.

File and hanging folders can be purchased at office supply stores. Just place hanging folders inside the milk crates and then place your file folders inside. The hanging folders keep the file folders from slipping and allow you to keep many files together. While most of your files will remain in your classroom, it's nice to have portability so you can do *fun stuff* like correcting from home on a Friday night.

Binders

Binders can be used in place of or in addition to milk crates and file folders. The advantage is they allow you to keep all of your information in the one spot; keep in mind the disadvantage is they allow you to keep all of your information in one spot! A binder is a good thing to organize with, but a bad thing to lose.

Plastic tubs

Plastic tubs can be used to store a number of items in your classroom. Because of the variety of sizes to choose from, they can hold everything from learning centers to textbooks.

Now that you've purchased letter trays, milk crates, file folders, binders, and tubs, what do you do next? You can use all of these tools, or combinations of them to set yourself up for organizational success. A checklist has been provided at the end of this section to help you track which organizational tools you wish to use.

Setting up Letter Trays

Letter trays come in handy for keeping yourself organized as well as the students. The trays should be labeled and assigned spots at the beginning of the year. Place your trays where they are easily accessible for the students, such as along a counter, on a teacher work table, or along the top of a bookcase.

Beware... Having organizational supplies does not lead to organization— but having a system does.

TRAY #1: NOTES FROM HOME

Let's start with all those papers that come in from home every day. On any given day you might find notes for you, notes to the Parent Teacher Organization, notes for the office, lunch menus, et cetera. Many of these notes will include money, or may be written on small pieces of paper that can easily go missing if you are not organized. With the exception of the notes for you, most of these papers will need to be distributed to other people in the school.

- Set up a place in the classroom for your **Notes from Home** tray and instruct children to put all notes and papers from home in there.

- Remember students learn routines quickly. Once they learn where they are to put the notes, you'll reduce the number of

Make sure you sort through the "Notes from Home" letter tray each morning as part of your own morning routine.

Organizing Your Paper Trail

students asking you "Where do I put this note?" Setting up a drop spot for notes from home will also eliminate a lot of anxiety and wasted time for students who might wonder where to put things.

- If you are a kindergarten teacher, you may want to show the parents where the drop tray is at the beginning of the year. This will keep them from trying to hand you papers directly.

TRAY #2: NOTES GOING HOME
Any time you have notes from the office, student work, book orders, or any other information that needs to go home, place it in this letter tray. At the end of the day distribute these papers to students to place in their daily folder.

Classwork travels through four stages. During each step it's helpful to have the work together in a tray that you can take home, or pull out when you have a few minutes. You will need to have the following classwork trays:

TRAY #3: WORK TO BE CORRECTED
Have students place finished work that needs to be corrected here. You can either have one tray for all finished work, or a tray for each subject. Having a tray for each subject will save you time when it comes to correcting assignments.

Once the students have put the work in the proper letter trays during the day, you can take the papers to your teacher work area and begin correcting. Once you've corrected the work, transfer it to the proper tray. If it's graded work that needs to be noted in some way in your gradebook, lay the papers in your **Work to be Recorded** tray. If it doesn't need recording, place in the **Student Work to Go Home** tray.

TRAY #4: WORK TO BE RECORDED
When you have a few minutes to spare, you can pull this tray and record whether work is missing or incomplete, as well as transfer any grades in your gradebook or on your grading sheet. When finished, lay the papers into the **Student Work to Go Home** tray. From there, papers can be distributed to the students, and then placed in their student file or directly into their daily/weekly folder.

TRAY #5: WORK TO GO HOME
Once you've graded papers and recorded the grades, you'll be ready to give the work back to your students. Together you'll review

Not all work needs to be graded, but all work should be looked at and corrected by you.

the work, and then it can be sent home for parents to see, sign and return.

TRAY #6: WORK TO BE FILED
Once work has been signed by parents and returned to school, you'll want students to place the signed work in a **To be Filed** tray. The work will then go into each student's private work file, accessible only by you and your assistant.

> *Only the teacher should distribute papers containing a student's grade.*

Setting up Crates, Folders, and More

We're going to assume that your file cabinet space is limited or nonexistent and that you will be using milk crates and hanging folders to store files. If you're lucky enough to have a file cabinet, think "file cabinet drawer" in any place where you read about using a milk crate.

You will need to break down your milk crates (or file cabinet) into the following sections:

Teaching: All files pertaining to instructing students in your classroom go here.
Non-Teaching: Files and papers that do not relate directly to instruction go here.
Outside class: All files pertaining to activities and duties outside your class go here.
Student work: A file folder for each student belongs in here.*
Private: Student files to which only you have access belong here.*

*Once these crates are set up they require very little maintenance from you.

Teaching Crate

Any paper that has to do with the teaching that occurs in your classroom should be in this crate. Here are some file folders that you will want to have included:

- **September–June folders**
  As you teach you will accumulate activities and papers that relate directly to each month—Halloween ideas, Christmas projects, et cetera. Keep monthly folders as a way to organize seasonal material, lesson ideas, and information about monthly holidays.

- **Skill-specific or Subject folders**
  A dilemma for many teachers is whether to organize their teaching files by skill or subject (as presented in their teaching manual).

Organizing Your Paper Trail

No matter how you are asked to record the grades, you should always keep a backup grading sheet for each subject in its own folder.

Organizing by skill works best because if you change jobs and/or relocate to a new school, you won't need to re-organize your folders. Examples of skills include addition, reading strategies, or subject/predicate whereas examples of subjects could would include: math, social studies, grammar, et cetera.

- **Theme folders**
  When teaching themes, keep all papers, tests, and overheads together, and place them in labeled folders in the order in which you'll teach them. Examples of themes include The Civil War, The Rainforest, and Inventors of the 20th Century.

- **Lesson plan folders**
  If you don't use a lesson plan book, keep copies of blank and completed lesson plans in a folder. If you end up teaching the same grade more than once, reviewing past lesson plans can help you determine what you will and won't teach again.

- **Substitute plan folders**
  You should have two folders for substitute teachers. The first should contain important information such your class schedule, daily routines, and classroom procedures. The second folder should contain activities the substitute can use if he needs additional work to give the class. If you know you will be out sick, leave the folders along with your lesson plans out for the substitute. If you're out unexpectedly be sure another teacher or a responsible student knows where your substitute folders are.

- **Grading sheets and subject grade folders**
  You need to determine how your school maintains its recorded grades before you can decide how you will maintain your daily grading records. More and more schools are turning to computers to keep track of grades, but there are still many schools that record grades using the old fashioned gradebook.

  Keeping all grades in one gradebook (either paper or computer based) without a back-up could be disastrous if your gradebook got lost or your school's computer system crashed. However if you keep grading sheets for each subject you teach in separate files, you'll always have a record of your student's performance.

- **Things to be copied folder**
  Some schools let teachers photocopy whatever they want whenever they want. Many schools have a special person whose job is specifically to make copies, while still others will only allow you to make a set number of photocopies per week. If there's something

you want copied, put it in your "To be copied" folder immediately. This way, all your copies are together and ready to go at a moments notice. Also, if there is a limit to the number of copies you can have, you'll be able to prioritize. Keeping everything you want to have copied in one folder will save you time.

- **Completed photocopies folder**
  You can keep completed photocopies for upcoming lessons in this file or put the copies into your daily folders for the day you think you will use them.

- **Future tests folder**
  Keep tests in their own file, separate from your other papers. That way, if you need a student to get something from the crate, the test won't be seen. You can keep tests in the back of your filing cabinet or in the milk crate in an unmarked folder.

- **Items-to-be-filed folder**
  Most teachers have a tendency to stack papers that need to be filed. Instead of having a huge pile, keep a separate folder for anything that needs to be filed away and do your filing as often as possible so it doesn't get out of hand.

  Things to be filed might include students' work, important notes from home, original copies of tests, ideas from magazines, or copies of lesson plans. If you don't have time to keep up with your filing, at a minimum make sure you file away those items pertaining to students' work or any communications with parents. It's always helpful to be able to grab a student's work or the results of your last parent conference at a moment's notice.

Remember: Make extra copies of tests so you'll have a key for correcting.

Non-Teaching Crate

Here you will keep the files that are not directly related to teaching, but that still relate to your classroom. You will want to keep the following folders:

- **To do folder**
  No matter where you're teaching there will always be forms to be completed. Whether the forms are for administration, parents, other teachers, or staff members, the paperwork can sometimes seem endless. Keep a "To Do" file close by your desk and, once you've place something side it, leave it there until it's 100% completed. This type of work is easy to take home and complete if you can't get to it at school, but if you don't organize it you'll risk never getting it done.

Organizing Your Paper Trail

Nightmare is the word that best describes my first book order experience. After collecting all the students' orders, it took me ages to figure out how to complete the master order form. Then it was off to the office to battle with the fax machine. Once I finally figured out how to get the fax machine working, I sent the fax off and tossed the children's order stubs into the garbage, thinking I was ahead of the game because I had everything on the fax master sheet. The book order arrived, but it took so long that many kids had forgotten what they ordered. Other children didn't know which books were theirs because their parents had completed the order. And to top it all off, the book club had made substitutions so I couldn't figure out what book belonged to which child. I'll take writing report card comments over completing book club orders any day!!

- **Book order folder**

  Book orders seem to be more popular with students at the beginning of the year, which makes them a great way to get your classroom library going, but completing book orders can be time consuming if not done correctly. However, a few simple suggestions will save you a lot of time and headaches.

  o Send home a note to parents with clear instructions regarding payment and due date for book orders. Tell them that payment should be made in the form of a check to the book club company and *not* the school. If parents do send in cash, either keep it and write your own personal check or send the money back home requesting that the parents resubmit the order with a check.

  o When the money comes in, make sure the student's check matches the order amount (one incorrectly calculated order can mix up the entire class bill), and ensure the student's name is included on the order stub.

- Before you've mailed or faxed the master book order, make a copy. Also, keep the individual student order stubs until the books arrive, so that the books can be easily distributed.

Keep everything (the master book order copy, your fax confirmation, and the children's stubs) for that month's book order in a folder so you can check off names when the books arrive. Completing book orders can be time consuming, but the points you earn towards building your class library can make it worth the effort.

- **Future events folder**
  This folder should include:
  - master copies of the school calendar
  - master schedule of faculty meetings
  - all field trip information
  - schedules and information pertaining to all school events

Keeping track of what's going on at the school is very important. You can count on some type of event to disrupt your schedule on a weekly basis. Every school has its book fairs, school performances, guest speakers, and field days, so don't be surprised if during the holiday season, before a break, or at the end of the year there are two or three events happening a week!

Have a system to track missed work for absent students.

Make sure you keep master copies of any schedules you receive from the office. If you receive an update regarding a school event, write it on your calendar and then file it in this "Future Events" folder. File papers chronologically from front to back, so you can easily locate event information. After an event has taken place, remove its paper from your file, so the next school event will be in the front.

The future events folder and your teacher calendar are probably the best way you can keep track of what's happening in the school.

- **New student folder**
  Keep copies of whatever papers you sent out at the beginning of the school year to your students. Be sure to include medical and emergency information, school policies, a supply list, lunch information, and any information from the specialty area teachers. This way, if new students transfer in during the year, you can simply pull out the papers and send them home.

- **Missed assignments folder**
  Having a student absent is very frustrating, especially when you have to keep track of the work he's missed. The more students that

Organizing Your Paper Trail

are absent, the more complicated it becomes to track individual assignments.

To make this process easier, use a "Missed Assignment" paper. Just place a folder on the student's desk with a "Missed Assignment" paper stapled to the front. As you assign work during the day, write it down on the sheet; if you hand papers out during the day, drop them on the desk. At the end of the day, gather all the papers and put them inside the folder.

When the student returns, give the folder with the missed assignment schedule to the student. Be sure to keep a copy of the schedule for yourself. As the student completes the work missed, he can check it off. Once everything is finished, the student can hand in the sheet and the folder so you can correct all the work.

Make sure you've established a policy from the beginning of the year regarding how long you'll be giving students to make up the work. A general guideline is two days for every day missed. Obviously you can make accommodations on an individual basis, but it's best to have a policy in place from the first day of school.

- **Class communication folder**

  In this file, keep a parent phone number list, as well as copies of volunteer schedules, room mom information, and copies of classroom letters that you have sent to parents.

- **Field trip folder**

  In this file keep copies of upcoming trip itineraries, permission slips, and office papers that relate to field trip.

Outside Class Crate

Meetings, conferences, communications with other teachers on staff, workshops, all these are part of your job and will likely take place outside of your classroom. To keep track of papers and other details, set up the following folders in your crate or cabinet drawer:

- **Specialty area folder**

  You may receive information from the librarian, the music teacher, or other specialty area teachers. It's easiest to keep all of this information together.

- **To the office folder**
  Keeping yourself organized means getting all correspondences to the appropriate parts of the school. At the beginning of the year, find out which papers go where—in some schools lunch menus go directly to the office, in others they go to the lunchroom.

- **Items for others folder**
  There will be things that you will need to give to other teachers or other staff members. If there is email in your school, then most correspondence will take place through the computer. If not, you can utilize the teachers' mailboxes to distribute notes, memos, or other papers to staff members. Keep a separate folder for these items and take the folder with you when you go to the office. This way you get all your mailing done at one time. Even if you do have email, maintaining this folder is a good idea. Often parents send in notes for their child's other teachers and ask you to pass them along.

- **Grade level folder**
  A grade level folder can easily be brought to meetings, and contains any information you want to share with other teachers in your grade. Smaller schools may have only two teachers per grade level whereas larger schools can have many more. Whether the teachers work as a team or not, you'll probably have information and papers you'll want to share and questions you'll want to ask.

- **Workshop folder**
  When you are at workshops you're usually bombarded with handouts and other kinds of printed materials. Afterwards, you'll often receive correspondence and follow up materials. Keeping a file allows you the chance to look through all the papers later.

- **Information for parents folder**
  During the year you'll come across papers you may wish to give to parents regarding their child—articles from magazines, information about learning styles, or just something you think a particular parent may be interested in. Keep these papers together in a file until you can get them to the parent.

Student Work Crate

Keep a work file for each student in this crate. After you distribute tests and papers during the week and review it with students, have them place it in their work file. At the end of the day or week, students pull the file and pop everything straight into their daily or Friday folder.

Student work crates allow you to keep all papers going home organized and easily accessible.

Private Crate

Here you will keep files to which only you and your assistant have access. For these files if you don't have a filing cabinet, we recommend purchasing a small lockable one. If you must use a crate, keep it separate and secure from the others by storing it in a locked cabinet, or underneath your teaching desk. You will need to keep the following files in this crate:

- **Student file folders**
  Keep two files for every student. You will need a **Personal file** to hold all report cards, conference forms, notes from parents, student evaluations, emergency and medical information, and any administrative concerns regarding the student. You'll also need a **Graded work file** to hold any of the student's work that you've decided to keep to show at parent-teacher conferences.

- **Parent information folder**
  This file contains parent phone numbers, addresses, email addresses, schedules, volunteer information, et cetera. Use these files at the beginning of the year to create your emergency contact index card ring.

Binders

Most of the above mentioned folders can be organized inside a binder just as easily as they can be placed in a crate. Though binders won't be practical for all your organizational needs, here are four binders that will keep everything in its place (be sure to use dividers and page protectors where appropriate):

- **Personal binder**
  Use a personal binder to keep important information at your fingertips. Make separate sections for: your grading information; any upcoming events (file your master copies of the school calendar, the faculty meetings, and the school events schedule here); relevant parent information, schedules and information for the school's specialty area teachers, master copies of grading sheets, missed assignment papers, and other frequently used forms; master copies of new student papers for new students; and any memos or updates from the administration. You can even include your personal calendar in this binder.

- **September–June binder**
  Create a binder with all your monthly holiday activities, seasonal teaching ideas, and other lesson ideas.

- **Skill-specific or subject binder**
  Keep all worksheets, tests, and ideas for the various subjects you teach organized in one binder. Keep the folder organized from September to June and you'll be ready to go the following year.

- **Theme binder**
  When teaching themes, keep all papers, tests, and overheads together, placing the materials in the binder in the order in which you'll teach them.

Plastic Tubs

Not everything is going to fit in a file, milk crate, or a binder. There will be many items that you'll want to keep together in one place, safe from water, heat, mold, mice or anything else that may be lurking in your classroom. Plastic tubs come in a variety of shapes, sizes and colors. They can be purchased inexpensively at large retail stores and are a good investment due to their durability. You can use them for:

- **Everyday storage**
  Over time you will collect supplies to use for projects and activities. Smaller items such as beads, thread, and stickers are easily lost, so use small plastic baggies or containers to store them individually. If you keep one big supply tub with the individual baggies or containers inside, you'll always have your arts and crafts supplies together.

- **Student supplies**
  Backpacks and lunchboxes are often items that end up on the floor if a coat closet is not part of your classroom setup. Use a large plastic tub to store the students' backpacks and lunches.

- **Learning centers**
  You will most likely change your learning centers throughout the year based on the skills you'll be teaching. As the year goes on, you'll want to replace the games that you use for skills review at the beginning of the year with more challenging games to reflect new concepts the children have learned. To increase the life expectancy of your games, when you have finished with the activities, place them in a plastic tub labeled by month or activity, and put it away until next year.

- **Theme units**
  One of the best uses for tubs by far is to store your thematic units. If you teach a specific theme each year, you'll be collecting supplies that accompany it. Take all the supplies you use—your books,

---

Growing up in an area that had snow, I was used to having a spot in my classrooms where students could hang up their coats and store their boots, backpacks and lunches. When I moved to a warmer climate I found there weren't any coat closets in the room, which eliminated a place for students to store their backpacks and lunches. I was very frustrated the first few weeks of school because no matter how hard students tried, backpacks and lunches always seemed to be on the floor and I always seemed to be stepping over them. To avoid this safety hazard in the classroom, eventually I went out and bought two big plastic tubs. As part of their morning routine, the students unpacked everything they needed from their backpacks and put their backpacks in the tubs; lunches went in a separate one. I was able to keep the tubs under the computer tables so they weren't in the way. Those tubs were one of the best investments I ever made!

magazines, maps, overheads, artifacts, videos, music and thematic binder—and place them inside the tub. As the theme comes around each year, all you need to do is pull out your tub and you are ready to go.

If you do plan on using tubs, storage may be an issue for some of the over-sized ones. If you have items which you will not need access to on a daily basis, consider storing these tubs at home or in an onsite storage facility at school (if possible). Smaller tubs can be easily stacked and placed in cabinets, drawers or on top of counters and cabinets. For larger tubs, where you'll be storing textbooks, backpacks and art supplies, look for out of the way places near your desk and under tables or counters.

"Darn it!! Foiled again by a plastic tub!!"

As a Last Resort

It's true: file folders, crates, tubs and binders are the best ways to organize your classroom. This whole *chapter* has been dedicated to using them. But there are those who will never achieve organizational nirvana. If you decide to do nothing else, at least start by getting yourself a tabbed notebook that is divided into sections. Keep memos, a calendar, and important phone numbers in there, and staple any loose papers that you need to hold onto inside. You can bring this notebook with you to meetings and conferences and use the lined paper inside to take notes. It's a small step towards being organized, but it's still a step nonetheless.

 Be careful when storing papers and books at home— humidity can ruin them so make sure your storage containers are air tight.

Organizing Your Paper Trail

Chapter 11

Organizing Your Students

Teaching students organizing strategies at the beginning of the year will save you time in the long run.

Now that you've organized yourself, it's time to get your students organized. The suggestions below can be used for students in all elementary grades, but you may need to simplify some of the procedures for kindergarten and first grade. You'll find that the majority of strategies involve you establishing the system while the students maintain it.

Being organized yourself helps teach students about responsibility. If your classroom is not organized you will find yourself wasting time and energy that could be better spent on other tasks. If you are over-organized, you run the risk of taking responsibility for tasks that should be the responsibility of your students (tracking their folders, keeping tabs on their supplies). You need to set guidelines that enable students to be both organized and accountable for their belongings.

Using Agendas

Most schools today provide students with agenda books to keep track of assignments. Assuming that your school does provide these books, there are various ways that agendas can be utilized: as a daily log for recording homework, as a communication vehicle with parents and as a tracking tool for missed work. In any event, here are some points to consider when using agendas in your classroom:

- Be sure you write down all homework and long-term assignments in the same spot in your classroom each day. Most teachers use their black boards but some use chart paper—pick one and be consistent.

- If homework is not due the following day, leave the information on the board until its due date. For long-term assignments, write the due date on the class calendar and write periodic reminders on the board.

- Decide when the students should write down their assignments. Some teachers write all the homework on the board first thing in the morning while others wait until the end of the day to post it. The most effective method is for you to write down the homework on the board as it is assigned during the day, and have the students write it down during their afternoon pack-up routine

- In the beginning of the year you may want to check agendas, especially in the lower grades, to make sure the students are writing everything down properly. Often teachers initial agendas and have parents do the same. Teachers have different policies on signing and checking agendas, so unless there's a school mandate, the choice will be yours.

- If you say you will be checking agendas then make sure you follow through with it. Parents often use the agendas to write notes to you and you always want to respond to a parent's question as quickly as possible.

- Agendas are a great place for you to record missed work so that the parent can see it's been missed. Remember, if you are going to write notes to parents in the agenda, be sure that you check it for the follow-up response.

- Encourage students to check off assignments in their agenda as they are completed. This simple step will aid them in keeping track of their work.

In addition to using an agenda for organization, have students use the monthly calendar, often included in the front of most agenda books, to plan the stages of a long-term assignment.

If your school does not provide agendas, you should have your students purchase one on their own or utilize a notebook or small pad for writing down assignments. A calendar-type notebook could work; also, as a last resort, a special notebook or writing pad for homework only will get students started on the right track.

If you use agendas for communicating with parents, be sure to check the agendas daily.

Organizing Your Students

Following Homework

During my first year of teaching I taught fifth grade. I remember the first time an angelic-looking child told me he had handed in an assignment and didn't know why I didn't have it. I turned the classroom, my house, and even my car upside down looking for it, to no avail. The following day I got a phone call from the child's parent. I was fully prepared to accept the blame for having lost the assignment... imagine my surprise to learn the assignment had never been completed to start with! I was shocked that a student had deliberately misled me. Ever since then, I've had a homework drop spot, and all homework goes into that spot. The students know where they need to put their homework, and when I collect the papers I check off each student's name. If the paper is not there, I don't have it.

Submitting Homework

As part of the students' morning routine, they should have to turn in their homework. Homework may be in the form of loose papers, workbooks, or notebooks. You may not always be able to check over homework the same day, but you should have procedures in place to ensure that the students have completed the assignments. You don't want to find out on Thursday that an assignment due last Tuesday was not turned in. Here are some suggestions for keeping track of homework.

Use letter trays for submitting homework, finished work, or work-in-progress.

- **Loose papers**
  The best way to collect homework is via a drop tray—when the students arrive, they drop their loose homework in. A standard letter tray works nicely, and if you'd like, you can have stacking trays for different subjects. Once they've deposited their homework, you collect it from there. Quickly count the assignments to ensure all work has been handed in.

- **Homework notebook**

    If you'd rather not have to deal with loose papers at all, have students staple loose homework papers into a homework notebook.

- **Notebooks and workbooks**

    You can have students leave their note or workbooks (open to the appropriate page) on their desks in the morning, so you can do a quick visual check to see if the assignment has been completed. Alternately, you can assign a homework space in the classroom where students turn in their open books allowing you to see right away who has completed the assignment.

Following Classwork

Because of the demands of the job, you won't always get to correct work as soon as students have completed it. If you need to delay correcting, you need to keep the papers and work from getting out of control.

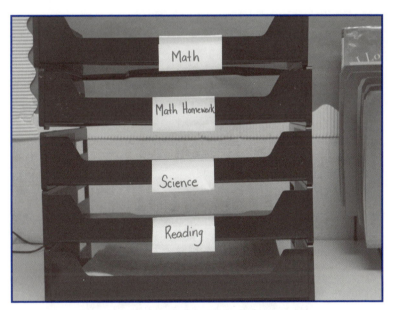

Use clearly labeled trays to help organize and track the students' classwork

To this end, have the children drop their completed loose papers in a clearly labeled letter tray so all the papers are together when you need to correct them. Use either one tray or a tray for each subject—the choice is yours. For note or workbooks that need to be corrected, simply have the students stack their books—open to the appropriate page—in the pre-assigned spot. When the books are closed, it means that you have corrected the material and the children need to check the pages and fix any mistakes.

Organizing Your Students

Another simple strategy to help you through correcting is to use bookmarks. At the beginning of the year, maybe as an art activity, have each child decorate several bookmarks with his name on them. Tell the children to clearly label the top of one side with the word "Finished" and the other with "Corrected." Students flag work that needs to be corrected with their "Finished" bookmark and you flip the bookmark to the "Corrected" side once you've checked the work.

Storing Student Materials

Supplies

At the beginning of the year students will arrive with pencils, glue, crayons, scissors, markers, et cetera, and they will all be wondering where to put their supplies. **No matter what the grade, each student should be responsible for having three sharpened pencils, an eraser, and a ruler ready to go at all times.** For all other supplies, there are a few options that can work in your classroom:

- **Shared supplies**
  Because it fosters sharing, a shared supply system is common in kindergarten and pre-kindergarten. In this system students' supplies are grouped together—and used by all the class. Some parents are not fond of this especially if they have purchased more expensive supplies for their child to use. To avoid this, be upfront at the begin-

Student supplies can be grouped together and shared, or kept separate with each student being responsible for his own supplies.

ning of the year about your supply sharing policy, explain why it works, and provide a detailed supply list so that parents have the option to purchase the same supplies for their child.

- **Grouped supplies**
  Supplies are grouped together by item but each child uses only the items belonging to him.

- **Individual supplies**
  Each student keeps his own supplies in his desk or supply bin. This approach is more common in older grades—a good rule of thumb being the older the student, the more responsibility they have for their supplies.

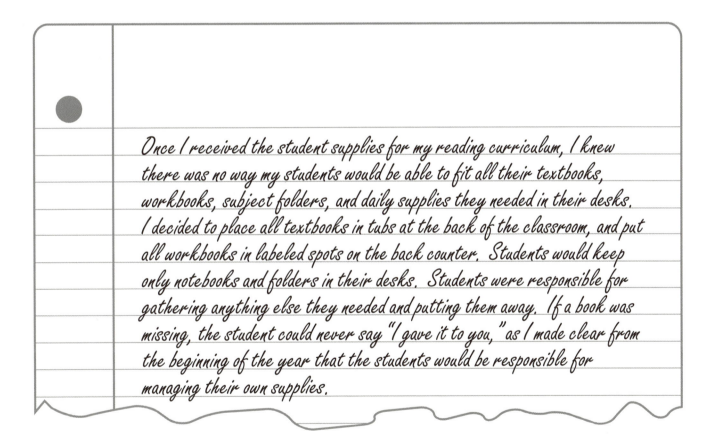

Once I received the student supplies for my reading curriculum, I knew there was no way my students would be able to fit all their textbooks, workbooks, subject folders, and daily supplies they needed in their desks. I decided to place all textbooks in tubs at the back of the classroom, and put all workbooks in labeled spots on the back counter. Students would keep only notebooks and folders in their desks. Students were responsible for gathering anything else they needed and putting them away. If a book was missing, the student could never say "I gave it to you," as I made clear from the beginning of the year that the students would be responsible for managing their own supplies.

Books

In addition to all the other things they have for school, students will have text, work and notebooks to keep track of. In older grades, lockers serve as a way of storing all of these, but very few younger grades have lockers. In your classroom some storage options to consider are:

Organizing Your Students

- **Individual storage**

  Students keep everything in their desks; however few desks are big enough to accommodate all the books, folders, notebooks and workbooks that a student will need, so this technique rarely works well.

- **Group storage**

Assigning a specific location for supplies (such as notebooks) keeps them out of the way until needed.

Have all folders color coded by subject.

You assign text and workbooks to each student, but store them somewhere in the classroom. Students hand out the books as needed, and then return them to the storage spot when not in use.

- **Crate/bin/tub storage**

  Crates, bins, or tubs are used to store the notebooks and folders, which are handed out to the students as needed.

You'll probably find that a blend of all three storage ideas works best.

Using Pocket Folders

Students need pocket folders to track loose papers, notes from teachers, and handouts for different subjects. Some folders can be kept in the students' desks, while others should be kept in a crate and handed out as needed.

When having your students set up folders, have all folders for the same subject the same color. It's often faster to find a missing folder when you know what color to search for.

If you don't have control over the supplies that come in at the beginning of the year, first see if the school will supply you with color folders. If not, purchase color stickers to place along the spine and front of the folders that students bring in. This will aid in quick and easy identification. Also make sure that students write their names and the subjects in black magic marker on each folder. Students should typically have:

Make labels for students ahead of time. This way all labels contain the information you want.

Work-in-Progress Folders

There may be times when students are working on papers that aren't finished but that you don't want floating around. Here are three suggestions for keeping track of these work-in-progress (W.I.P.) papers.

- Have students keep a W.I.P. folder which stays in their desks (some teachers refer to this as a desk folder). Any loose papers, especially if they are incomplete, go in there. Using one folder keeps all incomplete assignments in one place. This system also helps prevent students from forgetting to finish their assignments.

- Have a class tray for work-in-progress. This way, all work is in one spot and you can easily look through it to see if any child is falling behind.

- Store W.I.P. folders in one of your milk crates, giving you easy access to all W.I.P folders, so you will know who has work that is missing or that needs completing.

Daily Folders

Students should have one daily folder for taking papers backs and forth from school to home. The daily pocket folder has several uses:

- **Homework**
  Students take home and return any homework papers or assignments in their daily folders. It's a great organizational tool because it keeps all homework assignments together. They can also use this folder to bring in notes from home or any money that needs to be turned in. You can incorporate students turning in homework and emptying out their daily folder as part of the morning routine.

- **Graded work**
  If you'd rather send work home on a daily basis instead of waiting until the end of the week, use the daily or homework folder for this procedure also. Just make sure students are returning the work that you want for your files.

Organizing Your Students

- **Notes**
  Put any general notes that need to go home to parent in the daily folder. You may want to utilize the student's agenda to note missing work or to raise a more specific question, but the daily folder is the place that you can send home any class notices.

Friday Folder

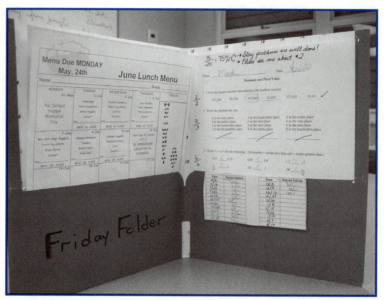

Use a Friday folder to send memos, classwork, and important notices home each week. Have parents initial the folder so you know they've seen what's inside.

Many schools have adopted the "Friday Folder." This is a pocket folder that goes home every Friday with all of the student's corrected work and is returned on Monday. If your school does not supply you with Friday folders it is an easy and extremely helpful procedure to implement in the classroom.

- Each child should have a folder designated as a Friday Folder.

- Inside the folder, staple a small piece of paper for the parent's signature, indicating that they've seen the work inside. There is a place to include the date for each Friday and a space for the parent's initials.

- To organize what's going home, you can use a milk crate and an individual folder to keep track of papers. Use one hanging folder for each student and organize them alphabetically. Whenever you have papers to go home during the week, put them in the appropriate hanging folder. Then, on Friday just transfer everything from the hanging folder to the Friday folder

- Everything that needs to go home at the end of the week should go in this folder. If you have an assistant in the classroom he can maintain the folders. If not, it will be up to you and the students. You can have a student be in charge putting anything that is not graded in the folders. Then all you have to do is distribute graded work to be placed inside. Remember: students should only handle their own graded work, and parent volunteers should never handle graded work.

- As you hand out and review graded papers during the week, have students place their own work inside their Friday folder. This cuts down on the "Friday Frenzy" because many papers have already been dealt with.

- Keep any items to be left at home on one side of the folder and anything that needs to be returned to school on the other. This helps parents when they are going through the folders over the weekend.

- Have a designated spot or letter tray for students to empty out their folders on Monday mornings. Once all the folders have been emptied, quickly look through them to make sure nothing has been left inside by mistake. The returned work can be filed at a later date.

- Remind students to place any notes from home, any money, or anything else that you need to see in its appropriate spot.

Papers on the left side of the folder get "left at home." Papers on the right come "right back to school."

When deciding whether to send graded work home daily or at the end of the week, consider the grade you're teaching: Parents in the younger grades like to see work daily whereas parents in older grades don't expect to check folders every night.

Other Folders

You can use however many folders you wish to help organize your students. Along with the work-in-progress, daily and Friday folders, we suggest you have students keep pocket folders for:

Organizing Your Students

You, not the students, should decide what folders need to be set up.

- writing (along with a writing workshop notebook with spiral binding)
- math
- reading and language arts
- social studies
- other content areas (can be added as required)

So that's it—organization in a nutshell. It may seem like a lot of work, but it's really just setting up and maintaining folders. The more organized you are the easier your first year will be.

Chapter 12

Organizing Your Time

Using Your Time Wisely

The Nine to Three Myth

During your first year, it's very easy to let school take over your life. You will have to spend more time during your first year than any other year on school work, but you need to keep a balance between work and your personal life. Decide how much time outside of your scheduled hours that you are going to dedicate to school work. Some teachers like to come to school early, others like to stay later in the day. Often teachers will take work home over the weekend, while others would rather stay late on a Friday to keep their weekend free.

Officially your day will begin about half an hour before the students arrive and will end about half an hour after students leave. Unofficially, it will start much earlier and stretch into night as you correct papers and plan lessons on your own time. Trying to get in a little earlier each day and then taking more work home to finish each night is an endless cycle that new teachers get caught in. While it might work to do this for a little while, you won't be able to keep it up. Start working within the time you have at school. If you use your time wisely, you can get a fair bit accomplished before students arrive and immediately after they leave. While it may be tempting to chit-chat in the morning or relax after a busy day, use this time to get yourself organized. Avoid the traps (the school office, the teacher's lounge, the hallways, or other teacher's classrooms) until you've finished what you need to do.

 Make sure you take time for yourself during the year.

Organizing Your Time 81

"Oh hi officer. I thought I'd just try and get a head-start on the day . . ."

Set a cut off time to keep school work from taking over your personal life.

Grade Level Cooperation

Making copies, laminating, getting papers to and from the office and the like are all things that take you out of your classroom. Creating tests, making a class newsletter, and gathering supplies are things that keep you in the classroom but eat up your planning time. Work with other teachers to minimize your efforts and maximize your results on these types of activities. Try dividing up:

- **Curriculum**
  If there's more than one teacher for the grade level, each teacher can be responsible for a curriculum area. Each teacher plans the lessons and assessments for his area then shares it with all the teachers. If you're really lucky you might be able to rotate classes so you just teach your area to all the classes on your grade level. Even without switching, sharing the curriculum gives everybody a break.

- **Special projects**
  If teachers on your grade level don't want to share subject area curriculum, thematic projects, book reports, or holiday activities are other areas that can be shared. If your grade level is going to be reading several novels during the year, each teacher can plan the activities and assessment for one novel and then share them with the other teachers. The same can be done with a thematic project or with activities planned for the holidays.

- **Administrative requirements**

    The administration often requires weekly newsletters, monthly updates, or term outlines for the grade level. If the requirements are the same for each teacher in your grade, sharing these responsibilities will cut down on the amount of time you personally need to spend on each one.

- **Clerical items**

    Making copies, laminating, or formulating worksheets and tests can be duties shared by teachers in your grade level. Arrange a rotating system where you each devote one planning period a week to make copies, check supplies, and other clerical tasks for your grade.

You may find yourself in a school where teachers are willing to cooperate on all or none of the above. If the latter is the case, try to find at least one other teacher with whom you can share some of these duties and you'll save yourself time in the long run.

Don't forget to utilize your parent volunteers in the classroom. Some might have half an hour after school while waiting for their child to finish an after school activity. Other parents, who may not be able to come into the classroom, may be willing to create games or activities at home. Don't spend your valuable time planning parties. Hand the task over to your room mom or other parents who are willing to help out, and simply supervise their preparations.

Getting a Helping Hand

First year teachers feel swamped, and if they say they don't feel swamped, they're lying! Accept the fact that you will never accomplish everything that you plan to do. Instead of feeling frustrated, use the first year as a learning year. Make notes to yourself after each topic you teach so you'll know what you can change for next year. Each year, pick a curriculum area to strengthen. Whether it's reading strategies, improving your writing program, or implementing more hands on activities in math, focus on one area and work your hardest on that. If you try to do everything to the best of your ability you'll wind up doing nothing well.

There are people around you that can help lighten your load at school. When starting out, make sure you get help from the following sources:

Mentor Teacher

Some schools have beginner teacher programs where you are assigned a mentor or model teacher who will guide you through your first year. If not, find one or two teachers who have been at your school for a few

You'll be eager to prove yourself as responsible during your first year, but don't give other teachers a free ride— you might burn out and they might expect even more from you next year.

Organizing Your Time

*"Welcome to Mountain Valley school.
I'll be your model teacher for the year."*

years. Introduce yourself and ask if you can use them as a mentor teacher. (You'll want a mentor teacher so you don't have to run to the principal every time you have a question.) The other teachers on your grade level will be busy enough trying to keep you up-to-speed on grade level matters so it's best to have somebody outside the grade level act as your mentor.

Teacher Assistant

A teacher assistant is a worker who is hired to help the teacher with tasks in the classroom such as copying, grading, and working with small groups of students. This is not to be confused with a teacher aide, who is assigned to one student with special behavioral or medical educational needs.

If your school does employ teacher assistants, you may have an assistant for your entire grade level, or you may have a part-time or full-time assistant in your classroom. Here are some basic guidelines for working with assistants in your room:

- Assistants should be treated as, and should conduct themselves as, teachers. Students need to have the same respect for assistants as they do for you.

- Assistants are not in the classroom to be the students' friend. They should expect the same behavior from the students as you do. You should feel confident when leaving your students in the care of the assistant, and not have to worry about his ability to keep control of the classroom.

- As the teacher, you are ultimately responsible for what gets done and what doesn't get done in the room. You should be aware of everything that goes on in the classroom, everything that gets marked or graded, and everything that goes home to parents. Therefore, choose carefully when assigning tasks to assistants. If an assistant grades your papers inaccurately, the final responsibility falls to you. You cannot say to a parent, "I had Mrs. Jones, our assistant, grade these and apparently she made a mistake."

- Do not have an assistant grade long answer or essay-type questions. If you are grading correctly, then you know what information is necessary for full credit. An assistant is not aware of a student's capabilities and cannot judge whether or not to give partial credit for answers.

- Establish the routine you want the assistant to follow each time he comes into your classroom. Even if you have an assistant that only comes in once a week or once a month, make sure you are ready ahead of time with very clear procedures for him to follow. Here are some suggestions on what to have assistants do:

    o Clerical work such as making copies, filing, or distributing notes to the office and other areas of the school

    o Work with small groups or individual children (under your guidance)

    o Check to see if all homework has been turned in

    o Grade simple papers, such as fill in the blanks, true/false, or multiple choice

    o Grade spelling words

    o Complete book orders

    o Make and rotate center activities

    o Organize the classroom

Each year that you teach, pick one curriculum area that you want to improve in.

Planning Ahead During the Year

Teaching the students is your main responsibility as a first year teacher. Simply put, your ultimate goal is to ensure that all of your students possess the exit skills in the areas of academics and personal growth they need to be successful in the following year. To do this, you have to examine and evaluate the curriculum. Don't assume that the methods suggested by the manual are the only way to teach the concepts—after all, you know your students the best, and need to be prepared to adjust the curriculum and your teaching methods accordingly. The most important thing is that the students learn the prescribed skill: how you get that across to them is up to you. Whether you follow the manual, use supplementary materials, or teach standing on your head—it doesn't make any difference as long as they get the skill.

Getting acquainted with a new curriculum is one of the most time consuming parts of teaching, but once you've done it you'll be ahead the following year. This book won't go into detail and provide you with intricate lesson plans or theme units, but will give you an overview of the types of planning you'll need to do. There are three levels of planning that will help you become familiarized with your new curriculum.

Year at a Glance

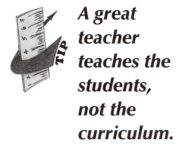

A great teacher teaches the students, not the curriculum.

Before the year starts, look through your entire curriculum and familiarize yourself with the skills the students will be expected to have at the start of the year, as well as the ones they will be expected to learn before the year is over. Try and create a scope and sequence that plots out what skills the students should master by logical points throughout the year. If you have other grade level teachers, do this together. Looking ahead helps you see places where you can plan for long-term projects, link chapters, or integrate other areas of the curriculum into one. Don't try to memorize the whole flow of each program. Right now you are just trying to give yourself a basic overview of the year so that you'll know which direction to head when you begin your term planning.

Term Planning

Each term, take the time to look through the material that you will be attempting to cover. Now is the time to focus and develop the specific projects, book reports, or other long-term assignments that you'll be having the students complete. Planning field trips, booking guest speakers and other meaningful learning experiences should all be taken care of in the beginning of the term so that you have a clear outline of not only what the curriculum entails, but also of how you are going to use outside resources to make it more interesting. When you are term planning, you'll have a better idea of what days you'll be missing due to school holidays, when you'll need to assign reviews and tests, and also when report cards are due. All these factors influence how much time you can allot to particular areas that need to be studied during the term, so you can make accurate lesson plans.

Lesson Planning

Most of your time is going to be spent teaching, so it's very important that your lessons are organized and well thought out. It's always better to over-plan, while accepting that you're not going to get everything done. Before you decide to teach a lesson you need to review and consider:

- the skill you are going to be teaching
- the outcome of the lesson for the student
- how the student will demonstrate that they have understood the concept
- how you will evaluate the lesson to see if it could be improved for future use

Know what your school requires for lesson plans. Some schools may just want you to note the manual pages you'll be using while others will want full blown behavioral objectives with a detailed outline of each lesson. In some schools, plans may need to be turned in each week for review by the principal, while in others, plans are simply for the teacher's use. No matter what your school requires, it is wise to keep detailed lesson plans for your own personal development. The more you've thought about the lesson and its outcome, the better your lesson will be.

Whenever deciding on a new topic to teach, remember to look at long-term goals and then work backward. Decide what overall skills you want the students to master and then examine how you can break these skills down into smaller sets of lessons. Don't, however, depend on the teacher's manual too heavily when you're creating your lessons—even though the manual may develop the lesson for you, these lessons should be used as a guide only. You know your students and you know yourself. If you have a better way to deliver the required skills to your students, do it. Although it's your first year of teaching, trust yourself.

Sections of a Good Lesson

To deliver a good lesson, you must ensure a bridging element, a body component, an application session and a wrap-up opportunity all exist in the available amount of time. Typically a lesson will be between 45 minutes and one hour. Often though you'll have a shorter amount of time and will need to modify your lesson. Regardless of the amount of time, it's important to include all elements. Here's a more detailed look at each aspect of a well thought out lesson.

- **Bridging**
  You should begin with about a five minute introduction to the lesson that ties together what the students already know to what they will be taught. The introduction should also peak their interest.

Keep a balance. The best lesson plans are well thought out and detailed, but can be modified the instant the teacher sees that students are not grasping the concept.

Improve your teaching by assessing the outcome of your lessons

Organizing Your Time

Stick to the important topic: don't try to do too much in the one lesson.

- **Body**
The body of the lesson should be about a fifteen minute lesson on the new topic. Students should be actively involved through discussion and exploration of the skill or concept.

- **Application**
Allow about twenty to forty minutes of work (depending on the grade) for the students to apply the skill they've just learned. During this time the teacher should be circulating to work individually with students who might be experiencing difficulty. You may want students to work individually, in partners or in groups.

- **Wrap-up**
Allow about five minutes where you bring the students back together and, as a whole group, have the students explain their understanding. Now is a good time to assess and see if there are any students confused about the new skill or concept.

 You need to constantly assess to see if students are understanding and ultimately mastering the concepts being taught. It is important to understand that assessment is not necessarily grading. Observation, verbal assessment, and classroom work are all quick assessments tools you can use.

Chapter 13

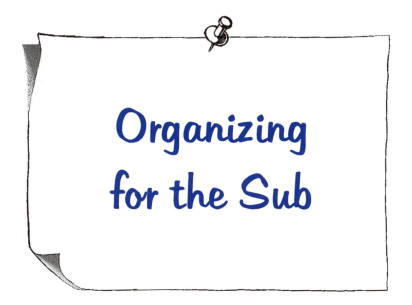

Organizing for the Sub

Every teacher, no matter how hard they try not to, will get sick or have to miss school at some point in their teaching career. Being prepared *before* the event occurs by creating a substitute folder, having back up lessons, and creating long-term substitute plans will help ensure things run smoothly if you can't be there.

What to Do When You Can't be There

Schools often ask for a set of substitute plans at the beginning of the year. Whether or not this is required at your school, you should prepare a set of plans for a substitute anyway.

Most likely you will know in advance that you are going to be out, but there is always the chance of an emergency. Simple tips to keep in mind are:

- The substitute's job is to carry out simple plans and keep control over your class. Therefore, your instructions should be simple and clear. Don't leave any plans that are confusing or require specific, uncommon knowledge about a subject. On the other hand, don't leave work that will only take a few minutes for students to finish.

- Try to cancel any parent volunteers scheduled when there is a substitute teacher. This may not be possible if your absence was unplanned, but in general it's best to avoid the added stress of a parent volunteer on the substitute teacher.

 Arrange with another teacher to check on the sub and students when either of you are out.

- At the beginning of the year discuss with the students the behavior you expect from them when a substitute is in your class—it should be no different than their behavior when you are there. Leave instructions for the substitute to write down the names of students who misbehave and the names of those who work hard and stay on task. Be sure to follow up with rewards and consequences when you return to school.

- Try to team up with a teacher in your grade level and agree to check on each other's classes when there is a substitute. Let the children know about the arrangement; chances are if your students know another teacher will be checking in, they will be more likely to behave.

The Substitute Folder

Keep a substitute folder full of important information and lesson plans.

Whether you know you will be out in advance or it's a last minute absence, preparing a substitute folder at the beginning of the year will save you time in the long run. Preparing a simple form with all your important classroom information in advance will serve as a quick reference for any substitute you have during the year.

Activities for a Substitute

Ideally a substitute will come into your class and be able to follow your original lesson plans for that day. Remember, the substitute is not you. If there is a specific skill or a new concept that you feel you should teach, then you need to leave alternative work to fill the time. Here are suggestions for just this kind of alternative work:

- Have a set of math problems for the substitute to write on the board for students to complete in their notebooks.

- Have *Weekly Readers, Time for Kids,* or other news articles designed for students saved for when you are out. Write up some questions to go along with the articles. The substitute can either make copies of the questions for the class, or he can write the questions on the board.

- Keep simple math games available.

- Copy a few logical thinking puzzles out of a book and leave it for the substitute. The students can work in small groups trying to solve the puzzles.

- Have the substitute rotate the students through four or five centers.
- Keep a chapter book that you are reading to your students available so a sub can pick it up and keep going.

Planning for Long-term Leave

Sickness, a death in the family, and other unforeseen circumstances may result in you unexpectedly having to leave your class on very short notice for an undetermined amount of time. In some cases that may mean you are out only for a week; in other cases you may be on indefinite leave. By most definitions, a long-term substitute is a substitute who is in the classroom for ten or more consecutive days, and will expected to take over all your duties. If you are out for an extended amount of time, keep in mind the following:

- You may have little say in what lessons are taught, or what occurs in the classroom once you are gone. In most cases, the sub will be guided by the principal (not you) to determine what needs to be done.

- If you can, offer assistance to make it a smoother transition for your students. Depending on how long you were in the class before your absence, you may need to help the sub with the report cards, handling parent-teacher conferences, and future lesson planning.

- Indicate specific things that you do not want altered (your behavior management strategy) but keep in mind that, for the time being, you are not the one in charge of the classroom.

Ideally, if you are out for an extended amount of time, the substitute will follow the teacher manual. However, you should prepare a set of long-term substitute plans to provide added support. When many teachers think *sub plans* they automatically equate them with worksheets. This doesn't need to be the case. During the summer or at the beginning of the school year create a complete set of math and reading sub plans. They shouldn't depend on the curriculum manuals in the classroom, (you won't know where you'll be in the curriculum when an unforeseen absence occurs) but the plans need to be appropriate for your grade level and should be able to be implemented by anyone taking over your class. You only need to create these plans once, and then you'll have them for as long as you are teaching that grade. Keep the plans in your long-term sub folder in your classroom, or give them to your principal to have "just in case."

Always stash away a few activities in a folder labeled "Backup Substitute Activities." That way, there will be items available if the sub runs low on things to do.

Organizing for the Sub

When developing long-term sub plans, it's wise to:

- Use a theme. Create lessons based on a theme that your class has yet to study. For each day, plan one math and one reading lesson, along with a social studies, science, and art activity. You might consider purchasing five story books that relate to your theme and structuring a full day of activities around each one.

- Pool with other teachers. Create a unit or a subject-specific set of activities. Give a copy to each member in your pool, and take a copy of the units they have created and place in your long-term sub folder.

- Collect activities. Keep a file folder labeled *Back-up Sub Activities*. Any time you get activity ideas from a magazine, a web site, or from another teacher, pop them into your sub folder. After a few months you will have a collection of back-up activities.

- Create a novel study—a unit of inter-disciplinary lessons that are based on one novel the students read in class. You can create the lessons yourself or, to save time, purchase set of novel study lesson plans from a teacher supply store. Watch for warehouse sales and pick up the novels so that you have a complete class set.

Summary Section Two

- In addition to teaching you will be expected to complete numerous tasks associated with your students, parents, other teachers, and administrators. In order to keep track of everything going on inside and outside your classroom, you need to stay as organized as possible.

- Whenever parents or administrators are expected in your classroom, be sure to have everything as organized and neat as you can, with any items needed for parent volunteers ready to go.

- Keep your desk as clean as possible. Having a small teacher work area for supplies is a great way to achieve this.

- Use daily folders to help organize daily teaching activities or meetings.

- Use a teacher calendar to remind you of any and all important events.

- Use a classroom calendar to help the students keep track of tests, project due dates, school events, field trips, school closings or anything else that pertains specifically to your students.

- Use letter trays to help keep loose papers together, and keep both you and your students organized. Always keep loose papers clipped together after you remove them from the trays so nothing gets lost.

- If you do not have enough file cabinet space in your room, use hanging files inside milk crates to store the variety of folders you'll need.

- Teach students how to use their agendas to keep themselves organized. Be sure your students are writing down their assignments each night. In addition, show them how to use their agendas to plan out long-term assignments.

- Have a plan for homework submission that is comprehensive enough to include notebooks, workbooks, and tracking loose papers. Remember to check all homework as soon as possible to make sure each student completed the assignments.

continued on page 94

Summary Section Two—*cont'd*

- Decide how to store student supplies, including textbooks, notebooks, and workbooks. Students will not be able to fit all their supplies in their desks, so only keep the most important items there and store the rest elsewhere in the classroom.

- Use folders for students to organize their work. The daily folder contains work that goes home each day while the Friday folder goes home on Friday and comes back on Monday. In addition, students should have a work-in-progress folder where they keep all the work they haven't yet completed, as well as folders for each subject area. Remember to have students label the outside of all folders clearly and to color coordinate the folders by subject.

- Once you set up a system and teach the students, the year will progress much more smoothly.

- There's no such thing as a nine to three school day. Don't get overwhelmed with all that has to be done.

- Use the resources around you and don't be afraid to ask for help from your grade level teachers, mentor teacher, and teaching assistant.

- Make sure you plan out what areas you will want your teacher assistant to help you with in the classroom.

- Plan effectively by looking at the curriculum to be covered for the whole year, then breaking the curriculum down into sections for terms and individual lessons.

- Don't get caught off guard: have substitute plans ready in the event that you are out for a few days.

- Create backup plans that can be used if you are away from school on indefinite leave.

Notes

Organizational Checklist

Item	Page No.	Yes	Not For Me	Comments
Daily Folder	53	☐	☐	_____
Calendar				
Teacher	54	☐	☐	_____
Classroom	54	☐	☐	_____
Teacher Board	54	☐	☐	_____
Letter Tray				
Tray #1 Notes from home	57	☐	☐	_____
Tray #2 Notes going home	58	☐	☐	_____
Tray #3 Work to be corrected	58	☐	☐	_____
Tray #4 Work to be recorded	58	☐	☐	_____
Tray #5 Work to go home	58	☐	☐	_____
Tray #6 Work to be filed	59	☐	☐	_____
Teacher Crate				
Folders for September—June activities	59	☐	☐	_____
Folders for specific skills or subjects	59	☐	☐	_____
Folders for themes	60	☐	☐	_____
Folders for lesson plans	60	☐	☐	_____
Folders for substitute plans	60	☐	☐	_____
Folders for grading sheets	60	☐	☐	_____
Folder for papers to be copied	60	☐	☐	_____
Folder for completed photo-copies	61	☐	☐	_____
Folder for future tests	61	☐	☐	_____
Folder for items-to-be filed	61	☐	☐	_____
Non-Teaching Crate				
Folder for things to do	61	☐	☐	_____
Folder for book orders	62	☐	☐	_____
Folder for future events	63	☐	☐	_____
Folder for new student	63	☐	☐	_____
Folder for missed assignments	63	☐	☐	_____
Folder for class communication	64	☐	☐	_____
Folder for field trips	64	☐	☐	_____

TIPS, Inc.

Organizational Checklist—*cont'd*

Item	Page No.	Yes	Not For Me	Comments
Outside Class Crate				
Folder for specialty areas	65	☐	☐	_____
Folder for items going to the office	65	☐	☐	_____
Folder for items for other staff members	65	☐	☐	_____
Folder for grade level meetings	65	☐	☐	_____
Folder for workshops	65	☐	☐	_____
Folder for information for parents	65	☐	☐	_____
Student Work Crate—Folders				
Folder for each student	65	☐	☐	_____
Private Crate				
Folder for students	66	☐	☐	_____
Personal folder	66	☐	☐	_____
Graded work folder	66	☐	☐	_____
Folder for parent information	66	☐	☐	_____
Binders				
Binder for personal information	67	☐	☐	_____
Binder for September—June Activities	67	☐	☐	_____
Binders for specific skills or subjects	67	☐	☐	_____
Binders for thematic units	67	☐	☐	_____
Plastic Tubs				
Tubs for everyday storage	67	☐	☐	_____
Tubs for student supplies	68	☐	☐	_____
Tubs for learning centers	68	☐	☐	_____
Tubs for thematic units	68	☐	☐	_____

TIPS, Inc.

Friday Folder Insert

Date	Parent Initials

Date	Parent Initials

Date	Parent Initials

Date	Parent Initials

Date	Parent Initials

Date	Parent Initials

TIPS, Inc.

Substitute Teacher Information

Student Procedures

Student arrival time and location:	
Student dismissal time and procedures:	
Morning routine:	
Specialty area classes and times:	
Lunch time and procedures:	
Recess time and procedures:	

Teacher Procedures and Resources

Helpful teachers:	
Helpful students:	
How to contact the office:	
Office extension numbers:	
Carpool days and procedure:	
Lunchroom days and procedure:	
Fire drill procedure:	

Behavior

Rewards and consequence procedure:	
Students to keep an eye on:	
Please list any students with good/poor behavior here:	
Comments:	

TIPS, Inc.

Reproducibles

Missed Assignments

Student: _____

Date: _____

Subject	Monday	Due	Tuesday	Due	Wednesday	Due	Thursday	Due	Friday	Due
Math										
Reading										
Grammar and Spelling										
Science										
Social Studies										
Other										

Bookmarks

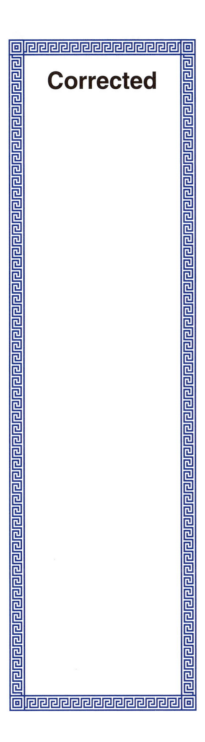

Corrected

Finished

SECTION THREE

The Good, The Bad, and The Ugly—Behavior Management in The Classroom

- ◆ Setting behavior expectations
- ◆ Combining praise, consequence, and meaningful rewards
- ◆ Motivating students with incentives
- ◆ Consequences for negative actions
- ◆ Handling disruptive behaviors
- ◆ Making adjustments for special circumstances

IN THIS SECTION

Chapter 14

The ABCs of Behavior Management

A simple definition of behavior management in the classroom is keeping the whole class under control on a daily basis, while at the same time dealing with and modifying the disruptive behavior of individual students. Unfortunately, there is nothing simple about managing thirty children in a classroom! Behavior management is complex—it not only involves how you handle disruptive behavior, but also includes how you run your class to minimize its occurrence. Your ability to properly manage your classroom will largely determine how effective a teacher you are. The most planned, hands-on lessons will be lost if you do not have effective control over your class.

 The less structure in your class the more opportunity you provide for off-task behavior.

You might think that class behavior depends solely on the *type* of students you have, but this is a misconception. Though every class may have students with particular behavior issues, the conduct of a class is not determined by the students—it is determined by the teacher. It starts with the kind of environment that you establish in your classroom.

- Is the classroom warm and welcoming?

- Do you greet the children each morning?

- Is there time during the day for students to share important news in their lives?

- Do you comment on student *effort* as well as *ability*?

- Have you set the standards for acceptable and non-acceptable behaviors?

The ABCs of Behavior Management

- Do children see you openly communicating with their parents?
- Are you modeling the behaviors that you expect to see from your students?
- Are the students aware of the class rules?
- And most importantly, through your actions and consistency have you established yourself as the person in charge in the classroom?

Effective classroom management results when a warm classroom environment is created by a teacher who sets and maintains behavioral standards. This is done by modeling acceptable behaviors, making your expectations clear to the students, and being consistent with rewards and consequences for appropriate and inappropriate behaviors. If a class is repeatedly engaging in disruptive behavior, chances are that one of these is out of place.

Positive interaction with students goes a long way.

The Power of Positive Praise

A smile, a wink, a kind word—sometimes teachers forget the smallest and easiest ways to reward a child. As you decide on what type of behavior plan you'll be implementing in your classroom, remember along with all the material reward and incentives, sometimes the simplest way to keep students on the right track is with a positive word. When you see a student working quietly or "doing the right thing," quietly tell the child you like the way he's working or catch his eye and give him a smile. Often this simple and gentle technique can keep a child on task. As well, positive praise goes far for the self-esteem of the child who is struggling academically. Remember, most students in elementary school care about what their teacher thinks, and a kind word or smile from you goes a long way.

Don't over do praise and offer it for every little thing because it will lose its meaning.

You as the Model of Behavior

You, not your students, set the standard for acceptable behavior in your class. A teacher who yells to get his students attention will have students who yell to get others attention. This means that you need to set the example for the behaviors you wish to see in your class.

Be a good role model for your students from the way you dress to the way you work.

Children will follow the example you set, even if it's a bad one.

> There are two things I do on the first day of school every year. First the children and I discuss class rules and come up with a class code. Then I tell them about a rule that I have never ever broken (of course they are always anxious to hear what comes next). I promise them that during the whole year, from August to June, I will never, ever yell at them, as a class or as an individual. I tell them that, in five years of teaching, I have never broken that promise to any class. And that, in return, I expect they will never, ever, yell at me. As well, I will never ever speak rudely or say anything that will hurt their feelings, and that I expect they will never speak rudely or say anything hurtful to me or their classmates. I remind them of this rule every day for the first week of school, and then periodically during the year. While the reminders are important, the most important thing for success is that I stick to the rule and model it—and I do, five years no yelling and counting . . .

The ABCs of Behavior Management

Chapter 15

From the First Day of School

Establishing a Class Code

During the first day of school, gather your students and establish a class code—a set of rules that the students try to follow. Some can be rules that you volunteer, like "No running in the classroom," while others can be suggested by the students. At the end, vote on six rules to keep and use to create a display board.

As new situations arise during the year, modify the rules, but always make sure the class code is in clear view for every student.

Determining a System for Your Class

During the first week of school students should be introduced to and accountable for the class behavior system. Your system should be clear, the rules concise and a consequence should be in place for those occasions when the rules aren't followed. In the first few days you'll need to explain:

- what system the class will use (positive or negative, public or private, individual or class)
- how it works and any incentive plan included
- how students can earn or lose on the system
- the time frame it covers
- the goal students are working towards

Display photos along with written class rules as a visual reminder of the rule.

108   You've Got the Job—Now Keep It

> *At the beginning of the year I explain to my students my most important rule: I call it 1-2-3-Out! It goes like this: The first time I notice a student doing something he shouldn't, I will give him a non-verbal reminder such as the "look," or a gentle touch on the arm. (Check your school's policy on this—some adhere to a strict no touching students rule. If so, do the "look" only.) The second time, I will say his name and remind him about what he should be doing. The third time, he will be asked to leave the classroom, and be sent to another teacher's room. That way each student knows they have a few chances to straighten out before they have to go. Often all it takes is a quick reminder of the "1-2-3 Out Rule" for students to think about what they should be doing and get back on task.*

> *On our class rules display, I include not only the rule, but a photo of children using that rule as well. Having a visual reminder next to the rule helps children see at a glance what they should be doing.*

- when the goal is redeemable
- the consequence for anyone caught cheating

You'll need to decide what time frame you want your behavior management system to cover. Running a behavior management system on a Monday to Friday basis can be difficult, as those are the days that are missed most often due to long weekends. If you want to use a weekly based system, have your week go from Tuesday–Tuesday, or Thursday–Thursday.

Follow the three C's for behavior management: be clear, be concise, and have consequences.

Parents should be made aware of how you plan to handle behavior in your classroom. You will need their support for your system and many parents will want to continue or follow up on your behavior management at home. Discuss your behavior plan during open house and send home a letter explaining it in detail. This will cut down on questions during the year.

Making Your Expectations Clear

As an inexperienced teacher, you may think that students have to be quiet all the time. With experience, you'll realize that there are times when some noise is acceptable, and times where absolute silence is required. In order for the students to know the difference, you'll need to tell them! For instance:

Absolute quiet time:	When tests are being taken, when someone else is talking, when it's reading time, when a guest speaker is present, during seatwork, during a fire drill, during all transition times (walking from one class to another)
Moderate noise:	During group work, a class discussion, or seatwork time
Loud but controllable:	During a class party, during recess

What Behaviors to Permit

Student Behaviors

Acceptable behavior is a personal issue that is different for every teacher. Some teachers don't mind if they call a student's name and the students replies "Yeah?" or "What?" however others do, and may make a rule that students try and answer with "Yes" instead of "Yeah." Others make it a point to ignore children that interrupt, while some teachers don't think about it one way or the other. Whatever rules you make, you must be sure and follow them—if you don't the students won't either.

There are small behaviors that you'll encounter every day that will take away from your teaching time. Create a plan of action for dealing with these interruptions. In the beginning of the year consider the level of action you will take for some of the following:

- tattling
- talking about other students/telling secrets

- interrupting
- disrespectful behaviors such as sighing, eye rolling, or shoulder shrugging when you are speaking
- copying other students work
- not listening
- talking all at once

There are certain behaviors that should **never** be permitted in class and that must be dealt with in the toughest way (a phone call to the parents, sent out of the classroom to another teacher's room, or in some cases straight to the principal's office) to discourage them from happening again. These include behaviors such as:

- physical violence (punching, hitting, biting)
- verbal threats
- stealing
- back answering/smart mouthing the teacher
- swearing

Students will only take rules seriously if you model the desired behavior and follow through with the consequence when a rule is broken.

Teacher Behaviors

New teachers sometimes expect that children will be well behaved and quiet at all times. But when behavior and noise escalate (as is bound to happen), a new teacher may panic at the loss of control and feel unsure as to how to redirect the class. Just as there are inappropriate student behaviors, there are inappropriate teacher behaviors as well. Getting frustrated, losing your cool or even yelling is something teachers find themselves doing, no matter how hard they try not to. Though you are bound to yell sometime in your career, there are alternatives ways to get students' attention that will save your voice and sanity, such as:

- flicking classroom lights on and off
- clapping a rhythm and having students clap back it back
- playing a piece of music that signals ATTENTION
- standing absolutely still, remaining silent, or staring at the clock or your imaginary wrist watch

Keep a bottle of water on your desk— staying hydrated will prevent you from losing your voice.

Having set rules and consequences doesn't make you mean, it makes you fair.

From the First Day of School

- ringing a bell

- mouthing your words and using exaggerated hand gestures—the students will stop what they are doing because they think they can't hear you

- showing an object that the children know means you need their immediate attention

- standing and counting wasted minutes which the class then pays back from their free time, play time, or other activities

It was before the Christmas break and my third grade students were excited, restless, and getting harder to handle. Finally, one afternoon, after spending all day trying to settle them, redirect behavior and get their attention, I had had enough. At 2:25 I stopped what I was I doing and wrote them a letter on the board. I explained that I was very disappointed in their behavior and that I expected much better of them, and that my disappointment was so strong I simply could not teach them any more that day. I instructed them to clean up, prepare to go home, and at 2:50 to dismiss themselves. When I completed the letter, I sat at my desk with my chin resting on my hands and watched them. They were instantly quiet. They went about their business, packing up, and being careful not to talk to other students. When anyone asked me a question, I simply refused to answer. I did not stand at the door, say goodbye, or anything. I just nodded towards the door at 2:50 and watched them trudge out, with sheepish looks on their faces. The next day everything was back to normal, I did not mention the event, and students' behavior was not a problem again. I didn't have to yell or loose my cool, and I know that my actions made a lasting impression on the students.

Chapter 16

Using Behavior Management in Your Class

We've all heard stories from our parents about the "good old days" when the teachers ruled supreme and students who didn't fall into place as soon as they set foot in the schoolyard were few and far between. Back then, children would come to school, do their classwork, and go home and do their homework. A quick look from the teacher, a verbal reminder to "straighten up," or the fear of getting sent to the principal's office was often all it took to get a student back on the right track. Refusing to do classwork, talking back to the teacher, or not completing homework was unheard of. Children had more respect for their teachers, and a bad report from school meant trouble once they got home.

The relationship between parents and teachers was different too. Years ago, teachers had more support from parents—the idea that "What the teacher says goes" was upheld in the classroom and reinforced at home.

Fast forward to the present, where teachers' responsibilities have gone above and beyond teaching. Any teacher with thirty or more years experience will tell you that today's students are different from the ones of years ago. More and more students are seeing school as a chore instead of an opportunity, and, unlike in the past, parent support for the teacher and the school is no longer assured. Because family structure and parenting styles have changed over the years, teaching responsible behavior and accountability often falls to the teacher. When a teacher has to spend more time concentrating on discipline than teaching, it can interfere with the students' learning. As such, teachers need

Always check you school's policy when designing rewards and consequences as part of your behavior management system.

Using Behavior Management in Your Class 113

Make sure parents are aware and on board with your behavior management system. It will cut down on problems if you have their support.

effective ways of managing behavior in their classrooms to minimize lost teaching time.

Guiding Behavior—Using Positives, Negatives, and a Reward Based System

Every effective teacher has a means by which to guide behavior in the classroom. Most use positive praise and class rules, but these alone are not enough. Focusing on positive praise doesn't allow you to deal with a negative behavior when it happens. "I really like it when you're not kicking Timmy" does **not** have the same impact as "Kicking Timmy is not allowed." And class rules cannot cover every behavior you wish (or don't wish) to see in your class—if they did, you'd have one hundred rules instead of five or six. Effective behavior management combines the use of positive praise, negative consequence and class rules with a reward based system.

Like most issues in education, there are two sides to the debate of using positive praise and rewards in the classroom to effect behavior. Without getting into the debate, suffice to say that balancing positive praise with negative consequence is a logical approach. After all: negative consequences are a part of life. Getting to work on time, driving the speed limit, and obeying the law all are real life responsibilities that, if ignored, result in negative consequences. It only makes sense that in school, positive actions and negative consequences will go hand in hand. Regarding rewards: either embrace the idea that rewarding students improves their behavior, or agree with those who believe that rewards devalue accomplishments by creating the expectation within students that unless they are rewarded, the task is not worth doing.

It's All about Balance

If you decide to use a rewards based system, **children should not be rewarded for every little thing that they do.** You want to reward students for doing the right thing, and for making improvements, but not for tasks that are part of their student responsibility. In real life, no one rewards you for getting up out of bed and going to work—it's part of your responsibility as an adult. You need to strike a balance. Don't confuse students by rewarding tasks that should be part of their school responsibilities.

Strong classroom management is a telltale sign of a good teacher.

Rewards work best when students know they *can* earn them, but are unsure of exactly *when* they will earn them. It can be a rather subjective area, but here are some points to keep in mind about rewards:

"All done—painted the walls, waxed the floors, and fixed that broken light socket. Do I get a reward?"

- **Save your voice**

    It's easy to reward students when they do exactly as they are asked, but it's better to reward them when they do something without having to be told (i.e. the whole class lines up quickly and quietly without any teacher direction).

- **Don't reward copy-cats**

    Sometimes you will see a child performing a task, unaware that you are watching. You reward that student and suddenly five others quickly do the same thing, hoping for a reward. They shouldn't get one.

- **Catch them being good**

    The student who is working while those around him talk, the child cleaning up a mess he did not make, or the child helping another without being asked are all candidates for rewards because they are performing a task without the expectation of reward.

- **Expect the eager beavers**

    Some students are motivated only by the reward, and will make a point of letting you know what they've done (i.e. "Ms. James, I cleaned the whole back counter without being asked.") A simple "Thanks" here is reward enough.

In any case, it is your classroom and the final decision is up to you. This section aims to provide you with the basics of how a behavior management system works, so you can decide what is best suited to you and your students.

Using Behavior Management in Your Class

Design your behavior management system based on the needs of the students in your class.

Students will learn your strategies quickly. What works with one student may not work with others, and what works one time may not work another, so while your system needs to be consistent in application it should be dynamic in nature. If you are going to use a behavior management system, before the students come through your door, you need to decide five things:

- when to use a positive or negative based system
- when to use a public or private behavior modification system
- when to reward students on an individual basis, in teams, or as a whole class
- what to use as the incentives for students
- what the consequences are of negative behaviors

Positive vs Negative Systems

Positive systems reward students for following the class rules, showing effort, and making good choices. Reinforcements are distributed when students are doing what they are supposed to do. Those that reach the goal by the end of the specified time period get a reward.

In a negative reward system the students start out with a set number of reinforcements which they strive to keep until the end of the specified time period. If they don't follow the rules, they can lose the reinforcements, but can (usually) earn them back.

Some teachers combine both systems, allowing students the chance to earn and lose reinforcements, based on adherence to the class rules. Other teachers practice positive only, based on the belief that you cannot take away a reinforcement that has been previously earned. In this system, instead of taking reinforcements away, the student just doesn't earn any more until the behavior improves.

Public vs Private Systems

A public behavior system is a system in which a student's behavior status is physically visible in the classroom. Examples of a public system include:

- **Class chart**
  Each student is assigned a name card and placed in the level of the chart that represents the desired behavior (The charts usually rank behavior from *Excellent* down to *Fair* and then *Poor*.) Their

> *Our whole school used a positive token-based reinforcement system. In the classes, the children were divided into color teams, which changed every term. The team colors matched token colors, and were called "Token Teams." Students could earn tokens for being polite, sharing, following the class rules, or any behavior that should be encouraged. Any teacher in the school could give any student the appropriate color token. As soon as the child was awarded a token, it went into a locked coin drop box. Each Friday the tokens were counted by the class counter and the totals for each team were sent to the office. The secretary added up all the team totals from across the school, and the team with the most tokens got extra recess—regardless of whether the members were in kindergarten or sixth grade.*
>
> *When I left that school and started a new job, I used the token system with my class. Even though the rest of the school didn't use it, it still worked wonderfully.*

standing in the class can move progressively down the chart until they reach *Poor*. Once they've reach that, they need to serve a consequence before their name card can be placed back at the top of the chart. In lower grades, many teachers use a green light → yellow light → red light system or a series of smiley faces ☺ ☺ ☹ to depict the three levels of behavior.

- **Board list**
  Write the name of anyone who is misbehaving on the board. Once the consequence is served, the name is removed.

- **White cards**
  A white index card is laid on the desk of any student whose behavior is unacceptable. The consequence is served as soon as possible, and the card is returned to the teacher.

In each of these examples, all the students and anyone else who enters the class (from the principal to the parents) can see which students have been "in trouble" just by looking at the chart or the name list. This is a convenient way to manage a class—the charts and lists are easily accessible, and, can serve as a deterrent for students who might act out. On the other hand, it can be very embarrassing for the students, and as the teacher, your main goal is to effect change in the students' behavior without humiliating them. **We do not advocate a public system. We feel it is degrading to students' confidence and self-esteem. There are better ways to effect change in a student's behavior.**

A private behavior system is a system in which the student's behavior status is only known by you and the student. At any given time, the student is mostly aware of his own behavior, not how he is behaving in comparison to other classmates. A private behavior system can be used for the whole class, but the receiving of reinforcements is between you and the individual student. Physical objects are used as reinforcements that the student accumulates and turns in for a reward. Examples of private behavior systems include:

- **Tokens**
  Children keep a plastic baggy in their desk. Poker chips are used as tokens to validate good behavior. A target number is set, and those that reach it by the end of the cycle earn a reward.

- **Pipe cleaners or stripes**
  Each student starts the cycle with three pipe cleaners or "stripes," (laminated construction paper that has been cut down into strips) which can be kept in a plastic cup in the student's desk or in a plastic baggy. A target number is set, and those that reach it by the end of the cycle earn a reward.

- **Tickets**
  Raffle tickets are given to students who are behaving well. Students put their name on the raffle ticket and hold them in a baggy, turning them in at the end of the week to be redeemed.

- **Index cards**
  Each student is given an index card. During the week students earn stamps or stickers. At the end of the week, a full card is redeemable for a reward.

- **Teacher bucks**
  Students earn "money" in an account tracked by the teacher. At the end of each term students bring in objects from home for a class garage sale and use their "money" to pay for items.

Individual and Class Systems

Once you decide on either a public or private system, choose the ways in which children can participate:

- **Individually**

  Each student is responsible for his own behavior and he gets the reward.

- **As teams**

  The class is divided into teams. The team with the most reinforcements (i.e. tokens, stripes) gets the reward.

- **As a class**

  The whole class works together to attain the goal.

You may decide to use all three. No matter what combination you choose, you should always have a class system. A class behavior system is especially important because:

- There are many times when you will want the students to be working together as a whole, and therefore will want to reward the class without singling out any particular student.

- A class system can apply positive pressure on a student who is not interested in participating in a personal system. He knows his classmates are depending on him to help earn the reward.

A class reward system is especially useful for group activities such as working on a class project, walking to and from areas of the school in a quiet line, working as a group during instruction time, preparing for dismissal, or when students are getting supplies ready for an activity. A class system is a great way of reinforcing cooperative group behavior. Examples of both positive and negative reinforcements for the class are:

Positive

- **Marble jar**

  Each time the class is working well together or receives a compliment, a marble is dropped into a glass jar. Once the jar is full, the class receives its reward.

- **Popcorn jar**

  A scoop of popcorn kernels is added to a jar each time good class behavior is noted, and when the jar is filled children have a popcorn party.

- **Links**

  Use construction paper to start a paper chain that hangs from the ceiling. Positive class behavior earns links that are added to the chain. When the chain reaches a certain point in the classroom, the students receive a class reward.

- **Seasonal**

  Use paper cut outs of leaves, snowmen, Valentine hearts, et cetera, and tape them onto the top or bottom of the board. Once they stretch across the board the class gets a reward.

Negative

- **Three stripes**

  Three stripes are marked on the board at the beginning of the day. If disruptive behavior occurs, half or full lines are erased. Once the stripes have disappeared, the class loses something of value.

- **Three times out**

  Any time you have to ask your class a third time for something (their attention, to line up, to be quiet) the class loses something it values.

Most of the time you will use positive reinforcement, but don't be afraid to use a negative reinforcement to get the class back on right track. If the entire class is getting out of hand, put your foot down. Pulling a big ticket item like refusing to continue a fun activity, shortening recess, or canceling free time shows the students that you're serious about the type of behavior you expect from them.

Incentives for Your Students

Before you implement any behavior strategy, you need to determine what goal your students will be striving to reach. Making students aware of the goal will help effect the desired behavior. Here are some suggestions for rewards that are quick, easy, and inexpensive:

Individual Rewards

- Extra free reading time.

- Extra recess: coordinate this with another teacher. One teacher takes the students who have earned extra recess outside, while the other teacher reads aloud to the remaining students or supervises "finish work" or "center" time.

- A night without homework.

I use two kinds of reward systems in my class—individual and whole class. Every Tuesday morning, each student gets three tokens when they arrive. During the week they try to earn extra tokens for a total of 15. Any child with 15 tokens by the following Tuesday gets extra recess in the afternoon. At the same time, I might add in something I want the class to make a stronger effort in remembering to do, such as have their agendas signed by a parent each night. Every day that all students come with a signed agenda the class earns three links on the paper chain I've mounted on the ceiling. When the links stretch across the classroom the class will receive a movie treat.

- Permission to sit at the teacher's desk.
- Treasure chest: students get to pick something out of a grab box filled with dollar store items.
- Magic pens: students may use glitter pens to complete their work during the day.
- Lunch with the teacher: set aside a day for students who have earned the privilege to eat their lunch with the teacher, principal, or librarian.
- Freedom to draw on the board.
- Permission to invite a friend from another class in for lunch.
- Letting the child be a kindergarten helper.
- Being allowed to get a drink without asking.
- Letting the child eat a healthy snack from home during class.
- Moving a desk to anywhere in the room.
- Sitting or lying anywhere safely during the day.
- Chewing gum or having candy during part of the day.

- Fifteen minute freebie: allowing children to do free choice activities for fifteen minutes.

Class Rewards

- Popcorn party: allow students to eat popcorn during a class, or serve it as a special treat at the end of the day.

- Cookies at recess: purchase a bag or two of cookies and allow each child a couple of cookies at recess.

- Movie: show a G-rated movie during a Friday afternoon.

- Clubs: coordinate with other teachers and pick an activity to teach the students such as tye dying, paper plane making, or kite building. Let children sign up for the activity of their choice.

- Give extra time at recess.

- Implement a "No Homework" night.

- Friend from home: students can bring in a stuffed animal or other toy to keep on their desk for the day.

- Themed free time: class decides on theme and each student brings in something relevant from home.

- Community treats: many restaurants and stores offer vouchers or coupons for classrooms and students. Check in your area to see what's available.

A Word About School Based Systems

A school based behavior system is one where the whole school shares the same behavior management strategy. You'll find the same system and the same incentives being used in grade one through to grade six. If you are lucky, you will walk into a job where the whole school follows a system that both the teachers and the principal have found effective, and all you have to do is implement it.

While school wide behavior systems are common in England, in Canada and the United States some schools use school based systems, while others leave the choice of behavior management completely up to the individual class teacher.

In our school we have a system called the Headmaster's Book. A student's name can be placed in the headmaster's book by any teacher in the school for many positive reasons: showing effort in class, helping another student, trying hard to overcome a problem area, making improvements in personal growth, or any act the student has performed for which the teacher feels he should receive recognition. Once a week, students who have been added to the book have their names announced during a school assembly, and their picture is taken and placed on a display board outside the office. At 2:15 the following day, these students are invited for tea and biscuits in the Headmaster's office, where they spend half-an-hour chatting with the headmaster while having their special treat. The children love this, and I find it fosters communication between other teachers when we discuss with each other why we have recommended a particular student to the Headmaster's book.

Chapter 17

Serving the Time—Consequences for Negative Behaviors

Once the consequence has been served, don't bring up the incident again.

Students should be aware of what the consequences will be if they choose not to follow classroom or school rules. The consequence should come as quickly after the behavior as possible, if not immediately after then certainly during that same day. You should always follow through on what you say: if you tell a child he has lost some playtime, then you need to make sure he sits it out. Below are samples of negative consequences frequently used by teachers we surveyed. Always check with your school to see what consequences are permitted for the grade you are teaching.

- **No reward**
  Students lose the chance to earn a reward.

- **Time out**
  Students are removed to another area to have quiet time to reflect on their actions. They rejoin the class when they're prepared to behave, once they've cooled off, or after a predetermined time interval has passed.

- **Send out**
  Find out where you can send a student who needs to be removed from your class. Typically, the options are another teacher's classroom, to the office, or to the principal's office. If possible, make a reciprocal arrangement with another teacher at the beginning of the year for any children needing to be sent out; and know when it's expected that student will be sent to the principal instead of being merely "sent out."

- **Missed playtime, recess time, or free time**
  Some teachers take away parts or all of these activities, depending on what happened. If a student is missing playtime or recess, **NEVER** take away food (snack, lunch, et cetera) or bathroom privileges. Allow them to have their food while they sit out.

- **Contact home**
  Send a note home or make a phone call to a parent to advise them of their child's behavior.

- **Extra homework**
  Assign extra work that the child must complete at home.

- **Detention**
  Keep the student after school either in your class or another supervised classroom. The child can complete a letter detailing what she was doing that resulted in the detention, and how she can prevent it from happening again.

There is a difference between humiliating a child and providing a child with time out to think about his actions.

If a student misbehaves, don't hold a grudge—it's immature and unprofessional. A really good teacher allows the child to serve the consequence, and never brings the incident up again. Once the consequence is served, that's it: the issue is finished, the slate is clean, and everything returns to normal. The student won't be thinking of positive behavior if you are constantly focusing on the negative behavior.

What to Do With a Disruptive Student

Knowing how to handle a disruptive student can distinguish you as a first year teacher who is in control of his class, instead of a first year teacher that the students feel they can "get one over on." Your goal with a disruptive student is to stop the behavior and get the student back on task as quickly as possible. When a student becomes disruptive you should:

- redirect the student towards positive behavior with a look, a touch on the arm, or a verbal reminder of the behavior you'd like to see. *"Macy, I'd like to see you working quietly like you were this morning."*

- remind the student she needs to make a positive choice or there will be a negative consequence. *"Macy, if you can't work quietly at your table I will have to move you to another spot."*

- remove student to another part of the room, and deal with the situation one-on-one. Discuss what is going on without being

Serving the Time—Consequences for Negative Behavior

You don't need to embarrass a student to get him to change a behavior.

confrontational. *"Macy, please take your books to the desk next to the teacher table and I will talk with you shortly,"* could be followed up with, *"You seem to be having a problem. What's going on?"* It should never be followed up with something like, *"What the heck are you doing?"*

If the student has, despite your redirection, continued to disrupt the class and your teaching, stop everything. Instruct the class to read, or finish seatwork and direct the disruptive student to meet you in a more confidential area of the classroom. Your choices here are:

- remove the student by sending him to another classroom
- send the student to the office
- call in assistance by sending two student messengers to the office with a note asking for another member of the staff to come and escort the student to another location.

No matter how badly a student gets under your skin, never lose your cool. If you need a break, ask another teacher to watch your class, or call the office and request someone to relieve you so you can cool off. Take a walk around the school, get a drink of water, and just remove yourself from the situation until you've had a chance to get yourself back together.

Know the chain of command at your school when requesting help in dealing with a disruptive student.

"I dunno. She said she needed a minute to relax..."

When the Schedule Changes, So Will the Behavior . . .

Events

Children are used to coming in the classroom with a set expectation of how the day will progress. When that schedule changes, due to a fire drill, an assembly, a class party, a school play, or a field trip, the children's behavior will often change too (and not always for the better). While this is natural due to the excitement associated with any out-of-the-ordinary-event, you still need to maintain control. This calls for pre-emptive measures to stop the problem before it starts. Before any class outing, or any other out-of-the-ordinary event, pull the class together for a quick chat:

- Let them know what is happening during the day, *"Instead of language arts we will be going to see the fifth grade play at 10:30."*

- Be **clear** about the behavior you expect to see, *"I am expecting that everyone will be sitting correctly and remaining silent."*

- Ask students to volunteer behaviors that would not be acceptable, *"Standing up during the show; talking to friends; calling out during the play; moving around in seats."*

- Determine what will happen to those students who don't follow the rules, *"You will get one warning from me, but if the behavior continues you will be sent back to another teacher's classroom."*

No matter how many parents are present, you are still in charge of discipline and student behavior.

Parent Volunteers

Parents are an asset in any classroom. Unfortunately, some children tend to act up when their parent is in the room.

There are some actions you can take with both student and parents to ensure that parent volunteering runs smoothly for everyone:

- Remind students that when a parent comes in, it is a chance for them to show the parent how grown up and responsible they are.

- Remind the class that parent volunteers are there to help the teacher and *all* the students, not just their child.

- Remind the children that anyone who can't follow the class rules will be sent to another classroom, even if it is their parent who is volunteering.

Serving the Time—Consequences for Negative Behavior

I love having parents in the classroom, but some children tend to act differently with their parent in the room. I remember one student in particular would undergo a total metamorphosis and revert to particularly babyish behavior whenever her mother showed up. Suddenly she was no longer a capable second grader but a child who spoke in baby talk, couldn't tie her own shoes, and had to be fed by her mother during class parties! While this behavior might have been okay at her house, it was not okay in our class. Afterwards, the other students teased her about the way she had acted while her mom was in. I had to speak to both her and her mother to resolve this situation.

- Remind volunteers that the purpose of being in the classroom is to help you with whatever you need help with, and not just to assist their own child.

- Tell the volunteer that the children will still be expected to follow the class rules, which you will be enforcing, so parents don't have to worry about disciplining a student. Telling the volunteers this up front also conveys that you won't be "bending" any of the rules just because they are in the classroom.

Chapter 18

Dealing with Special Situations

Adjusting Your System

What works with some of your students won't work with all of them. In certain cases, you may need to adjust your management system to meet the individual needs of a student. One child may need to work extra hard on using good manners, while another may be working on improving listening skills.

Some children have chemical imbalances, syndromes, or medical situations that affect their behavior, and make certain goals harder to attain (i.e. children with Asperger's Syndrome have a very difficult time being organized). In your class you will likely have students that are receiving medication, assessments, or some other outside of school intervention to address specific behavioral concern.

Regardless of whether the focus is to help a student reach a short-term goal or help a student deal with a behavior that is beyond her control, you will find that you need to change your behavior system so that it is beneficial to that particular student. This is where an individual system is handy because these adjustments are private—between you and the student (and, of course, the parents). Try:

- **Choosing behaviors**
  You, the parents, and the student should choose one or two specific behaviors on which to focus. Students with special situations may need a different goal to work toward in order to make the modification attainable and meaningful.

- **Double reinforcements**
  Allow this student the chance to earn double reinforcements when he tries to work on a particular skill.

- **Shorter cycles**
  Allow a child with behavioral difficulties to have a shorter time to reach his goal. The weekly cycle, while fine for the rest of the class, may be too long; consider charting the student on a day-to-day basis. Set the goal each morning and reward its achievement at the end of the day. Gradually you can lengthen the cycle time.

- **Using a behavior modification chart**
  Create a behavior chart that's easy to use and maintain. For younger students stamps or stickers can be used. For older students, a rating scale or point system can be used. Below are two sample charts.

Student's Name: _____ **Date:** _____

Completes work on time	Sits quietly during instruction
Is kind to classmates & teacher	Cooperates with others during play

Student's Name: _____ **Date:** _____

Behavior	A.M.	P.M.
Unpacking and starting morning work		
Packing up with all necessary supplies		
Raising your hand for a question.		

The last chart was used for a third grade student focusing on improving three behaviors. The important elements of this chart are:

- The expected behaviors were discussed with parents and students, and were specific.

- The student knew the number of points he could earn and the points were connected to a class reward system.

- The points earned in class worked in unison with a reward system at home.

- The teacher only had to record information once or twice a day.

The most important point to remember with any behavior modification system is *consistency*. Without consistent reinforcements and feedback, the system won't work. Therefore make sure whatever plan you put into place, whether it is for the entire class or an individual student, is one you can manage with consistency.

In situations where you are considering asking for outside help for a student or it has already been requested, you may be asked to record, observe or keep a behavior chart for medical or psychological purposes. You may even have to do this for more than one student. If this is the case, try the following to help you keep track.

- Decide on a time each day to make notes about behavior. Two five-minute breaks to make notes might be better than trying to record your observations at the end of the day.

- Pick a format that works for you. While the doctor's office might need a chart, it may be unrealistic for you to have this chart with you at all times. Maybe keeping tape-recorded notes, using sticky notes, or making a quick phone call home would be better. Only commit to what you are prepared to follow through with.

No child is perfect. All children, even the "best behaved" will push limits in order to find out where the boundaries are. Your job is to establish and uphold those reasonable boundaries. And like adults, children go through hard times with issues like family, adolescence, friends, and more. Knowing your students and their pattern of behavior will enable you to know when a student is just goofing around, or when they are seeking attention for a much more serious reason. Educate yourself about the student's situation at school and at home, and consider this when dealing with the child. Being as aware as possible about all aspects of a student's situation *outside* the classroom will provide insight into behaviors taking place *inside* the classroom.

Dealing with Special Situations

Summary Section Three

- Behavior management includes how a teacher controls the class as well as how he modifies the behavior of disruptive students. The classroom environment you create will determine how your class behaves overall.

- You need to be in charge, set the rules and boundaries, model the desired behavior and set the expectations for your class.

- Set standards for acceptable student behavior and follow them yourself. If you don't want students yelling, interrupting, using sarcasm or being rude, then you shouldn't be either.

- Don't forget that verbal praise is a powerful tool, and should be used first in your behavior management system. A smile or a kind word can go a long way.

- When deciding on a behavior management system, consider which type of system you will use. Will it be a public or private reward system? A positive or negative system? A system based on the individual or the whole class system? Or, some combination of all of these?

- Some schools have school wide behavior management systems, some schools have grade level systems, and some have neither. If your school already has something in place, follow their lead. If not, be sure to create whatever system works best for you and your class. Be sure your approach doesn't violate any school policies.

- Although behavior management systems should be primarily positive in approach, you need to decide how you will deal with negative behavior, what the consequences will be. Be consistent. If you tell students there will be a specific consequence you must follow through.

- Some students with special needs may require their own individual behavior modification systems. Don't commit to any behavior management plan that you cannot follow through with consistently.

- Finally, remember as with most areas in education, behavior management is all about balance. Balance your system with verbal praise and rewards, positive incentives and consequences for inappropriate behavior.

Notes

Behavior Chart #1

Student's Name: _____ Date: _____

Behavior #1	Behavior #2
Behavior #3	Behavior #4

Behavior Chart #2

Student's Name: _____ Date: _____

Behavior	A.M.	P.M.

TIPS, Inc.

SECTION FOUR

The Students Arrive—Thriving During the First Weeks of School

- **Establishing classroom structure**
- **Ice breaking games and activities**
- **Getting the parents onboard**
- **Making homework less of a hassle**

IN THIS SECTION

Chapter 19

Smooth Sailing from Day One

Establishing Yourself as the Teacher

From the very first moment the students walk through the door you need to have a plan for your day and your daily routines. This includes the rules of the classroom, emergency procedures, classroom jobs, morning and afternoon routines and any other daily occurrences in your room.

Your job as a teacher is to teach. You are the adult in the room. No matter what grade you teach, you are **not** there to be friends with the students. They have friends; they are called classmates. We all want our students to like us. No teacher wants a student to go home and say, "Mrs. So-and-so is not nice," or, "I don't like my teacher," however, it will happen, so you might as well accept it.

During the first week spend extra time with your class focusing on rules and routines.

Creating Structure During the First Week of School

Many teachers treat the first week of school like the last week of summer, focusing more on games and getting acquainted than on teaching. While you'll want to do a few fun activities for the whole "getting to know you" part, it's important that you treat the first week of school like any other—with an added focus on schedule, expectations, and class rules. Children will arrive in your classroom anticipating some rules, anxious to know how the new grade operates, and expecting to work—after all, summer is over and school has begun. The best way for your

During my years as a teacher, I've learned the importance of creating structure and getting the children to follow the classroom rules and routines from the moment they walk through the door on that very first day. On the first day of school I place an interest inventory sheet and a student survey with a pencil on each desk. As the students come in, I welcome them, say hello to the parents, have them drop their supplies on the back counter and have them get to work. This helps get parents out of the room quickly, gets the students settled down, and introduces them to my routine of having morning work each day. I've learned that the rules and routines I want students to follow throughout the year need to begin that first day.

class to learn about your expectations is to have standard procedures in place. Here are some tips for making the most of the first week:

- **Do it from day one**

  If you want your students in alphabetical order when they line up, don't wait until the second week of school to try it out. Have all your operating procedures in place and start them from the first day.

- **Teach on the first day**

  It may sound obvious, but you should start delivering your curriculum from the first day of school. Even if your fellow teachers don't, teach at least a math, reading, and writing lesson each day during the first days of school. Having a schedule and knowing what to expect will lessen the anxiety for many students and make the transition into your classroom smoother.

- **Balance fun with curriculum**

  It's fine to play a few "getting to know you" games, but just choose a couple and play them first thing in the morning or at the end of the day—or even both. A few games and a few recess periods is all it takes for most of the students to learn names and get acquainted.

Mrs. Larskin was pleased she'd remembered everything in time for the first day . . .

- **Use time wisely**

    You would never spend a whole morning any other time of the year having children label folders, so don't do it during the first week. Instead, have children write their names on supplies (like glue, crayons, and ruler) at home, and label in class materials (notebooks, folders, textbooks) **as they use them** during the first few weeks. It's much better to spend two minutes at the beginning of the first social studies lesson labeling a green folder than to give up a whole hour where children sit and label folders for all their subjects.

- **Be polite but firm with parents**

    Unless you want parents to be in your classroom each morning, unpacking their child's lunch and supplies, have them leave their child at the door from the first morning onwards. In the younger grades, this seems to be much harder (for both children and parents) and you might want to let parents in on that first morning; however, by second grade parents should say goodbye at the door and that's that! Experienced teachers will tell you that having a parent stick around the first few days makes it worse—not better—for the child.

These few points are only the tip of the iceberg, so to speak. Read the following chapters for a more detailed examination of all the things that you'll need to consider to make the year run smoothly.

Smooth Sailing from Day One

The student-teacher relationship has to be established before learning can occur.

Establishing Class Rules

Rules are an important part of setting up your classroom and are critical to your daily procedures. Remember what we said earlier about having routines and procedures in the classroom? Students expect them and a classroom without rules can quickly spiral out of control.

If you start the year with strict rules you can always ease up as the year progresses. But if you start too lenient, it is very difficult to tighten the reins once the tone for acceptable behavior has already been set.

Some rules to consider for the classroom are:

- Be respectful of others.

- Raise your hand AND wait to be called on. Many teachers forget the second part of this rule and consequently so do the students.

- Come in and leave the classroom quietly.

- Keep your hands and feet to yourself.

- Listen carefully and follow directions.

- Line up quietly

There are plenty of other rules you can include but remember your classroom rules should be the general rules that create a safe and productive environment each day.

Many teachers believe that students should have a part in creating the rules for their classroom. Before you do this, know what rules you want to include so you can guide the discussion appropriately. If you want students to participate in creating the classroom rules try following this procedure:

- Write the students' suggestions on the board.

- Ask students questions that hint at the rules you want, yet let them formulate the rule themselves. You could phrase a question such as, "Should we all just jump up and stand in a big clump when we leave the classroom?" hoping to elicit a response from the children like, "No, we should make a straight line."

- If the students miss or decide against a rule that you want included, simply tell them that it is important and include it in the list.

- Once all the suggestions are on the board, have students vote on the most important rules. Having five to six rules works best.

Know what rules you want for your classroom before the year begins.

140   You've Got the Job—Now Keep It

When creating my class rules bulletin board, I photograph children demonstrating the rules. The photograph goes on the board along with the rule and serves as a visual reminder of what the children should be trying to do.

Establishing Procedures

Giving Directions

Before giving students an assignment to complete independently you must make sure they understand what needs to be done. Giving directions to your class sounds easy enough, but it's not. No matter how well you explain a task, there will be children who didn't hear the directions or didn't understand the assignment. To avoid repeating directions to dazed and confused children, try these tips:

- Make sure you have everyone's attention before you start. If you find that you are giving directions while students are moving around, stop talking. Wait for the students to settle down and then start again.

- Be clear and concise.

- Before students begin, ask a student to repeat the directions.

- Ask if anyone has questions or is confused about the assignment.

- Write the directions on the board. This is especially helpful when assigning multiple tasks, or when the class returns from recess, lunch or a specialty class. Instead of trying to get their attention, simply say, "The directions are on the board," and expect the children to start.

Morning Routine

When the students arrive in the morning, there should be an established routine for them to follow. **Parents should not be allowed to**

help with the morning routine. You may find there are parents who like to come into the classroom and help their child put away homework, supplies, or books. During the very first week, you need to gently explain to parents that the children must put away their supplies and prepare for the day on their own. Even in the younger grades, the children can learn routines very quickly and be responsible for putting away their own items in the morning. Be sure to mention this during open house to drive the point home.

A good morning routine should take approximately five to ten minutes—depending on the age of your students—and include:

- unpacking backpacks
- handing in notes from home
- putting away homework and lunches
- sharpening pencils
- starting morning work

Having a set morning routine is important for several reasons: it gives the students focus and keeps them from socializing too much; it gives you time to take attendance, sort out lunch monies, and handle any problems that might arise when the students walk through the door. Finally, and most importantly, it leaves very little work for you in getting the class ready to start the day.

Find a spot for students to drop notes from home. A basket, bucket, or decorated bag will do nicely.

Keep in mind that students will want to talk and catch up with their friends the same way you like to chat with fellow teachers first thing in the morning. Allow time for this when they arrive and are unpacking, but have a set time when students know they must be in their seats, ready for morning work to begin.

MORNING WORK

You should have work posted each morning for students to begin as soon as they come in and are settled—this is "morning work." It should take about 20 minutes, depending on your schedule, and it should be posted in the same place every day. Many teachers will conclude their morning work message with directions such as, "Be ready for math at 8:50. Have your math textbook and notebook on your desk." This way the students know what subject they will have first, what they'll need on their desks and when they will need to be ready.

There are many ways to handle morning work. Morning work should be meaningful and relate to the curriculum. Avoid using activities like worksheets, word jumbles, and crosswords that don't serve a true educational purpose. Morning work is a great opportunity for students to spend some time:

- developing their creative writing
- finishing work from the day before

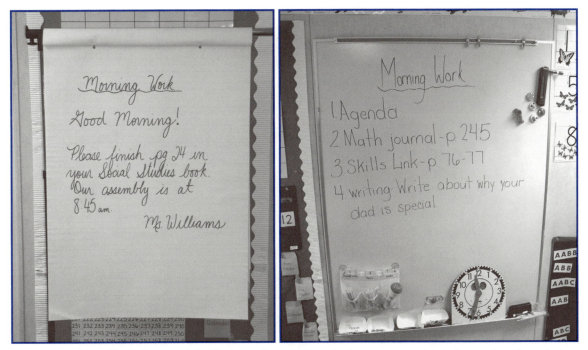

Post morning work in the same location each day to get students focused and ready to go.

- solving a riddle or brain teaser
- solving math equations/word problems
- proofing sentences/paragraphs for writing errors
- practicing for standardized testing
- working on a project for class
- participating in center activities

Always have something students can do once they finish their morning work. Activities that are quiet or are easily cleaned up work well as students can get ready quickly for the first subject of the day.

Daily Schedule

Along with posting morning work, many teachers list a daily schedule in the classroom for students to view. You can write the schedule on the board each morning or use laminated sentence-strip cards. You can arrange your schedule based on time or by classes. Displaying a schedule cuts down on questions such as, "When is the assembly? What time will we start math? When is recess?" While schedules are especially helpful for those students who need structure, a posted schedule helps students know what to expect throughout the day and can eliminate surprises.

A picture schedule works well for kindergarten children. In addition to keeping the daily schedule straight, if you include the different activities in printed format, the schedule can function as a reading aid as well.

In the older grades, where schedules may follow a similar pattern each day, you may find it sufficient to simply write down any schedule changes for the day. For example if your recess is usually at 10:30 but the class must attend a performance at that time, note only the schedule changes on your board.

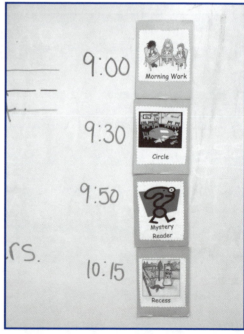

A picture schedule helps keep younger children on track during the day.

Afternoon Routine

The afternoon, when students are preparing to leave, always seems to be the craziest time of the day. This doesn't, however, need to be the norm in your classroom. Always start the year by giving the students plenty of time to clean the class and their desks, to note their homework, and to pack their bags. During the first week this may take as long as 20 minutes, but as the weeks progress, give the class less time. Once the children have mastered the routine, the class shouldn't need more than 10 minutes to clean, pack, and be ready to go.

To help ensure cleaning up at the end of the day goes smoothly in your classroom, know the answers to the questions below before the school year starts.

When will students fill out their agendas?

Have students write down their homework at the end of the day. Writing homework down in the morning creates a problem if the homework assignment is changed or cancelled, and having students write their homework throughout the day can be disruptive to the lesson you are delivering.

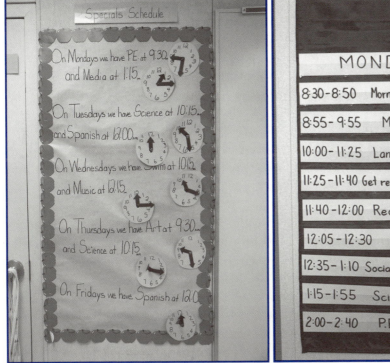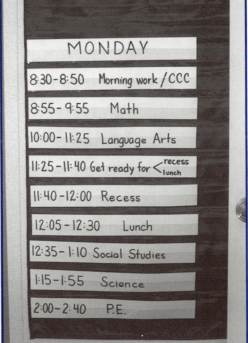

A class schedule keeps your students on track during the day and eliminates any surprises.

Smooth Sailing from Day One

Will you be signing agendas?

Signing agendas is a personal philosophy. Ask other teachers in your grade level what they do. Some guidelines are:

- For second grade and lower, initial the students' agendas.

- For third grade and above, initial agendas at the start the year so you can get a feel for which students are going to need monitoring and assistance, then, as the year progresses, stop initialing and give the students the responsibility of knowing their homework assignments.

- Be sure to check the agendas of those students who need a bit more help with organization.

- If you plan to use the agenda as a communications tool with parents, be sure to check the agendas each day for notes or comments from home.

Who passes out papers to go home? Who cleans up the class library?

Assign classroom jobs to your students. Have any papers that go home ready in a designated spot so students don't come looking for them at the end of the day.

Do you want students doing their jobs before or after they are ready for dismissal?

Have students complete classroom jobs after they are packed and ready to go.

What should the teacher do during pack up time?

In addition to monitoring what's going on, helping students who need the extra guidance writing down homework, and getting ready to go home, you should try to use this time to straighten your desk and other work areas.

Once you've decided on the routine, set a time limit. For the first week or two, give the students 15–20 minutes to pack up. Then start scaling back on the time until you're down to about ten minutes. This is all the time it should take students to get straightened away.

A fun and motivating way to get students to pack up is to play music. Play the music in the background for the first two weeks while you give directions on what to do. As the weeks progress, turn the music up and step back. Pick a different song every month if you'd like, but make it something completely different from what they usually hear—perhaps a fast paced song from the fifties or a disco song from the seventies. Classical music is another excellent choice as one classical piece can take up the full ten minutes. Pick something upbeat and fun and you'll see how quick and easy afternoon clean up can be.

What should students do while waiting to be dismissed?

Most teachers find themselves with a few extra minutes at the end of the day after the students have packed up and the classroom has been straightened out. As well, there are always small pockets of time during the day where you and your class have nothing to do. Whether you're waiting for dismissal, to board a bus, or waiting to change classes, instead of letting those few minutes go to waste you could always:

- read part of a chapter book
- read a selection of poems
- play a mental math game
- do a quick review of the day so far
- practice addition/subtraction/multiplication/division facts
- practice spelling words
- sing a song
- play a fun game
- tell jokes and riddles
- allow students to socialize

Daily Routines

You will also want to institute some day-to-day procedures and routines in your classroom. We've already discussed a few of these routines, such as where students put their homework, notes from home, and notebooks. You might not think you'll need to bother with such small details, but consider the case of Mr. Thompson and his second grade class:

Smooth Sailing from Day One

Mr. Thompson was a first-year teacher in second grade and decided that having his students line up systematically was too infantile. During his first weeks of school he just let the students line up randomly. Students were complaining, arguing, pushing and shoving in their attempt to be first in line or to stand next to a friend. He quickly found out that he was spending too much time each day dealing with problems when the children were lined up. He realized he needed to implement some type of procedure and, by the third week of school, Mr. Thompson had assigned a line leader, a door holder and implemented a line order for all the students.

LINE ORDER

The above case of Mr. Thompson shows why you need to implement some type of system to line students up—hence "line order." We suggest you have line order no matter how old the students are. Fifth graders will push, shove, and argue just as much as first graders when it comes to lining up. Here are some quick tips for creating line order:

- Alphabetical order is fast, easy and impartial because children line up in the same order as they appear on your class list. Put any new students at the end of the line.

- If you don't want to line them up in true alphabetical order, line the children up alphabetically backwards (so those with a surname starting with Z are first). It still keeps the students in an easy to manage order, and your class list (albeit backwards) is still an accurate way to track them.

- If you don't like lining students up alphabetically at all, give each student a number and line them up numerically. Be sure to write down the students' numbers so you will know where each child should appear in the line.

- No matter which ordering system you choose to implement, the first student is the leader of the line and the second is responsible for holding the door.

Classroom Jobs

Your classroom will run smoother if you have jobs for the students. The cooperative and collaborative air helps foster a sense of togetherness among the children. The jobs you choose for your students will vary depending on school policies, your classroom set-up, and the grade you teach. Below are some common classroom tasks primary and elementary aged children can manage competently:

- line leader
- door holder
- office messengers
- fire drill bathroom monitors (only for bathrooms in the classroom)
- paper distributor
- paper collector
- computer monitor
- counter/center cleaner
- librarian and/or book monitor
- class cleaners
- office aids (taking notes or walking students to the office)

You don't want to burden the class with too many jobs, but most jobs don't take long to perform. Classroom jobs, and the little sense of empowerment they provide the students, help create a feeling of "our classroom" instead of "the classroom."

Assign many students to one job: you can never have too many classroom cleaners.

To distribute the classroom jobs and keep them organized, there are several approaches to choose from. No matter which approach you go with, you'll need a chart or job board listing all the jobs you will be using in your class. You can assign jobs using one of the following methods:

- Rotating assignment: Write student names on clothespins, craft sticks, or Velcro name tags. Place names on the job chart following a predetermined order (alphabetically, numerically, et-cetera) and assign the first name to the first job, the second name to the second job and so on. Once all the jobs are filled, place the rest of the names in order else where on the chart (i.e. along the bottom or in a spot that designates they're on break from performing a job). To change jobs, take the first name and place it at the end of the list. Then move all the names up one place. Many teachers use this same system as a means by which to line up their class. The first student on the job chart is also line leader, and the second student on the chart is then door holder. Once the jobs change, the line order for the class changes too. The first student in the line goes to the end and as does his name on the job chart. This way everyone has a chance to complete all jobs during the year. If there are students without a job, they can either have a break or better yet, they can help clean up the general areas of the classroom.

- Random assignment: Write all students names on craft sticks (or clothespins) and put them in a plastic cup, jar, or coffee tin labeled "Next Time." Start with the top job on the chart, pull a name, and assign that student to that job. Keep pulling names until all the jobs are assigned and place those names either on the chart as you go or in a cup labeled "Job Helpers." Those names left in the "Next Time" cup will be selected first the next time. The only problem with random picking is that it doesn't ensure that all the students will have a chance to perform every job.

- Behavior based assignment: You can assign jobs based on your behavior system. The student who you think "deserves" to be line leader due to improved behavior or overall consistent positive behavior can be line leader for the week. This takes a bit more tracking on the part of the teacher, because it's important not to assign the same jobs to the same students.

There are many ways you can rotate students through jobs. Here are three ways to consider:

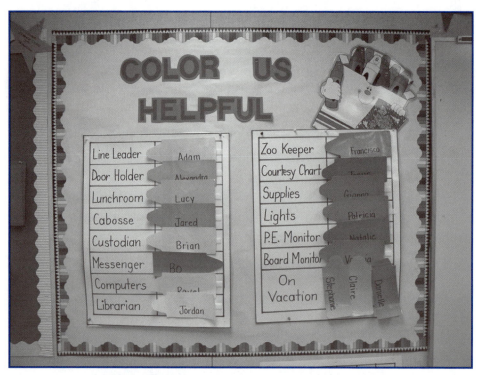

Keeping students names in order ensures that students get the opportunity to perform each classroom job.

- Daily rotation works well for younger children who may find it difficult to wait for their turn at a new job if a weekly rotation is used. However, it is time consuming for the teacher to change the jobs daily and can be difficult for a child to remember his or her job for the day when they change so frequently.

- Weekly rotation works well because it allows each student a comfortable amount of time to perform her job. Unfortunately if there is a short week due to holidays, some students will not get their full turn.

- Biweekly rotation works by rotating students every other week. This type of rotation works well because if there is a short week, the students still have another full week to keep their jobs. Second, because the job chart changes only twice a month, it's not as much work for the teacher. However, rotating every two weeks means students without a job have to wait longer to get one.

Decide how you'll handle students being absent or on vacation. Having a predetermined schedule enables you to reassign a job if you know a student will be on vacation the week she is supposed to be line leader. Pulling jobs randomly using sticks allows you to put an absent student's name back in the pile for later. The bottom line? It's up to you whether or not you will hold jobs for students who are absent. Decide what you'll do and let students know how absences will be handled.

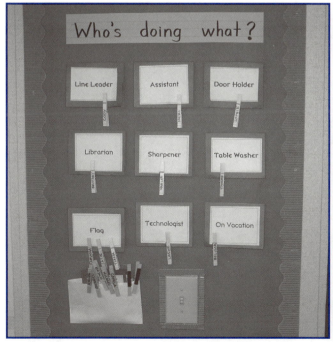

Writing students' names on clothes pins allows you to clip them to charts, job boards, and plastic cups.

Smooth Sailing from Day One

Additional Routines

STUDENTS LEAVING THE CLASSROOM

Throughout the day students will come and go from your room for a multitude of reasons: music lessons, speech therapy, resource room, gifted and talented class, doctor's appointments, bathroom, water and the list goes on. You need to keep track of where all your students are at all times.

- Check the school policy because some schools do not allow children to leave the classroom without another teacher or a buddy. Some schools utilize hallway passes. **Never let a student leave the classroom alone.** If one child needs to go to the office, send *two* friends along with her. That way if the student needs to stay in the office the friends walk back to the classroom together.

- Once your student leaves the room with Mrs. Jones the speech therapist, that student becomes her responsibility. However, it is your responsibility to know that Billy is with Mrs. Jones or that Billy is in the bathroom, at music lessons or having lunch at home.

- Tape a sign-out sheet somewhere in your room, preferably near the door (the corner of the blackboard is a good spot). After students tell you they are leaving, they write down their name, the time they left and where they are going. When they return to your class, they put

Use a sign-out sheet for students leaving the classroom, especially for a large class.

"I'm in the middle of something here—just make sure you sign the sheet on your way out."

a line through their name. This system helps you monitor where your students are and is easily transportable in the event of a fire drill. Posting a new sign-out sheet each morning can easily be included as one of your class jobs.

FIRE DRILL PROCEDURES

- When leaving the class, you can choose to have your students line up alphabetically in their fire order number, or they can line up in whatever line order you use regularly in the classroom. Either way works fine as long as they know, in advance, which way to assemble when the alarm sounds, and which way to group themselves in the pre-arranged meeting spot.

- Make sure you always bring a class list with you on a fire drill. Many schools require this.

- Grab your list of students who have left your classroom. You'll need to be able to account for every student in your class, even if they are with another teacher in a different part of the building.

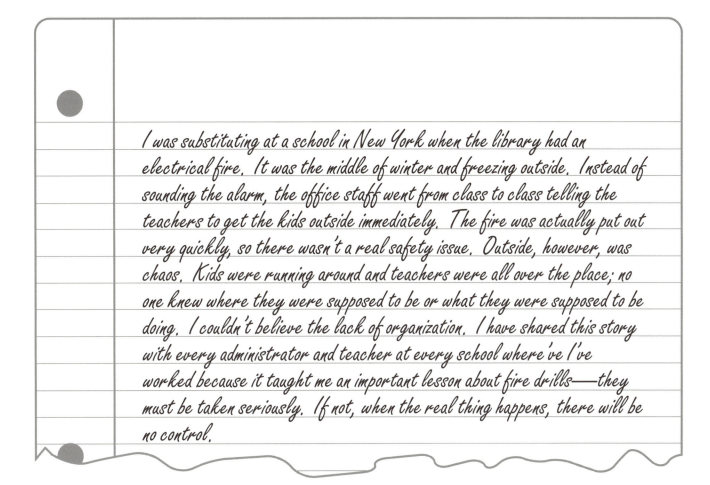

I was substituting at a school in New York when the library had an electrical fire. It was the middle of winter and freezing outside. Instead of sounding the alarm, the office staff went from class to class telling the teachers to get the kids outside immediately. The fire was actually put out very quickly, so there wasn't a real safety issue. Outside, however, was chaos. Kids were running around and teachers were all over the place; no one knew where they were supposed to be or what they were supposed to be doing. I couldn't believe the lack of organization. I have shared this story with every administrator and teacher at every school where've I've worked because it taught me an important lesson about fire drills—they must be taken seriously. If not, when the real thing happens, there will be no control.

- If you have a bathroom in the classroom, assign two students for the entire year to check the bathroom before lining up. You'll need two students as one may be absent or actually in the bathroom at the time of the drill.

- Do not permit any talking during a fire drill until the class is safely back inside the classroom. Explain to the students that this is a safety issue because they must be able to hear (and follow) directions. Be consistent with this point and establish a serious consequence (phone call home to the parents) for students who break this rule.

- When you've safely led the children to the pre-assigned meeting place for your class, quickly check to ensure all students are present. This vital step is obviously going to be much easier, faster and accurate if you have silent children grouped in a systematic and sensible manner. Be a role model. If you don't want the students talking then don't chit-chat with other teachers. You may find that other teachers chat and let their students relax during a fire drill, but don't be intimidated. Though it may only be a "drill," if a real crisis were to occur—because they've had the proper training—you'll be able to count on your students to be ready and listening for directions. This is just what you want because you're ultimately responsible for those children while they are in your care.

Keep a class roster near your classroom door to be used for fire drills.

- Remember the power of positive praise: compliment your class on a job well done.

Most schools have strict procedures for fire drills and you may find that all of the above suggestions are already in place at your school. If not, make sure you implement a fire drill procedure in the beginning of the year. Most schools like to have a fire drill during the first few weeks of school.

Chapter 20

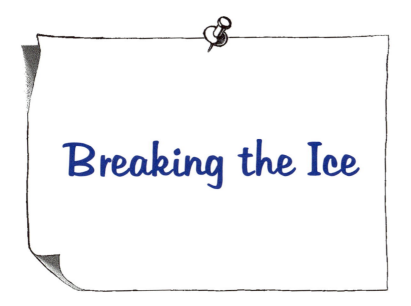

Breaking the Ice

Getting to Know You

During the first few days of schools, you'll want to get to know your students both personally and academically. It's also important for the students to become acquainted with each other. While many of your students may already know each other, there may be some children who are new to the class or who have been separated from their closest classmates. Generally, the bigger your school the more likely your students will not know all of their classmates.

To help everyone get to know one another, try some fun games and activities.

Games

WHO'S MISSING?
Choose one child to be "it" and have her cover her eyes. Choose another child and have her step out of the room while all the other students mix themselves up at their desks. The child who is "it" will have three guesses to figure out who is missing.

WHAT'S IN A NAME?
Have the students sit in a circle. Each student must think of a descriptive word that starts with the same sound as her first name. The first student says the word and then her name, followed by the next student. It might sound something like this:

Beautiful Brittany
Hello beautiful Brittany, I'm silly Sally
Hello beautiful Brittany and silly Sally, I'm tall Terrance
Hello beautiful Brittany, silly Sally, and tall Terrance, I'm excited Eddie

Continue this around the circle until all the children have had a chance to say their names. The students may want to go around the circle more than once to see if they can remember everything.

Activities

RIDDLES

Have each student fill out a short questionnaire. Collect all the papers, and pose the answers as riddles to see if the children can guess who you are talking about. When developing your questionnaire, keep the questions simple if you are teaching young children; if you have an older class, try to make some of the questions introspective.

A sample questionnaire could include:
What is your pet's name? What is your favorite TV show? What is your favorite subject in school? Something people might not know about me is _____ If I could learn about anything it would be _____.

Sample riddle:
I have a pet rabbit, my favorite color is purple, and people might not know that I can sing. Who am I?

As a bonus, answer one of the questionnaires and create a riddle about yourself. Mix it in with the students' riddles and see if students can guess that it's yours.

CONCRETE POETRY

What better way to start off the new school year than with poetry? Have students write down as many words or short phrases as possible that describe their physical and emotional traits. While they can use words such as friendly, helpful, or shy, they cannot use sentences or negative words or phrases such as *hate my brother.* Have the students trace the outline of their hand on construction paper and write the words or phrases along the outline. Students can decorate their hands and write their names on the back. Hang the poems on a bulletin board for all the students to read throughout the week. They'll have fun guessing which hand belongs to whom. Leave the hands on display for parents to see.

Concrete poems allow students to be creative while exploring poetry.

GRAPHING

In this activity, students gather data by questioning other students. This is a great way to get the class interacting and to introduce graphing. Brainstorm questions students want to ask other students such as favorite pet, favorite food, number of siblings, et cetera. Pick one and brainstorm related categories. Create a tally chart on the board to track answers for each category. Make one bar graph together with the class and then split the students into groups to create their own questions, tally charts and graphs. Display the completed graphs on a bulletin board. This is a great way to fill up a bulletin board as well as showing off students' work in the first week.

CLASS COLLAGE

Use butcher paper to create a class mural. Have students create self portraits and underneath, include their name and one skill they are looking forward to learning in the grade. Display the completed mural in classroom or hallway.

USING HIEROGLYPHICS

This activity uses hieroglyphics to create a representation of the student. Draw parts of the face on the board. Create a key using each part of the face to represent an aspect of the student's life. A face may have five eyes, no nose, or three ears, depending on how you set your key. Children create their face based on information about them. Display completed faces and a key for interpretation as a bulletin board for parents and students to guess the glyph.

During the first week choose activities that can fill bulletin boards and showcase the students' work.

Breaking the Ice

KEY

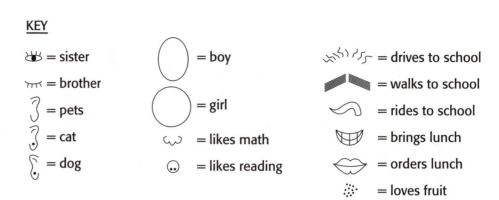

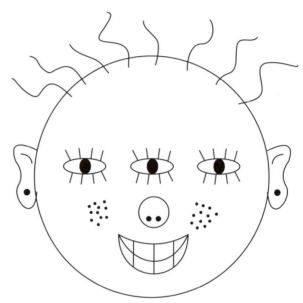

This student is a girl who likes reading, gets driven to school, has 3 sisters, a cat and a dog, brings lunch, and loves fruit.

MYSTERY STUDENT

Provide each student with a large paper bag and a student mystery questionnaire to take home. Students complete the questionnaire, put samples of the objects in the bag, and, with their name written on the bottom of the bag, return the questionnaire and bag to school. During the first few days of school, randomly select a bag, read the questions and hold up the objects. Have students try and guess who owns the bag.

Mystery Student Questionnaire

This is my favorite book _____.
(place sample in bag)

This is my favorite color _____.
(place sample in bag)

This is a picture of my favorite food _____.
(place picture in bag)

My favorite word is _____.
(write on paper and place in bag)

I have a pet _____, here is the picture.
(place in bag)

I do this in my free time _____.
(include photo or clue)

I do not like _____.
(place sample in bag)

Breaking the Ice

Chapter 21

Bringing the Parents Onboard

Sending the Important Stuff Home

During those first few days of the new school year, parents receive tons of paperwork from the school. That's why it is important to send home only the most vital information in the first few days and to keep your letters brief.

"This is Sylvia's teacher. Have you finished filling out those few papers I sent home?"

Try to spread the various letters and forms out over the first week or two so the parents have enough time to actually read and absorb all the information they are receiving. Remember some parents may have several children, so they'll be receiving much more than just your paperwork.

Create a checklist to track which students have returned important forms.

Even if you already sent out a letter at the end of the summer, send home a welcome letter during the first week of school as well. In this letter, include:

- **General information**
  Let the parents know how to reach you. Give your school email address, telephone number and work hours. Do not give out any personal information such as your home address, telephone number or email address. Although there are teachers that do not mind supplying this information to parents, it is not wise to give out any personal information.

- **School Schedule**
  Note school hours, drop off and pick up times and locations, and the general school dismissal policy. As well, let parents know about procedures for students that are arriving late or leaving early.

- **Class schedule**
  Attach or include your classroom schedule. While many teachers send home a full schedule with times for all subjects, other teachers prefer not to commit to a set schedule. Unless your school mandates that you send out a complete formalized schedule listing the times for all your subjects, you can just send out a simple overview of subjects that are based on a school wide schedule, and therefore unlikely to change times, such as P.E., music, and art.

Class begins:		8:20
Monday	Spanish	10:20–11:00
Tuesday	Library	9:00–9:40
Wednesday	Music	1:00–1:40
Thursday	P.E.	12:30–1:10
Friday	Art	10:30–11:10
Lunch		11:30–12:00
Recess		12:00–12:20
Dismissal		3:15

Bringing the Parents Onboard

Spread out letters and forms that get sent home over the first two weeks.

You can also copy your schedule onto a monthly calendar template and send it home to parents. Many teachers create calendars on a monthly basis which contain test dates, assignment dates, and school wide activities. These calendars are used mostly for kindergarten and first grade. If you plan on sending home a calendar each month, make sure you are extremely organized and can plan an entire month ahead of schedule. As they are unfamiliar with the curriculum and the time frame it takes to complete assignments, most teachers in the older grades find it very difficult to create monthly calendars during their first year.

- **Homework policy and information**
  Briefly explain the homework policy and explain that a complete homework packet will be going home later in the week.

- **Emergency contact and medication form**
  Attach an emergency contact sheet. Although the school will be sending an emergency contact form home, you should have one on file in your classroom also. Along with the emergency contact sheet, send home an index card and ask parents to include all the emergency and contact information on it as well. In your letter, explain that the index card is kept on a key ring so it can be easily brought along on any field trips the class takes, allowing you quick and easy access to the pertinent information in the event of a real emergency.

- **Volunteering**
  Decide whether or not you'll want classroom volunteers, and if so, let parents know that you'll be following up with a separate, detailed letter in about six weeks.

- **Supply list**
  Include a list of specific supplies that your students will require for school. Check to see if your school or your grade level already has a basic student supply list.

Sample Welcome Letter

Dear Parents,

Welcome to the third grade. We are looking forward to a busy and exciting year in our classroom. Here is some information to help you and your child during the first days of school.

The Third Grade Team

The third grade is being taught this year by Mrs. Smith (3A), Miss Barnes (3B), and Mr. Clarke (3C). Our assistant is Mr. Adams.

We will be working together in our team planning and creating collaborative learning activities, and are looking forward to meeting all of the students in the third grade.

Our Schedule

Below is an overview of our weekly schedule. Notice that class begins at 8:30. All students are expected to be in class at that time to begin their morning work. Students who are tardy may have difficulty completing their assigned morning work on time.

Class begins:		8:30
Monday	Spanish	10:20–11:00
Tuesday	Library	9:00–9:40
Wednesday	Music	1:00–1:40
Thursday	P.E.	12:30–1:10
Friday	Art	10:30–11:10
Lunch		11:30–12:00
Recess		12:00–12:20
Dismissal		3:15

If you need to take your child out of school early, please send a note indicating the time of dismissal. Similarly, if your child will be going home with another student, a note is required in the office.

continued on page 164

Bringing the Parents Onboard

Homework

I will be sending home a complete homework policy packet tomorrow. Included in this packet is my complete homework policy, a suggested list of supplies to keep at home, strategies for parents and students to make homework a less stressful time, and a contract for the students to sign regarding their homework. The contract must be brought back to school signed by both the student and parent or guardian no later than Monday.

Please be sure to read and review the packet with your child. We have gone over the homework policy in class, so the students are already familiar with the information. Homework is a very important part of school and should be taken seriously. After reading the homework policy, please feel free to contact me with any questions.

Parent Volunteers

Parents have already been inquiring about volunteering. Before I can have parents come into the classroom to help out, we must get the school year underway. Volunteering will begin around mid-October. In the meantime, please watch for my volunteer letter that I will be sending home soon. Parents are welcome to volunteer in our classroom, and I look forward to working with you in our class.

Finally, please feel free to contact me throughout the school year with any questions or concerns you may have. You can reach me through email at teacher@tips.com, or by phone at 888-8888 ext. 876. Please leave a message with your phone number and let me know the best time to reach you. My school hours are from 8:00–3:30, but I'm often here before and after school so I can return messages.

It is my hope that we can work as partners throughout the year in order to ensure an enriching and fun school year for your child.

Sincerely,

Miss Barnes

Sample Emergency Contact Sheet

Please complete the following information on this sheet AND on the attached index card. The completed sheet and index card should be returned to school by Tuesday, September 2nd.

This information is imperative as it relates to medical concerns. All information is kept confidential. The index cards will be used to take on field trips in case of an emergency. This is for my records and does not replace any other official emergency contact sheet you may receive.

Thank you for your cooperation.

_____
Child's First and Last Name

_____   _____
Mother's Name (or guardian)   Father's Name (or guardian)

_____   _____
Mother's Home Number   Father's Home Number

_____   _____
Mother's Cell   Father's Cell

_____   _____
Mother's Work   Father's Work

_____   _____
Pager Number   Student's Date of Birth

Allergies: _____

Treatment: _____

Other Medical Concerns: _____

Medications to be taken during school:_____

Emergency Contact Information—Please provide one contact other than parents.

_____   _____
Name   Relationship to child

_____   _____
Home Phone   Work Phone

_____   _____
Cell Phone   Pager #

Your Email Address_____

Bringing the Parents Onboard

Volunteering in the Classroom

In some schools, parent volunteers are only required for school wide events. However, most elementary schools have parent volunteers in the classroom. The older the grade, the less likely that parents will be volunteering. No matter what the grade or how many volunteers you plan on having, we have some straightforward suggestions on how to incorporate parent volunteers into your schedule.

- At the beginning of the year, send out a letter to parents with clear-cut guidelines for volunteering. Ask the parents to let you know what type of volunteering they would like to do. Some parents want to be in the room working in content areas with students, while others would rather just help with arts and crafts. Keeping track of their preferences will help you with your parent volunteers in the long run.

- Decide how you want to schedule the volunteers. Some teachers choose to keep a list of volunteers and call them ahead of time. Other teachers prefer to have volunteer times designated for the same time each week. This way, they can then assign parents to the slots and send out a schedule for the month.

During my first year teaching kindergarten I was very enthusiastic to have parents come in and help out in the classroom. I told the parents if they wanted to come and volunteer to simply call me when they were available and I'd work something out. One morning a parent left me the message that she had some extra time and would be stopping by in the afternoon to volunteer. Needless to say, I was unprepared to have a volunteer that afternoon and was embarrassed when she showed up because I had nothing for her to do. I know I appeared unorganized and unstructured, and as a first year teacher, that was the last impression I wanted to make. From that day on, I changed the way I dealt with scheduling volunteers!

- Try not to schedule parent volunteers on Mondays or Fridays. Volunteers require preparation and you might not want to use your weekend this way, meanwhile Fridays are often good days to catch up on things that may have accumulated during the week.

- There are many ways in which parents can volunteer. A parent as a guest speaker is a terrific way to include parents in your classroom and involves them in their child's educational experience.

- Have a very clear plan for what the volunteer will be doing. Whether it is reading a story to a group of students, working individually with a student in a content area, or working with the class on a project, make sure you have the activity laid out from start to finish *before* the parent arrives.

- Have a time limit. Tell the parent you need a volunteer for a specific time frame and stick with it. If you can be flexible about the time of day, that's fine, but never leave the arrangements open-ended—it only makes things harder for you and the volunteers.

- Don't ever let parents volunteer to do any grading or perform any other clerical work that involves grades or other confidential information.

- Keep an eye on the group of students with the volunteer. Often parents feel uncomfortable disciplining students, and frankly it's not their job. If you see a child exhibit inappropriate behavior, quietly

"Thanks for coming in—would you rather paint or do paper mâché?"

Bringing the Parents Onboard

Let parents know ahead of time what they will be doing when they come in.

take the child aside and speak to her. If the behavior continues, remove the child from the group; don't leave it up to the parent.

- Parent volunteers are a great help when you are rotating groups. You can have a group doing seatwork, a group doing centers, a group working on a skill with you, and another group working with a parent on an activity.

- Along with arts and craft projects or centers, parents can play math games, they can read aloud, or work with small reading and math groups, they can help students with computers, spend some one-on-one time with students that need extra help or enrichment, rotate displays or change bulletin boards, or even come in as guest speakers.

- Enjoy having parent volunteers. Some teachers look on parents as an intrusion, when parents simply want to share their child's daily experience. Having parents in your classroom helps take the mystery out of what you are doing on a daily basis and will often give them greater respect for what you do.

Finding a Classroom Mom

Many teachers enlist the help of one parent to be the classroom mom, a sort of head volunteer who helps you co-ordinate parties and events in the classroom. It could be a dad, but in most cases it will be a mother who volunteers for this job. At the beginning of the year, sit down with your room mom to see what she is interested in doing and what she will have time for. You may want to have two or more room moms who share the responsibilities between them—especially if they are juggling jobs, careers and family.

How much you allow your classroom mom to do is up to you. There are teachers who want to be in charge of every aspect of what goes on the classroom, but other teachers gladly give up the responsibility of planning parties, contacting other parents for field trips or other activities. Here are some suggestions to help you decide what your classroom mom can do.

- **Classroom parties**
  Once you've given your overall party policy to your classroom mom, you can let her contact other parents about food or helping out at the party. Unless you have specific ideas for activities, ask the mom for some suggestions. Let her arrange as much as she is willing to take on.

Sample Volunteer Letter—A

Dear Parents,

Throughout the coming year I will be looking for parents to volunteer in my classroom. If you are interested in volunteering, please fill out and return the form below so that I can fit your interests with our classroom needs. If you will be volunteering, please remember to contact me as soon as possible if you cannot come at the arranged time.

Thanks so much.

Sincerely,

Mr. Green

I would be interested in volunteering for the following:
(Please check all areas of interest)

Working with individual or small groups of children in reading _____
Working with individual or small groups of children in math _____

Helping students on computers using:

The Internet _____
Word processing _____

Making activities for learning centers (cutting and pasting) _____
Helping out with arts and crafts projects _____
Helping out with classroom parties _____
Going on field trips_____

I cannot help in the classroom, but can volunteer from home (making learning center games, cutting and pasting, and making phone calls). _____

Student's name _____

Parent's name _____

Phone number and best time to call _____

Bringing the Parents Onboard

Sample Volunteer Letter—B

Dear Parents,

Throughout the coming year I will be looking for parents to volunteer in my classroom. Volunteer times are **Tuesday and Thursday afternoons from 1:30–2:45.** Please fill in the form below—and check multiple areas of interest if you wish—so that I can fit your interests with our classroom needs. Once all papers have been returned, I'll prepare and send home a volunteer schedule. If you can't make it in at your time, feel free to switch with someone else. If you've switched times or you can't come at all, please contact me. Thanks so much.

Sincerely,

Mr. Green

I would be interested in volunteering for the following:
(Please check all areas of interest)

Working with individual or small groups of children in reading _____
Working with individual or small groups of children in math _____

Helping students on computers using:

The Internet _____
Word processing _____

Making activities for learning centers (cutting and pasting) _____
Helping out with arts and crafts projects _____
Helping out with classroom parties _____
Going on field trips _____

I cannot help in the classroom, but can volunteer from home (making learning center games, cutting and pasting, and making phone calls). _____

Student's name _____

Parent's name _____

Phone number and best time to call _____

You've Got the Job—Now Keep It

- **Field trips**

  As most room moms end up being incredibly helpful to you throughout the year, give them first choice on which field trip they'd like to chaperone. Then, let them contact the other parents in the class to arrange chaperones for the remaining field trips. If you have a behavioral issue with a certain child and need his or her parent to attend, just tell your class mom that the parent is already scheduled and will be coming along.

- **School events**

  Often your school will hold an event for which the teachers will be asked to arrange volunteers. Let you room mom make the calls.

- **Weekly volunteer time**

  If you have regular volunteer times set up in your classroom, you can have your room mother contact people to fill the volunteer slots.

You may want your room mother to do all of the above or you may want her to handle only a portion of the activities. That decision is up to you. If for some reason no one has volunteered for room mother, ask if there is a parent who would be willing to help out with parties. Parties take the most planning and are what you'll appreciate the help with most. Often the thought of being room mother is overwhelming because of the time constraints. If you break the jobs down, you can have different parents doing different parts of the room mom job.

Hosting Open House

Many teachers dread open house (also known as back-to-school night), usually held during the first few weeks of school, but you shouldn't and here's why:

Open house is your chance to sit the parents down and give the straight skinny on what will be going on in your classroom. Parents, when surveyed informally as research for this book, were asked specifically about what they wanted to learn during open house. Surprisingly, they did not put curriculum at the top of the list.

Below we've listed information you should include in your open house talk. Remember to keep your explanations short—you'll probably have less than an hour to speak. That may sound like an incredibly long amount of time, but it will go by very quickly. Some teachers do cute activities with the parents during open house, however, this is not advisable. Open house is your time to explain your policies and

Provide parents with a handout of your outline so they can take notes during open house.

procedures. Take advantage of this time, and provide parents with an agenda or outline of the topics you plan to cover.

Here are some of the areas parents want information about:

- You, your background, your education and any past teaching experience will be big areas of interest to the parents of the children you're teaching. While it's alright to tell them about your hobbies and interests, do not give out any personal information that you wouldn't want the entire school (including your students) to have.

- If parents ask questions that seem to indicate they are concerned that this is your first teaching assignment, assure them that you have the support and guidance of your administration and colleagues and play up the fact that, as a first year teacher, you're extremely motivated and looking forward to doing wonderful inventive activities in the classroom.

- Explain the basic morning and afternoon routines and the structure for the day.

- Parents will want to know about your teaching philosophies and the teaching methods you employ. How will you be teaching during the day? Will you teach the whole class or deliver the lesson to small groups? Will you use textbooks or rely on your own teacher created activities? Briefly explain your plan for teaching the curriculum, and be prepared to give a few examples of your techniques.

- Homework and your homework policy are often other big areas of interest and concern for parents. You will find they will have a lot of questions so know what your policy is, stand your ground, and be prepared to answer questions about quantity, consequence, quality and grading scheme. Parents also want to know how much parental help is expected or advised, and the number of book reports and special projects that will be expected during the year.

- Your behavior policy and that of the school's is often queried at this time. Explain your rules, any reward and consequence system you use and articulate your plan for handling recurring behavior issues.

- Let parents know how they can expect you to communicate with them and vice-versa. Tell them if they can anticipate newsletters, emails, expect phone calls or rely on the more traditional paper-based note system.

- As a teacher, you'll have goals for students to reach by the year's end, as well as skills you will expect your students to have mastered by this time. Curriculums often change, so cover the basics of the major skills to be taught and mastered by the end of the year with the parents

- The class schedule your share with parents at open house should just include the times for recess, lunch and any special events (such as library or music). Don't box yourself in by giving parents a specific schedule for content areas unless your school dictates you must.

- Your approach to fun activities such as field trips, class parties, and birthdays can also be handled at open house. Mention any policies that you or the school may have such as the distribution of birthday invitations during school hours.

- Discuss how you handle absenteeism and missed work. A good guideline for students who are out sick is two days to make up work for every day missed.

- Parent volunteers are often encouraged by schools these days and they perform many valuable functions. Open house is a great time to cover the basics: what parent volunteers do, how a parent can become a volunteer, and what your expectations of the parent volunteers for your class are. You may even want to include your parent volunteer form with your open house outline.

Remember that open house is your time to show the parents that you know what you're doing. Even if you're more nervous than you've ever been in your life, pretend that you're not. The more you've planned and practiced what you're going to say, the easier it will be. Remember, have your policies and procedures in place and be prepared to answer questions about them. Putting together an agenda or an outline for the parents that covers what you will be discussing is often helpful. Parents can use it to follow along and take notes if they wish.

At the beginning of your talk, explain that this is a general overview; if parents have specific questions or concerns about their child they should make an appointment to speak with you. If during open house, a parent is monopolizing time it is perfectly appropriate to say, "I can't go into that at this time, but if you'd like to make an appointment to speak to me further about it, that would be fine." Or, "I have many items to cover tonight; if you need further clarification I can speak to after open house or sometime tomorrow."

At open house have extra copies of all forms you sent home during the first week available for parents.

Bringing the Parents Onboard

Finally, don't be frightened. Open house is not bad. For the most part, parents sit and listen to you tell what the year will be like and most of their questions are about homework. It is very rare that a parent gets upset or confrontational during open house because, frankly, most open houses are held within the first month of school and there's very little for parents to be angry about. Try to look at open house as a great way to get to know the parents, for them to get to know you, and for them to understand what their children will be doing in school.

Chapter 22

Helping with Homework

No matter what you tell parents, you will not be able to control how much help they actually give during homework. Whenever you discuss homework help, try using the word "guidance" instead of help. The difference is subtle yet important because while it is okay for parents to guide their children when necessary, they shouldn't be delivering the answer or defining the process by which the students solve a problem or complete a project.

 *Be clear with students and parents about homework expectations.*

When it comes to homework and parents, providing an explanation of your policy, doing your part to make homework run smoothly, and giving parents tips to help make homework less of a hassle will help reduce problematic homework situations during the year.

Explaining Your Homework Policy to Parents

Set up your homework policy at the beginning of the year, explain it to the students, and provide each parent with a copy. The homework policy should detail clear, concise expectations and consequences about completing homework. To develop your homework policy, you'll need to be clear about your expectations and consequences as well as any reward systems you may want to implement. Some examples of the type of expectations and consequences that you can include in your homework policy are:

- Students should read 10–20 minutes per night.

- In addition to 10–20 minutes of reading, homework should take about 10 minutes per grade level per night.

- Homework will only cover concepts already taught in class.

- Homework needs to be handed in on time.

- All homework must be handed in neatly. Torn, stained, crumbled papers or papers without proper headings will not be accepted.

Have a place for parents to sign and return important notices sent home.

- Students are not allowed to return to the classroom after 3:30 to retrieve a forgotten book or assignment. (This helps children understand they're responsible for organizing themselves when packing up. If they forget a book, they have to suffer the consequences of a missed homework assignment.)

- Homework that is faxed or from a copying machine will not be accepted for the same reason as mentioned above. However, students can call a friend and have the friend read the assignment over the phone. (This will not happen often because friends will get tired of having to do this.)

- Once the school day has begun, parents cannot deliver homework that has been left at home.

- Students who don't complete homework will miss five minutes of recess.

Break down the homework packet into parts to be sent home each day.

- After a third missed homework in a semester the student will have a 30 minute classroom detention.

- If all students remember their homework the entire class can have a reward. You can reward them on a daily, weekly, or monthly basis.

These are simply examples of what you can include in your homework policy. You need to decide on a policy that best suits you and your class and is consistent with what your school permits.

Sample Homework Policy Packet

Homework Policy for Mrs. Stevens' Third Grade Class—Part One

Dear Parents,

Welcome to the start of a brand new, exciting year. Homework will play an important part in teaching students about responsibility this year, and I will be assigning homework on a regular basis. As I won't be assigning any work that we've not covered in class, I expect students to do their own work and to ask for guidance only after they have given their best effort. There may be times I send work home that is challenging, but I will indicate this on the assignment paper. Please guide you children only when they need it, and do not do the homework assignments with or for your child.

Here are some tips to help homework run more smoothly at your home.

- Make homework a priority at home.

- Find a quiet place to have your child complete homework, away from TV, radios, or other interruptions. Completing homework in the car on the way to softball practice is not the best habit.

- Help your child decide on the best time of day to do homework: right after school, before dinner after they've had some playtime, or immediately following dinner. If possible, include your child in this decision so he or she has input in the homework issue.

- Keep supplies close at hand. Please see the attached suggested supply list. Having supplies ready will help eliminate procrastination.

- Make sure your child has the phone number of several other children in the classroom. If he needs clarification on an assignment, he can call a friend.

I'll go over the homework directions in school at the end of each day, encouraging children to ask any questions that they might have. When children need help at home, it's often because they've misunderstood the directions. Ask them to explain the directions to you and you can then read the assignment to see if they are on the right track. If they know what they need to do but still have questions, try guiding them though a problem only after they've attempted it on their own first. If your child is still confused, have him or her phone a friend for clarification. If you do feel it's necessary to assist your child, please drop me a note, email, or call me the following day and let me know that help was provided. This way I can be sure to review the assignment with your child to see where the confusion was.

Helping with Homework

Completing homework neatly, completely, and handing it in on time are all part of a student's responsibility. Because I know that we all forget things from time to time, students will be given three chances before a detention is given. If this happens, I will contact you and let you know. If, due to unforeseen circumstances, your child is unable to complete the assignment, please send in a note letting me know why the homework is incomplete.

Also, it is my policy that students will not be allowed back into the classroom after school hours, and faxed or photo-copied homework will not be accepted. Students are given ample time to pack up at the end of the day. Having to face the consequence of not remembering a book or an assignment will help students to become better organized in the long run.

Thanks for taking the time to read this, and feel free to call me if you have any questions.

Sincerely,

Mrs. Stevens

For your child's study area at home, he or she will need a small tub, container or some sort of method for storing the following:

Writing Supplies	Paper	Books	Other
pencils, sharpener	loose leaf paper (lined)	dictionary	hole punch, scissors
erasers, rulers	unlined paper	thesaurus	glue, tape
	graph paper		coloring supplies
	scrap paper		

Please detach and return to school

I have read the above memo_____
                               (Parent signature)   (Date)

TIPS, Inc.

Homework Policy for Mrs. Stevens' Third Grade Class—Part Two

Homework: How can I help without doing the assignment????

- Make homework a priority in your house.

- Decide on a daily homework time. If your child is old enough (second grade and above) sit down at the beginning of the year and decide on a homework time together. Look at the extracurricular activities of everyone in the family to see what time is best—it can always be adjusted throughout the year if required. (In the car on the way to soccer practice is not the best homework time.)

- Make sure your child has a quiet area to work. No TV, radio, phone calls, or loud interrupting siblings. Hopefully all siblings will be doing homework at the same time.

- Any school-age children that do not have homework should read a book quietly or play away from the homework area.

- Keep supplies close at hand. Please see the attached suggested supply list. Having supplies ready will help eliminate procrastination.

- Have the phone numbers of two other students in your child's class, so that your child can call for last minute clarifications or directions.

- Use a timer or clock to help structure homework time. For children with attention issues, it's often helpful for them to know they will work for 15 minutes and then get a break. If they know a timer will go off, they will focus less on how much time they've been working and be able to focus a bit more on their homework.

- Provide guidance not the answers. Have your child read the directions to you and explain what they think they need to do.

- Decide how much guidance your child actually needs. Children should be able to work on their homework independently at home, unless they are too young to read directions or have special needs. If your child is in kindergarten or first grade, he or she may need help reading and understanding directions and may even require help to complete the assignment. By third grade however, your child should be able to complete all aspects of his or her homework independently.

Helping with Homework

If your child has a learning disability (or you suspect this is the case), a more hands-on approach with homework may be required. We can work together to come up with a solution that will still allow your child as much independence as possible.

- Make sure you have your child's attention before giving a direction.

- Explain directions if necessary in short, concise steps. If further assistance is needed try assisting with the first problem only.

- Don't "sit down" (literally) with your child—stand. Sitting down tells your child you're there for the long haul.

- Start the school year off firmly and tell your child that you will not be completing homework together. Assure him or her that you will be there to give guidance and make sure that directions are understood.

- If you are checking homework, do not to point out individual mistakes. Instead say, "I've found four mistakes on this page. You need to find them and fix them." This allows you to check work without actually changing any of your child's work or giving them the answers.

- For longer projects, break projects down into parts (if not done so by the teacher) and help your child decide when each part should be completed. For example, chapters one–three should be read by Friday or the rough draft must be completed by Wednesday, October 15. Helping your elementary age child plan out long-term assignments using a calendar will be beneficial to her as she progresses through the grades.

- Don't feel that you need to become the homework police. If you feel your child has not put his or her best effort into the assignment, tell your child you think it should be redone. If he chooses not to redo the assignment then (without your child knowing it), contact the teacher and let him or her know your feelings. Together you can create consequences for incomplete homework or rewards for a job well done.

- Breaking the "doing homework together habit" may be a lot like getting your child to sleep through the night. In the beginning you'll have to ignore a lot of whining, but if you stand your ground your child will begin to complete homework without your assistance.

Homework Policy for Mrs. Stevens' Third Grade Class—Part Three

Parents—this is a copy of a note that your child received during the first few days in my class this year.

Homework Contract for Third Grade

I, _____, understand that homework is a very important part of _____ grade. I promise to put forth my best effort when completing my homework. I understand that homework is my responsibility. I know my parents can give me guidance but cannot sit down and complete homework with me or do my homework for me.

Date _____ Signed _____
(Student's signature)

Signed _____
(Parent's signature)

Avoid Morning Madness—Make a Sure Spot!!!

Have you ever heard yourself say "I did my homework, but I forgot to bring it" or "I know had my gym clothes ready to go, but I forgot to put them in my bag . . ." Teachers have heard it all!!! Make sure you never forget your homework again by creating a "SURE SPOT" in your house—a place where you will put your bookbag each night once you are sure that you have everything you need to bring to school inside. Always keep your bookbag in the same spot. Once you've finished your homework, check your schedule for anything else that you might need for the following day, like your band instrument, or your gym clothes. Gather everything (homework included) and place it all into your bookbag and put the bag in your "SURE SPOT." Now there is no more morning madness, where you run around like crazy trying to get everything together! Your teacher will love the idea and your parents will thank you!!!

My Sure Spot is: _____

Helping with Homework

Making Homework Hassle Free: What a Teacher Can Do

Teachers are sometimes partially to blame when parents become over involved with homework; either because of the type of work the teachers assign or because the directions they send home are incomplete or confusing. Follow the suggestions below to help make homework less of a hassle:

- If you don't want parents to help, don't send home complicated homework. Remember, you should not be using homework to introduce new concepts.

- Be sure that you've gone over the directions for the homework assignments and that all the students know what they need to do. If you feel that you want to send home something that requires a bit more brain power, put a note at the top of the page that says "Challenging: Parents, please do not help."

- Be very clear with your expectations regarding how the finished homework will turn out. Most homework assignments in the elementary grades are not very difficult, but make sure you know what outcome you want before you give the assignment.

- Be willing to adjust homework assignments. If you've given a weekly homework assignment and find that it's too much for the students, scale it back or make a change. It's okay to change the requirements or due dates if most of your class is struggling.

- Build up students' self-esteem. Tell students that you feel confident in their ability to complete homework without the help of their parents.

- If students are confused about something, tell them it's okay to ask their parents for some guidance so they can get on the right track, but it's not okay to let their parents do the work for them.

- Model working independently in class. During the school day, students should be guided to solve problems on their own as much as possible. The more independent they become in class, the more confident they will feel completing homework on their own.

- If students ask you a question that you're sure you've already answered, instruct them to ask a friend. If further clarification is needed then have them come back to you.

- When assigning long-term projects, go over every aspect of the assignment with the students. If parents have questions politely tell the parent that the assignment was reviewed in class, but students are welcome to ask a friend and then you for further clarification. Be sure that you let the students know this also. If you take the attitude of, "I've already gone over this assignment so I won't answer any more questions," then you've left the parents no other option but to help.

- For longer assignments, give the students a rubric and explain how it will be used. A rubric helps them make sure they've included all the components necessary for the assignment.

- For long-term projects, consider including a sentence in the directions that says, "*You should receive no help from parents with this assignment. Your effort will be reflected in your grade.*" It might seem a bit harsh, but it sends the message that parents are not expected to participate in the project.

Parents have some very valid concerns once you tell them they can't help with homework. Some of these concerns are: their child will carry on and cry, their child will hand in garbage, or their child will do the assignment incorrectly. Since so many parents are concerned over homework issues, before telling them how to break the homework helping habit, reassure parents that you understand many of their concerns.

Here are some points that you can mention at open house so parents understand your homework rationale and can gently ease away from helping with homework:

- First, explain to the parents that students complete assignments all day long in class with very little guidance. They read directions and complete their work independently. As the classroom teacher, you do not sit down with children individually to complete each assignment; therefore parents don't need to sit down during homework time.

- Second, tell the parents that if they don't start stepping back, then they should be prepared for another entire year of providing "hands-on" help with homework. Homework help is not a condition children outgrow, it's a habit they grow into and it doesn't magically change once children hit a certain age—on the contrary it will only get more difficult because children will expect help as long as parents are willing to give it. (Obviously if you're teaching kindergarten or first grade, you won't be advocating a complete hands-off policy, but you should encourage the parents to let their child do as much as possible on their own.)

Helping with Homework

- Third, and this one drives home a big point, tell the parents that every time they sit down with their child to help with homework, they are silently reinforcing the message that the child is incapable of completing the work herself.

- If a student hands in messy or incomplete homework, that is your responsibility, and you will deal with it in the classroom, one-on-one with the student. This takes the pressure off the parents, because really, the responsibility of doing homework belongs to the student, not the parents.

- Finally, assure parents that when assigning homework you will make every effort to send home work that can be completed independently by the students. In addition, let parents know that they must also make every effort to ensure that their children are completing the work on their own. Refer parents back to homework policy package for helpful tips.

Remember, most parents do not want to do their children's homework. They simply want to make sure it gets done and gets done correctly. They want their children to always do their best. What you need to continually reinforce with parents is that the children must become responsible for their own work and face the consequences at school

> Every year at open house I tell parents that if they feel their children do not put their best effort into completing an assignment to send me an email, drop me a note, or give me a call indicating their concerns. I've found parents usually love this idea because suddenly we've become partners and they don't feel alone—it gives them a strategy and makes me their ally. Anytime the concern turns out to be justified, I create a consequence for the child at school. Nine out of ten times, this works and the student starts to take homework more seriously. This strategy is especially effective if the consequence at school is followed up with a consequence at home.

(which should be followed up at home) if they are not working up to their full potential. Homework policies that incorporate expectations from school and home will work best for all parties concerned.

Why Some Parents Don't Help at All

For all we've talked about parents being over involved in their children's homework, the opposite can also be true: you may have parents that take little or no interest in helping their children with homework at all. There are a variety of reasons why parents may have a hands-off policy when it comes to their child's schoolwork so don't be quick to judge the lack of attention these parents give. It's often not that the parents don't care, it's that there are other concerns in their lives that are taking precedence at that moment. Some of these problems might be:

- **Financial problems**
  Some families have very difficult financial problems where one or both parents are working more than one job. Often the parents simply do not have the time to commit to helping their children with homework or projects and their work schedules can conflict with school events and parent-teacher conferences.

- **Personal problems**
  All people go through difficult times and often families going through a crisis will put a child's school work on the back burner.

- **Personal view points**
  Some parents simply feel that their children should do all school work on their own. There are parents out there that will not help their children with homework or projects because they feel it is not their job.

Having parents who are uncommunicative or uninvolved is often just as frustrating as having parents who are over involved. If you have a student in need of some help at home but know that none is being given, ask the parents to come in for a conference and discuss your concerns. If conferencing makes no difference, try holding a "Homework Help" session after school one day a week—after all, most schools require their teachers to stay for up to an half an hour after dismissal, so you'll be around anyway. This way, the students who have no other options get the help they need.

Helping with Homework

Summary Section Four

- Establish yourself as teacher from day one. Accept only the behavior you plan to accept for the entire year.

- Create structure in your classroom. Decide on your classroom procedures before the students arrive at school. Spend the extra time during the first few weeks teaching students routines and procedures and making them follow through. The time you spend during those first weeks having students repeat tasks, redo unacceptable work, and learn routines will be time well spent.

- On the first day of school, establish and post the classroom rules. While you can decide on the rules as a class, make sure the important rules you want get incorporated too.

- Create a balance between curriculum and fun during the first few days of school. Spend a small part of the day involving students in getting-to-know-you activities as well as putting away and organizing supplies. Spend the rest of the time doing classwork.

- Send home a welcome letter containing general information about the school year during the first week of school. Also send a letter about volunteering and a packet containing your homework policy.

- Plan on having volunteers in the classroom. Be specific about the activities you want them to do and always be prepared with the supplies they will need.

- Invite one or two of the parents to be room moms to help plan parties, participate in school events, coordinate field trip chaperones and any other "non-teaching" activities you'd like help with.

- Open house is your opportunity to explain your policies and procedures to parents. If possible, outline what you will be covering and make copies for the parents. Know your policies and procedures, be confident and try to enjoy the evening.

- When assigning homework, set the students up for success. Make sure the homework does not introduce a new concept and provide the students with clear directions.

- Supply the parents with strategies to use at home so their child can complete homework independently.

Notes

Class Schedule

Class Begins	Subject	Time	
Monday			
Tuesday			
Wednesday			
Thursday			
Friday			
Recess			
Dismissal			

TIPS, Inc.

Emergency Contact Sheet

Please complete the following information on this sheet AND on the attached index card. The completed sheet and index card should be returned to school by _____.

This information is imperative as it relates to medical concerns. All information is kept confidential. The index cards will be used to take on field trips in case of an emergency. This is for my records and does not replace any other official emergency contact sheet you may receive.

Thank you for your cooperation.

_____
Child's First and Last Name

_____	_____
Mother's Name (or guardian)	Father's Name (or guardian)
_____	_____
Mother's Home Number	Father's Home Number
_____	_____
Mother's Cell	Father's Cell
_____	_____
Mother's Work	Father's Work
_____	_____
Pager Number	Student's Date of Birth

Allergies: _____

Treatment: _____

Other Medical Concerns: _____

Medications to be taken during school: _____

Emergency Contact Information—Please provide one contact other than parents.

_____	_____
Name	Relationship to child
_____	_____
Home Phone	Work Phone
_____	_____
Cell Phone	Pager #

Your Email Address _____

TIPS, Inc.

Reproducibles

Mystery Student Questionnaire

Fill in the questionnaire and put a sample of each item in a paper bag. Put your name on the bottom of the bag and bring the bag to school with all your samples (clues or pictures) inside. Each day we'll open a several bags and try to guess who the bag belongs to, so don't tell anyone what you're putting inside!

This is my favorite book _____. (place sample in bag)

This is my favorite color _____. (place sample in bag)

This is a picture of my favorite food _____. (include picture)

My favorite word is _____. (write on paper and place in bag)

I have a pet _____, here is the picture. (place photo in bag)

I do this in my free time _____. (include photo or clue)

I do not like _____. (place photo in bag)

? ? ? ? ?

Homework:
How can I help without doing the assignment????

- Make homework a priority in your house.

- Decide on a daily homework time. If your child is old enough (second grade and above) sit down at the beginning of the year and decide on a homework time together. Look at the extra curricular activities of everyone in the family to see what time is best—it can always be adjusted throughout the year if required. (In the car on the way to soccer practice, is not the best homework time.)

- Make sure your child has a quiet area to work. No TV, radio, phone calls, or loud interrupting siblings. Hopefully all siblings will be doing homework at the same time.

- Any school-age children that do not have homework should read a book quietly or play away from the homework area.

- Keep supplies close at hand. Please see the attached suggested supply list. Having supplies ready will help eliminate procrastination.

- Have the phone numbers of two other students in your child's class, so that your child can call for last minute clarifications or directions.

- Use a timer or clock to help structure homework time. For children with attention issues, it's often helpful for them to know they will work for 15 minutes and then get a break. If they know a timer will go off, they will focus less on how much time they've been working and be able to focus a bit more on their homework.

- Provide guidance not the answers. Have your child read the directions to you and explain what they think they need to do.

- Decide how much guidance your child actually needs. Children should be able to work on their homework independently at home, unless they are too young to read directions or have special needs. If your child is in kindergarten or first grade, he or she may need help reading and understanding directions and may even require help to complete the assignment. By third grade however, your child should be able to complete all aspects of his or her homework independently.

    If your child has a learning disability (or you suspect this is the case), a more hands-on approach with homework may be required. We can work together to come up with a solution that will still allow your child as much independence as possible.

- Make sure you have your child's attention before giving a direction.

- Explain directions if necessary in short, concise steps. If further assistance is needed trying assisting with the first problem only.

- Don't "sit down" (literally) with your child—stand. Sitting down tells your child you're there for the long haul.

TIPS, Inc.

Reproducibles

Homework—cont'd

- Start the school year off firmly and tell your child that you will not be completing homework together. Assure him or her that you will be there to give guidance and make sure that directions are understood.

- If you are checking homework, do not to point out individual mistakes. Instead say, "I've found four mistakes on this page. You need to find them and fix them." This allows you to check work without actually changing any of your child's work or giving the answers.

- For longer projects, break projects down into parts (if not done so by the teacher) and help your child decide when each part should be completed. For instance, chapters one–three should be read by Friday or the rough draft must be completed by Wednesday, October 15. Helping your elementary age child plan out long-term assignments using a calendar will be beneficial as he or she progresses through the grades.

- Don't feel that you need to become the homework police. If you feel your child has not put his or her best effort into the assignment, tell your child you think it should be redone. If he chooses not to redo the assignment then (without your child knowing it), contact the teacher and let him or her know your feelings. Together you can create consequences for incomplete homework or rewards for a job well done.

- Breaking the "doing homework together habit" may be a lot like getting your child to sleep through the night. In the beginning you'll have to ignore a lot of whining, but if you stand your ground your child will begin to complete homework without your assistance.

TIPS, Inc.

Homework Contract

I, _____, understand that homework is a very important part

of _____ grade. I promise to put forth my best effort when completing my homework. I understand that homework is my responsibility. I know my parents can give me guidance but cannot sit down and complete homework with me or do my homework for me.

Date _____ Signed_____
(Student's signature)

Signed _____
(Parent's signature)

- -

Avoid Morning Madness—Make a Sure Spot!!!

Have you ever heard yourself say "I did my homework, but I forgot to bring it" or "I know had my gym clothes ready to go, but I forgot to put them in my bag . . ." Teachers have heard it all!!! Make sure you never forget your homework again by creating a "SURE SPOT" in your house—a place where you will put your bookbag each night once you are sure that you have everything you need to bring to school inside. Always keep your bookbag in the same spot. Once you've finished your homework, check your schedule for anything else that you might need for the following day, like your band instrument, or your gym clothes. Gather everything (homework included) and place it all into your bookbag and put the bag in your "SURE SPOT." Now there is no more morning madness, where you run around like crazy trying to get everything together! Your teacher will love the idea and your parents will thank you!!!

My Sure Spot is: _____

TIPS, Inc.

Reproducibles

SECTION FIVE

Staying on Top—
The Importance of Grading

- Grading vs assessing
- What to grade—classwork, tests, and homework
- Determining your grading scale
- Keeping track of graded work
- Report card comments

IN THIS SECTION

Chapter 23

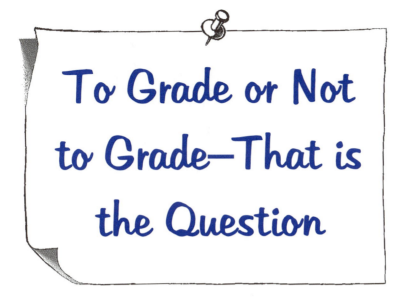

To Grade or Not to Grade—That is the Question

Grades seem to have become a tangible necessity yet, for most good teachers, grades aren't necessary to understand how a child is doing in the class. Moreover, a gradebook is not necessary to tell them the standard of work a child is producing. However, more often than not, grades are mandatory for teachers to measure how the students are doing, for parents to view and administrators to evaluate. So when you grade a student's work keep in mind its significance—grades offer solid evidence of a student's performance and give both the parent and the student an indication of how the student is performing against grade level standards.

"We should spend more time fertilizing and nurturing the flowers instead of measuring how tall they've grown."

—Author unknown

"This is all well and good, Mrs. Carter, but will it be on the standardized tests this year?"

The Difference between Grading and Assessing

When hearing the word assessment, many people think of grades. Performing an assessment is not necessarily grading. When you're assessing you evaluate whether or not students understand and can apply the skill or skills that you've taught them; when you're grading you assign a point value to the assessments. Assessments can be done in many ways.

- **Informal observation**

  Watch and listen to students while they work to gain insight about who is having problems.

- **Verbal assessment**

  Have students explain something to you instead of writing it down. Often students understand a concept but have a difficult time expressing their understanding on paper.

- **Cumulative assessment**

  Keep a portfolio, or any other long-term representation of work, so you can chart students' progress from the beginning of a project through to the end.

- **Classwork**

  Independent work should show progress towards the mastery of a concept. In some cases you may wish to grade certain work.

Mr. Riggs loved doing informal student observations.

- **Quizzes and tests**
  Pretest before a unit to determine what the students already know. Post-testing will measure how much the students have learned. Post-tests are almost always graded.

Deciding What to Grade

Some schools may have specific requirements regarding the types and amounts of assignments that need to be graded. Be sure to find out what the grading requirements are for your grade level, and use that to help you decide what work to grade. **Every piece of student work does not need to be graded.**

There are a variety of assignments or activities in school that can be graded. Before you give an assignment to students, you must consider the following:

Will the assignment need a grade?

Not all assignments need to be graded. Assignments can be corrected together as a class or by you alone, but they don't all need a grade. A check mark, smiley face, or comment is enough for probably 50% of the assignments that will cross your desk.

 As a teacher you will be constantly assessing students, but not necessarily constantly grading them.

Why are you grading the assignment?

Are you looking for comprehension of a story? Mastery of a math skill? Grammar and punctuation? Grade only those assignments that reflect a true assessment of the concept taught.

What will you be looking for in the answer?

Once you've decided *why* you are grading the assignment, decide what specific components you'll want in the answer and assign a point value for each. Make your students aware of the requirements for the answer. This is especially important for any essay type questions. For example, do you want a topic sentence? How many examples do you want the students to give? Will you be grading for spelling and grammar? These are all important points to consider.

Are you grading something only because it's easy to grade?

Be careful that fill-in-the-blank type papers aren't the only ones you grade. You will need to take time to grade more comprehensive papers also.

It is important to decide what you're looking for in an answer before you give and grade the assignment.

The list below contains assignments that fall into the categories of classwork, tests, and homework—the type of work that teachers assess and often grade. Before you start teaching you should think about which assignments on the list you would grade and how much weight you would give each assignment towards a student's overall grade.

Work done at home:
- daily homework
- book reports or other projects

Work completed in class:
- written reports
- oral reports
- work books
- worksheets
- written answers to questions from textbooks
- oral answers to questions from textbooks
- group projects or activities
- learning centers
- creative writing
- formal writing
- reviews for tests
- formal assessments (quizzes or tests)

When deciding a final grade, you should also take into account class participation, effort, and behavior.

Classwork

Classwork should be the main component of your grading scheme. The work that children do on a day-to-day basis best reflects their overall independent ability. Classwork can be a mix of the student's individual work, group projects, and class reports. Behavior and effort can also be included in the classwork grade. When grading classwork consider what we've already discussed about grading as well as the following:

Consider including marks for effort and class participation as part of all students' grades.

- Put comments on papers whenever possible. Comments are very important for students as they give them a sense of direction and understanding about your expectations. You needn't write long comments, simple comments to address the specific difficulties such as *"Missing topic sentence"* or *"Not enough detail"* are fine. Don't forget the positive comments too, they are just as important—especially if you see improvement in a child's work. As well, parents often appreciate comments (both positive and negative) on papers, and including comments tends to cut down on questions about how you arrived at the grade.

- Be sure to review any papers with students who have completely misunderstood the assignment or concept. If more than one child had difficulty, this can be done as a group review.

- Reflect participation and effort in a student's overall grade and, when necessary, use these to decide whether to round a student's grade up or down. Do not get into the habit of rounding grades up, unless the student has shown strong effort in that subject. (If you round a grade, you should include a comment on the report card about the student's effort being reflected in the grade.)

- Let students learn by having them correct their mistakes on graded work. When grading a paper, don't write the correct answers for the students. Instead, put an X, a circle, or some other mark near the incorrect answer. As part of the assignment, students can redo the work. You can even give them extra points if they can redo the problem correctly. The extra points motivate the students to redo the work while allowing them to see how they made their mistakes. You won't have the time to do this for all graded assignments so choose assignments where this type of review would be most beneficial.

- Any time you write a grade on a student's paper, you should include a fraction that shows the points earned over the total possible points, as well as the percentage the fraction equals. This allows

To Grade or Not to Grade—That is the Question

students to actually see how many points they lost on the assignment.

17/25 = 68% = D

Don't always include the letter grade. Instead, at the beginning of the year, let the students know what percentages constitute an A, B, C, D and F. Once they know this, most will be able to figure it out on their own.

Tests

Many teachers rely heavily on test grades, especially at the intermediate level. Be careful about putting too much emphasis on tests. Remember, many students that do well in class may do poorly on tests because of anxiety. The opposite is also true. Some students who do not do well on a daily basis do well on tests because they have practiced and have been drilled on the test material. In either case, the test score isn't a complete picture of the student's true capabilities. Final grades shouldn't rely heavily on test scores. While you'll have to abide by school policy, if you are permitted to assign weights to different kinds of assessments, test scores should represent only about 40% of the total subject grade. The remaining 60% should be made up of classwork grades, long-term projects, and effort.

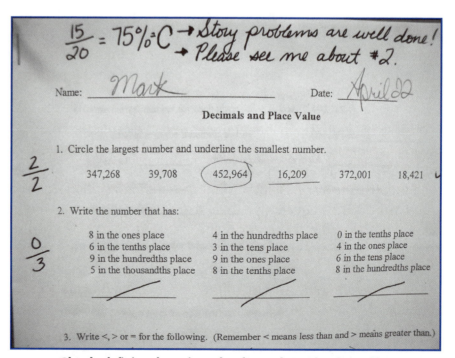

Clearly defining the point value for each test section makes correction easier, and allows students to see where points were lost.

ADMINISTERING TESTS

- Have the students complete a review paper at least three days before a test. This will give you time to go over the paper with the class and clear up any areas of confusion. It is a good idea to periodically grade review papers, but in general, reviews should be used simply to check for areas where there still may be confusion or questions.

- Be sure to allot enough time for the students to take the test in its entirety. If you **have** to split a test, give a specific section in the morning and then the rest in the afternoon. **Do not redistribute previously completed sections.**

- All students should be given the same amount of time to do the same amount of work. The only time this might not hold true is if you have a student who is getting some type of modification to the curriculum and is allotted extra time.

- Before the test starts, make sure students have all the necessary supplies—including reading material or quiet seatwork in the event they complete the test early. To minimize distractions, students should not be allowed to talk or get out of their seats during a test and they should raise their hands to ask a question. If you start these procedures at the beginning of the year, there will be structure within the classroom and the students will understand what is expected when the time comes to take tests.

GRADING TESTS

- Know exactly what you are looking for in an answer before grading the tests.

- Consider giving partial credit for answers. Some students are on the right track but don't quite put the whole answer together. In math, a student may do everything right from a process or problem solving perspective, and then in the end, add two numbers together incorrectly. Partial credit gives students credit for what they know, but shows them that next time they need to work more carefully, add more detail, or do whatever it was that cost them the extra points.

- Include a writing component whenever possible, even on a math test. When answering word problems have students not only show the mechanics of how they got their answer, but also have them write step-by-step directions on how they arrived at their final answer. They should include a final sentence such as, "After the markers were split up, there were three remaining."

- Make a "Don't Ask" policy amongst the students when it comes to grades they've received. When you review a test with the class make it clear that students are not allowed to ask each other their grades. The reason for this is obvious—the student who received a poor grade is not going to want to tell people his mark.

- While you may not review every graded classwork assignment, always go over tests so that students can understand what they did wrong. When reviewing tests, let the students complete problems on the board or read their answers out loud. When reviewing long answers it is helpful to call on a few students to read their answers. This lets the rest of the class hear answers that have been written several different ways, yet contain all the necessary details to get full credit.

Don't forget "the parent factor" when grading work done at home.

Homework

Most teachers will tell you that (if given the option) they would choose not to give homework on a nightly basis. Many teachers don't want to give homework because they feel it must be graded. Homework has become the norm in many countries, especially the United States, and is given out on a regular basis. In some cases the homework policy is strictly mandated by the school while in others it is left up to the teacher. In either case, quality over quantity is the objective.

Homework is beneficial when it's used for reinforcement, lesson review or extension, remediation, assessment, long-term skill reinforcement (i.e. multiplication facts or spelling words), and development of independent work skills and study habits.

Homework provides little value when it introduces brand new concepts, requires a large amount of parental input, is a source of frustration for students and parents, and monopolizes the children's free time.

Using homework as a graded assessment tool can be dangerous because of the "parent factor." You can usually tell by the quality of the work a student turns in if he is receiving too much help at home. If you suspect this to be the case you'll have to address the matter with the parents in question.

Homework falls into two categories: daily and long-term homework.

DAILY

Daily homework is just that—work that gets sent home one day and is returned the next. Whether or not you grade daily homework is up to you. There may be some daily homework that you'll want to grade such as spelling assignments or a math review sheet. However, for daily homework, you may want to consider just checking it and giving it a smiley face or a check mark. Remember, in order for students to value homework you must also, so make sure you review and return everything that is handed in.

LONG-TERM

Long-term homework is homework that gets completed outside of school over a longer period of time. Projects and book reports are the main components of long-term homework. As this type of homework often gets graded, suggestions on how to grade long-term homework assignments are listed below.

All homework does not need to be graded, however it does need to be reviewed so that students see its value.

- **Book Reports and Projects**

    Most parents help their child on major projects (such as book reports) that get completed at home. One way to offset this situation is to include five to ten points in the final grading sheet or rubric; so along with awarding points for content, punctuation, grammar, and neatness, award points for "reflects student's effort." Giving student effort a point value helps with several issues:

    First, you can deduct points if a student obviously did not put the appropriate amount of effort into an assignment. You'll know this because you'll know the capability of the student's best effort. Conversely, you'll know what he produces when he works quickly without much effort.

    Second, you can deduct points if you feel there was too much help given on the assignment. If your third grade student is using semicolons and colons correctly and has multiple compound sentences, there's some extra help going on (or you're teacher of the year). Similarly if drawings, maps or covers do not look the same as the student's normal classroom work, then you know that he had help.

    If a parent questions you on this part of the grading, explain your reasoning behind the deductions. Even the most critical parents will rarely argue with you on this point. It's not that parents help their children with the intention of doing something negative—

"Ummm, looks good Timmy, you sure you didn't have help with this?"

To Grade or Not to Grade—That is the Question

parents simply want their children to do the best possible work they can, and their help can run from providing some simple guidance to actually completing the <u>entire assignment</u> for their child. Get used to it, it happens all the time, and you've got to decide what to do about it.

- **Weighting long-term projects**
It is next to impossible not to grade an at home book report or project. No matter how much help the student received, he did put in the time and effort and a grade is both expected and deserved. Book reports and projects should count for no more than 10% of the student's overall grade for the marking period.

That may seem like very little credit for a long-term project however consider why book reports and projects are done. Book reports should be done to encourage children to read on their own and then show what they've learned from the book. At home projects should be assigned so that students can take what they've learned in class, blend it with information they've researched on their own and synthesize both to make a project demonstrating the knowledge they have gained.

When assigning book reports and projects be careful not to put too much emphasis on the artistic aspect of the project. Some children are not artistic and projects that involve making figures, 3-D models, mobiles, or buildings can be very challenging and may take the "fun" out of doing the project—some kids are even self-conscious about their drawings. Be sure to have a balanced project and grade accordingly for those students who are "artistically challenged."

Assign quality projects that are fun to complete so grades become less of a focus and learning becomes the priority.

Using Grading Scales

The grade you are teaching and the policy of the school will dictate what grading scale you use. Lower grades usually have a comment-based grading scale such as:

O—Outstanding
S—Satisfactory
U—Unsatisfactory
NI—Needs Improvement
P—Pass
F—Fail

Higher grades normally will follow a system such as:

Letter grades from A to F
Percentage-based grades
Number grades from 1 to 5

While your school may not follow the exact grading scale above, it will most likely be similar. Quite often schools have more than one grading scale, depending on grade level. Be sure to know what grading system is used by your school in your grade. If you are expected to put number grades (such as 76%) on report cards, then use the same types of grades when you grade your papers. However, we strongly suggest if you are using letter grades (such as A–F) that you include a percentage grade too. Students should know if they are receiving a low or a high A. There's a big difference between a 99% and a 90%. By giving both letter and percentage grades, students and parents know exactly where the student stands and there are no surprises at report card time.

> Several years ago I started teaching fourth grade in a new school. I had spent many years teaching fifth grade at my previous school where we used an A–F grading scale. When I started my new job I continued using letter grades when grading assignments. Wasn't I surprised when I had to do report cards and realized the school used percentages instead of letter grades. I never even thought to ask what grading scale was used and nobody ever mentioned it to me. It created some friction with parents who saw Cs coming home during the term and then saw 70% on the report card—I don't think they realized how low the C was. My advice to new teachers is to find out the grading system your school uses as soon as you start. Also, include percentage grades whenever possible because they're a clearer indication of what the grade actually is.

Chapter 24

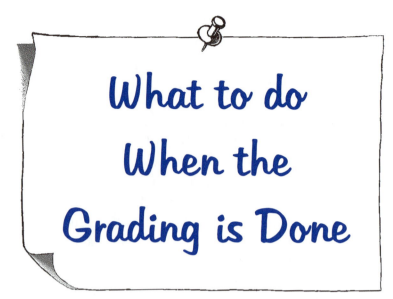

Tracking Class Grades

Once you've graded students' work, you can't just hand it back—the grades need to be recorded for report cards. Each teacher seems to have his own way of tracking grades, but grade sheets in combination with a master gradebook works best. Even if your school has a computer based gradebook, always keep a separate copy of the grades on paper. This way if something happens to one system, you know you can always rely on the other. (It's funny to note that many teachers refer to the paper gradebook as the backup system, while others refer to the computer gradebook as theirs.)

Using grading sheets may seem like extra work, but there is peace of mind in knowing that if your computer failed, or if your gradebook was missing, you are covered. Typically, it is best to have a grading sheet for each subject labeled and tucked inside its correspondingly labeled folder so that, before you give students back any graded work, you can easily record the grades onto the grading sheet first. Then, once a week, you can pull your grading sheets and enter grades into the computer or the master gradebook. Use some kind of a symbol on your grading sheets to indicate the grades you've recorded into the gradebook; use a highlighter to show any assignments still outstanding or work that has not been turned in.

Many teachers prefer grading sheets because:

- If you grade papers at home, you can record the grades on your grading sheet immediately and return assignments the next day—you don't have to worry about getting around to entering the grades in the gradebook or computer first.

- Grade sheets are easy to take home. Many schools won't let you take home gradebooks or digital copies of grades.

- The grading sheets allow you to see at a glance who has incomplete work. This is important information to have at your finger tips, especially if you have an unexpected visit from a parent or administrator.

- You can categorize your grading sheets by week or subject. (Categorizing by subject makes it easier to copy the grades into your master gradebook or computer.)

- The grade sheets serve as your back-up grades. Save them for the entire year, until that last report card is printed and mailed.

- Grading sheets are easy to make: include the date, the assignment, the assignment type (classwork, homework, or a test), the total points possible, and the points given. You may want to include an A for absent, M for missing, I for incomplete, C for completed, or E for excused. You can find pre-printed forms in books or on the internet, yet it may be more economical and convenient to create your own. The following is a sample of a grading sheet.

Deciding What to Keep

After parents sign and return work, you should keep students' work on file. Depending on the size of your class, keeping **all** work in a file may not be practical for you. You can either keep work and send it home at the end of each semester, or hold onto work for the entire year. Here are some suggestions of types of work to hold onto:

- **Keep all graded work**
  You may decide that you want to keep all the work that gets graded throughout the year. To help manage the large amount of paperwork you'll have, take the work out at the end of each semester and store it away (in a tub) until the end of the year. This serves several purposes:
    - If a parent or administrator questions a grade you can take the folder out and review the student's work, which had been sent home and signed by the parent. This happens more often than you think. Parents see a low grade on an interim report or report

What to do When the Grading is Done

Grading Sheet Sample

Subject: _____math_____   Term: _____1st_____

Name:	Date: 10/3 Assignment: Page 14 question 1–10 Assignment Type: Classwork Points: 50	Date: 10/7 Assignment: Chapter Two Assignment Type: Test Points: 100	Date: 10/12 Assignment: Workbook page 37 Assignment Type: Homework Points: none	Date: Assignment: Assignment Type: Points:	Date: Assignment: Assignment Type: Points:
Billy	37	88	C		
Susan	50	93	M		
Katie	48	100	Inc.		

You've Got the Job—Now Keep It

card and demand to know what is going on. If you keep the student's work you've got the necessary information to back up the grade.

o If you keep and store the work yourself, you can pull the folder during parent/teacher conferences. It's easier to explain the difficulties (or strengths) a student is having when you have specific examples of the work in front of you. It's also enlightening for parents to be able to compare work from the beginning to the end of the year, which can be done if you keep all the work.

- **Keep tests, low grades, or improved work**
  If you don't have the space to keep all the work, we suggest that at a minimum you keep tests, work with low grades, and any work that shows improvement. Request that parents sign either all tests, low grades only, or all graded work. Even if you only keep tests or work that received low grades, you will still have an adequate amount to show parents at conferences.

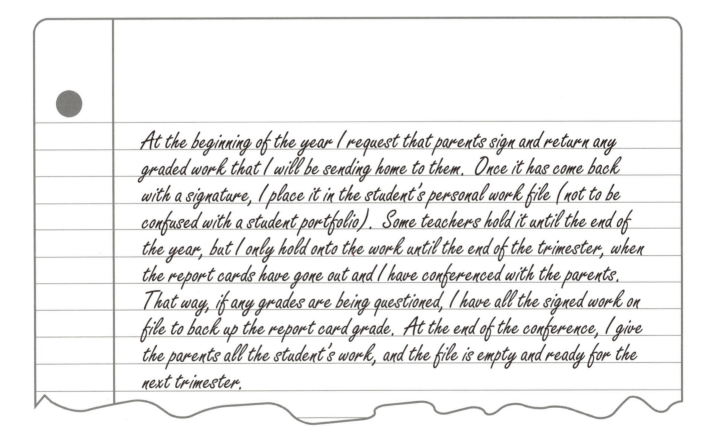

At the beginning of the year I request that parents sign and return any graded work that I will be sending home to them. Once it has come back with a signature, I place it in the student's personal work file (not to be confused with a student portfolio). Some teachers hold it until the end of the year, but I only hold onto the work until the end of the trimester, when the report cards have gone out and I have conferenced with the parents. That way, if any grades are being questioned, I have all the signed work on file to back up the report card grade. At the end of the conference, I give the parents all the student's work, and the file is empty and ready for the next trimester.

Chapter 25

Writing Report Cards

For most teachers, report cards are not at the top of the list when it comes to their favorite things about teaching. Depending on your school, report cards can be sent out between three to four times a year and there may be interim report cards to complete as well. When preparing report cards you'll need to make sure of two things: that you have enough graded assignments so the final grade truly reflects a student's work and that you write meaningful report card comments.

Avoiding the Crunch

In order to accurately reflect what the student is doing in the classroom and avoid a crunch at report card time, you should grade papers and other work regularly throughout the semester. There are many teachers who hand out lots of worksheets just before report card time to generate enough grades for their gradebooks. This is does not fairly reflect the student's work and is time consuming for the teacher. Grading won't be that bad if you implement a few simple suggestions:

- Try not to let your grading pile up and become unmanageable. Though it's easy to put student's work aside and not grade it for a week or two, try and get into the habit of grading daily or a few times a week.

- Let your assistant help you grade, but be careful. Make sure the assistant knows exactly what you are looking for and refrain from having him grade any long answer questions—only you know what specific information is needed for answers that earn top marks.

- Try to have three or four graded assignments per subject per week. This will give you a strong authentic sampling of the student's work.

- Consider dropping the lowest grade in each subject, unless it was from a test or major project, as this grade often does not reflect the student's true abilities. (Do, however, keep the work related to these poor marks in the student's file.)

Writing Effective Comments

You can buy published books that contain nothing but report card comments. If you choose to use these books be careful: they are fine to generate ideas (especially if you have never written report card comments before), but they are rarely specific enough. In reality, comments should focus on the child's strengths, discuss any weaknesses or challenges as specifically as possible, and state a plan of action that addresses the problem. If you have students who are doing well in **all** areas and you have no concerns, make sure you comment on progress made and areas in which you'd like to see them continue to excel.

Example One: Comment for student experiencing academic difficulty

Lola is very outgoing and has many friends in class. She is always available to lend a helping hand in the classroom. Academically, Lola is on grade level in reading but continues to struggle with basic concepts in math. She needs individual attention to grasp new skills and requires constant reinforcement to retain new information. I will continue to work with Lola individually and in small groups in math, but I suggest Lola receive tutoring outside of class for continued reinforcement.

Example Two: Comment for student experiencing behavioral difficulty

Robby works hard in class and is doing well academically. However, as discussed in previous conferences, socially he continues to have difficulty relating with the other students. During group work Robby tends to want to control the group and has difficulty compromising. In addition, he is being aggressive when playing during recess. I feel confident that he can work to improve his social skills, but I also feel a conference is necessary to discuss this issue in further detail.

Example Three: Comment for student experiencing no difficulties

Again this term, Jose has shown a solid understanding of all curriculum areas, especially math and creative writing. As he demonstrated a strong grasp of his times tables, I was pleased that he handled the challenge of two digit division, and eagerly helped other students who were experiencing problems with multiplication. His strong social skills have made him a friend to many, both inside the classroom and out. I encourage him to keep reading at home and writing excellent stories for next term.

Example Four: A poorly written comment

Maria is a sweet girl and is a pleasure to have in class. She works hard, is helpful and has lots of friends.

Some report cards either do not give a section for comments or limit what you can say by including only a small amount of space. If this is the case in your school, then you have no choice but to keep things short, as in: *John is doing well in all content areas but needs to focus on working independently.* If your report card does not have any space for comments, it's all the more important that you have written documentation for each student readily available during your parent-teacher conferences.

Report card comments should address what the student does well and where work is needed.

When addressing serious academic or social problems, it is very important that the report card is not the first time the parents learn about the situation. No matter where you teach, it is your responsibility to quickly inform the parent if a child starts to have difficulty in class. The report card serves as a formal evaluation of the child's performance during the semester, and is not a substitute for parent communication.

Remember, when completing report cards:

- use plenty of graded assignments to develop your final grade
- take class participation and student effort into account.
- avoid blanket comments such as *John is a sweet boy and is a pleasure to have in class*
- make sure the comments are clear but concise
- point out the child's strengths as well as any challenges he may have
- include a plan of action for any areas of concern
- choose your words carefully because parents take these comments to heart, reading something into everything you write

Summary Section Five

- When grading an assignment determine what skills you are assessing. Know what you expect to see in the answers before you begin grading.

- When determining report card grades, classwork grades should be the largest percentage since this work reflects what students produce independently in class each day. Tests should count as a smaller percentage and homework should count the least. Consider effort and participation when determining the final grades.

- All homework does not have to be graded but needs to be reviewed.

- Have a homework policy in place complete with clear expectations and consequences.

- Understand the grading system for your grade level at your school. Be sure to use the correct grading system from the beginning of the year.

- Don't let grading pile up. Try to get grading done daily or at a minimum once a week.

- When writing report card comments, don't write blanket comments; focus on the student's strengths, discuss any weakness as specifically as possible, and try to state a plan of action.

Notes

Grading Sheet

Subject: _____ Term: _____

Name:	Date: Assignment: Assignment Type: Points:	Date: Assignment: Assignment Type: Points:	Date: Assignment: Assignment Type: Points:	Date: Assignment: Assignment Type: Points:	Date: Assignment: Assignment Type: Points:

TIPS, Inc.

SECTION SIX

Say What You Mean and Mean What You Say–Effective Communication

- ◆ **How to communicate with co-workers**
- ◆ **How to communicate with parents**
- ◆ **Steps for effective meetings and conferences**
- ◆ **How to deal with the uninvolved parent**
- ◆ **Get it in writing**
- ◆ **Including students in conferences (or not)**

IN THIS SECTION

Chapter 26

Faculty Communication

As an employee, your first responsibility is to the school for which you work. When speaking about your school and your colleagues or other employees, you should portray both in a positive light. This is easier said than done, especially if you're caught in the heat of the moment and upset over a new policy, the latest procedure, or are having personal issues with another staff member. In these situations, the best thing to do is keep quiet. Never ever speak poorly of anyone at your school or the school itself, especially to parents—even if you feel you have a close relationship with them. It is unprofessional. Schools are notorious for gossip among both teachers and parents. Don't share any information that you wouldn't feel comfortable with everybody knowing.

Working with other Teachers

As a newbie coming into the education field, you are filled with wonderful ideas and are probably quite excited and eager to get into your classroom and teach the students everything. That's the best part of being a new teacher, the passion you have for teaching and for your students. Don't let the negativity of a burned out teacher dampen your enthusiasm.

Once you get into your new school you will begin to meet other teachers and staff members, many of whom have been in education for many years. Be cautious about what you say and how you interact with the staff. You do not want to come across as a "know it all," or as being "cocky;" on the other hand, you may feel that if you ask a lot of

TIP: Be confident, but not arrogant.

questions others may think you're unsure of yourself. Remember—everyone was new at something once, so don't be afraid to ask questions. You're new to the school and new to teaching so ask whatever questions you feel are necessary. Try directing your questions to some of the veteran teachers on staff.

Veteran teachers have a lot to offer you, so keep an open mind and pay attention to what they say and do. Many new teachers often make the mistake of seeing veteran teachers as stuck in their ways, unwilling to try new things, and boring. You must realize that most veteran teachers have seen the educational spectrum go full circle. They've been through the debates of phonics, whole language, open classrooms, heterogeneous grouping, homogeneous grouping and everything in between. They've had to deal with every type of parent, every type of student, every type of principal and every type of teacher. They know the ropes, the ins and outs, the pros and cons, as well as the ups and downs, and, because of this, most veteran teachers are an asset to you.

After teaching fourth grade for several years, I started teaching second grade in a new school. One of the other teachers had been teaching second grade for thirty years. When we sat down to discuss curriculum I found her lessons, for lack of a better word, boring. She wasn't doing any of the new and exciting concepts being touted in the educational field so I pretty much did my own thing that year. The following year she moved to another state and it was only after she left that I had realized the opportunity I missed. She had possessed so much knowledge about how to give children a strong foundation for the later grades, and although I found her method of teaching less than exciting, I had to admit that her students left her classroom in June with all the exit skills needed to be successful in the next grade. From that one experience, I've gained so much respect for teachers who have been in the field for a long time.

When You Have a Problem with Another Teacher

The two biggest complaints teachers have about other teachers are they don't pull their weight and they won't work as a team.

For the most part, when it comes to disagreements with your co-workers, you're going to have to put up with the situation as best you can. As a child, there were probably children in your class that you did not like. As an adult, there will probably be people in your workplace that you do not like. Do as your mother taught you and follow the "Golden Rule" to treat others as you wish to be treated. Your job is not to regulate what the other teachers do. Your job is to teach to the best of your ability—it's the principal's job to deal with the other teachers. Even if you think the principal doesn't know what is going on, she probably knows much more than you think.

If a situation with another teacher gets to the point where you absolutely can't deal with it anymore, the first thing you must do is speak directly to the other teacher. You never know, maybe the two of you can work it out. If, however, you can't solve the problem together, talk to the principal. Be as unbiased as you can as you explain the situation and be prepared to have the other teacher pulled into the conversation to solve the problem. But also be prepared for the fact that the problem might not get solved, and you'll just have to work around it.

Try to handle problems yourself first before going to the principal.

Communicating with the Principal

Think about the problems you might encounter in your room with the various students and their parents. Now multiply that by the number of classes in your school and you'll have a better understanding for what your principal has to deal with each day.

What you may see as a huge problem may be seen as something less important by the administration. When dealing with your principal keep these thoughts in mind:

- Don't run to your principal for every little thing. If you're constantly going to the principal with problems, you may be perceived as a complainer. Instead, use your mentor for advice on how to solve the problem.

- If you eventually have to seek your principal's advice be prepared to explain what the problem is, how you've tried to solve it and any other possible solutions to the situation you think viable.

- If an issue with a parent or student could escalate, let your principal know immediately. Parents or other staff members will often go

Faculty Communication

An emotional response is not a good first approach when dealing with your principal.

Introduce yourself to the office and maintenance staff.

directly to a principal if they have a disagreement with you, and you don't want your principal to hear about a negative situation in your classroom from someone else. Make sure you give the principal a heads up about any potential problems headed her way.

Communicating with other Staff

The staff at your school is not limited to your fellow teachers. It includes everyone involved in the daily running of the school. Make sure you introduce yourself to and establish a relationship with the person who runs the office as well as the head of the maintenance staff. As you work on developing a lasting relationship with these people, keep in mind that they usually work all year long, they don't get the same holidays as teachers, and they don't get near the appreciation and of accolades that they truly deserve.

During my first year teaching first grade there were four of us, all new to both the school and the grade. Three of us got along famously and had very similar teaching styles. The other teacher, however, was a different story. He wanted to stick solely to the curriculum, not do any outside projects, and had a worksheet-based teaching style. All four of us were concerned because it was a small school and we had been told from day one that we had to work as a team. For the longest time we all tried to work together, but I was becoming more and more frustrated with the situation. I also found I was compromising my teaching style because the other teacher didn't want to do the same types of projects as I did. Finally the three of us went to the principal because, despite the myriad conversations we had had as a four-person team, we felt we could not solve this problem on our own. We explained that although we all had tried hard to work together, the three of us were frustrated with trying to change our lessons and objectives to fit in with his teaching method, and we felt our teaching was suffering because of it. We were told to include the other teacher as best we could, but to teach how we wanted. We were also told that it was not our job to police the other teacher. Basically we just had to deal with it (which we did), but I also learned a valuable lesson: though you should always try to find a solution to your problem, there just might not be one and you'll just have to make the best out of the situation that you can.

Chapter 27

The Importance of the Parent-Teacher Relationship

Perhaps one of the most important relationships you will build during the year is the parent-teacher relationship. Surprisingly enough, parents are often as apprehensive as the students when the year begins, especially when a child has had previous academic or behavioral challenges.

Parents value open communication with and access to teachers when it comes to the components of a successful school year. Yet many parents feel nervous about contacting a teacher if there is a problem because they fear the teacher might "take it out" on the child. From a teaching perspective this is concerning. Parents and teachers should be partners in a child's education: both parties have the best interest of the child at heart and each one's unique relationship combines to give a much better picture of the child as a whole.

It is impossible to cover every situation you will encounter with parents. You will have parents that are too involved with their child's schooling as well as parents that are not involved enough. You will also have relationships with wonderful parents who support you and are willing to work at the teacher-parent partnership, while there will be other parents that can't wait to see you leave. The better the relationship you have with parents the easier your year will be and, most importantly, the better the school year the student will have knowing everyone is involved with his education.

Students as Jekyll and Hyde

You will find that you have students who are absolute angels in class, follow all the rules, finish their work, behave beautifully, yet, when you speak with their parents, you find out that their child's behavior is completely different at home. Of course this isn't true for all children. Some children's behavior remains the same regardless of the setting, while others behave perfectly at home but act out in school. So, when discussing student behavior with a parent, it's not unusual for a parent to look at you in bewilderment and say, "Are you sure you're talking about **my** child?" (It's also more likely for a child to perform a personality switch when the parents are present in the school setting, such as during a class party, when a parent is volunteering, or on a field trip.)

It's helpful to remember "Jekyll and Hyde" when talking to parents, because, when it comes to personality, the child that parents have at home may not be the same child that you see in school. As well, you see a side of their child that the parents don't often get a chance to see. The point to remember is that, as the teacher, you have something to learn about each student from the parents, so listen carefully.

Before discussing how to have successful communication with parents, you should understand what it's like to be a teacher as seen through the eyes of students and their parents.

The Relationship between Teachers, Students, and Parents

As a teacher of thirty students, you have to split yourself in thirty different directions. Ideally, each child should get 1/30 of your attention. There will always be certain children who will need more of your time and others who will require less, but overall it's your job to teach and treat all children fairly.

That is not necessarily how students and parents see the teacher's relationship with a child. If a teacher asks a student to draw a picture of herself in school, it's likely the picture will contain two people: her, the teacher, and no one else. That's basically the way children see you—you're their teacher, the other students are merely classmates. Although parents understand you have thirty students, they'll still be expecting you to give 110% of your attention to their child.

One year while I was teaching fourth grade, I had more children with challenges in my class than I had ever had before. In addition to several highly gifted students, there were students with impulse control problems, students with neurological disorders, and students who were far below fourth grade academic level. In addition, I had many involved parents wanting weekly updates who made it very clear that I needed to take the extra time required to meet the specific needs of their children. After all, as one parent reminded me, that was my job. She was right, that was my job, but I politely reminded her that it was also my job to look after the other students in my class too. She paused and replied, "I understand that but . . ." and continued on about how her child needed extra attention. I realized something important in that moment: as logical and intelligent as the parents might be, they still expect your main focus to be their child.

Coming from Different Perspectives

It is important to remember that although both you and the parent may have the same concerns for a child, you're both coming from completely different directions and thinking from completely different view points. Keep an open mind during meetings with parents, and you'll see how much easier reaching a solution can be. Both you and the parent want to solve the problem, so you need to take advantage of the synergy this can offer. Let's take the example of Mrs. Clarke and her son:

Mrs. Clarke's son, Harold, is having trouble with math. She and her husband have done everything they can but Harold is just not grasping even the simplest of concepts. As for the teacher, she has been working with Harold on an individual basis as much as possible, as well as re-teaching him in a very small math group.

Here's what both parties may be thinking:

MEETING

Teacher	Parents
I'm doing all that I can to help this child in the classroom.	We're doing all we can at home to help our son.
The parents are going to wonder why I haven't solved their son's problem yet.	The teacher is going to wonder why we haven't done more.
Why aren't the parents doing more at home?	Why isn't the teacher doing more in the class?
The parents are going to be upset and looking to me for the answers.	The teacher is going to be upset and look at us for answers.
How am I going to explain that perhaps their son needs further evaluation?	What if he needs something more?

As you can see, both sides are thinking along the same lines. Both are worried the other might think they're not doing their job to the fullest, or not doing everything possible to solve the problem. It's often a concern for both parties that the other will be passing judgment and making assumptions. This is not an uncommon fear.

There will always be parents who feel it is the school's responsibility, not theirs, to solve the child's academic problems. Similarly, there will be teachers who blame parents for a student's poor academic performance without taking any responsibility themselves, or teachers who give up on students, and don't go the extra mile. While this isn't the standard attitude of most parents and teachers, you **will** run across a few like this. What's important to remember is to not be judgmental or make assumptions when dealing with parents. Keep an open mind. Your goal is to work with the parents to find a solution to their child's problem, not against them.

Parent–Teacher Communication

A Word about Private vs Public School Parents

Public and private schools are both equally demanding of their teachers, however teaching in each school comes with its own unique set of challenges, especially when it comes to teachers interacting with parents. In contrast to a public school, whose sole purpose is to educate students, a private school has a dual role—to serve as a business as well as an educational facility. Teachers in private schools often feel more pressure by administrators to please parents in order to satisfy the number one rule of any successful business—always keep your customers (a.k.a. the parents) satisfied.

Regardless of whether you teach in a public or private school, you will still encounter all types of parents—from those that are very involved right down to the parents you'll never see. There is not one rule that determines *which* parents you'll find *where*. No matter what school you are in, it is important you understand the expectations placed on you by parents, and that you make effective parent-teacher communication a number one priority.

Chapter 28

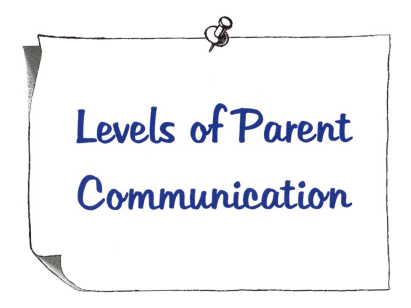

Levels of Parent Communication

Note: There is a running debate in education whether or not to include students in meetings and conferences with parents. Some schools have a policy about this, but most schools leave it up to the teacher to decide. Both teachers and parents have very distinct views on this subject. Whether or not to include students in meetings and conferences comes down to personal philosophy. There is no right or wrong answer, but you need to consider all the variables before making a decision. For now, this discussion focuses on communication with parents where students are excluded. Further in this section the pros and cons of including students in conferences are compared, and strategies for teachers who wish to involve students in parent-teacher conferences are included.

 Respond to parent concerns by the end of the 2nd day even if it's just to tell them you're aware of their concern and you are working on it.

Phone Calls, Meetings, and Conferences . . . Oh My!

Not every meeting with a parent will be formal. Sometimes you can solve a problem or answer a question through a note in the agenda or an email. At times, a simple phone call will suffice, while other times you will need to schedule a meeting to discuss a specific issue. Finally there are the term conferences and, in some cases, child study team meetings. These are the most formal meetings between parents and teachers.

The top of the triangle represents issues that need the least attention and the bottom reflects meetings that demand the most. This is not to say you shouldn't take notes, emails, or phone calls seriously. You'll need to deal with all parental concerns no matter where they fall in the triangle, however, issues on the bottom of the triangle will take up more of your time and will be more serious in nature.

The levels of communication are as follows:

- **Notes/email**

  If a parent sends a note or an email, you can usually respond in kind unless you've been specifically asked to call them to discuss the matter.

  Anytime you are communicating in writing or by email, however, you should be aware of the tone of your message. Tone is sometimes hard to convey through writing, so things likes jokes and sarcasm can be easily misinterpreted. Be careful what you write, and make sure what you've written means *exactly* what you wanted to say.

- **Unscheduled visit or phone call**

  Often you'll run into a parent in the hallway before or after school, or they'll drop by the classroom with a quick question. If you can answer the question at that time, do so. But if you feel it will need more time, schedule an appointment to have the parents come in. Likewise, if parents phone, call them back and answer their questions as quickly as possible. If you feel that a parent needs a more in-depth conversation, schedule a meeting.

- **Meetings**

    A scheduled meeting can be initiated by you or the parent, usually to discuss a specific item. Such an appointment might be made when there is a concern about test grades, homework assignments, overall work habits, or social problems in the classroom. Occasionally parents will want to meet and discuss something happening at home that they feel you should be aware of, such as the child not completing homework, or a more personal family situation. A scheduled meeting can also be an appointment to follow up from a prior meeting, or simply to inform the parent about the child's accomplishments in the classroom.

- **Term conferences**

    Term conferences are held at the end of the marking period to discuss the child's overall progress. Term conferences are the most in-depth, as it might be the only time during the year you'll see a child's parents.

- **Child study team meetings**

    Some matters may require a child study team meeting involving you, the parents, the principal, the guidance counselor, and possibly an educational psychologist. These meetings are often scheduled before or after school as they can be lengthy. A child study meeting can be requested by a teacher, a parent, a principal, or an outside medical professional. Be prepared to bring and share any information about the student that relates to the issues being discussed.

No matter the type of meeting, a parent may bring up an issue (or issues) that you did not expect to discuss. Don't feel pressured to respond right away. Instead, say to the parent "You've mentioned an important point. I'd like to make sure I've considered it from every angle, so I will have to get back to you tomorrow." This ensures you don't wind up saying something "off the cuff" that you'll wish later you hadn't.

How to Conduct a Parent-Teacher Meeting

Although there is no fool-proof plan for a perfect parent-teacher meeting, there are guidelines you can follow to help create a more productive conversation.

The paragraphs below illustrate an example of a teacher initiated meeting to discuss Cheryl, a student who is not finishing her classwork in a timely manner.

Background:
Cheryl's mother thinks her child needs more time to complete assignments because she is just naturally a slower worker. You feel that there is an appropriate amount of time allotted for the child to finish her work and that she needs to learn to use her time more effectively. The parent wants all incomplete work sent home. You are not willing to do this. How can you solve this problem?

Action:
Your first response may be to think the parent is nuts, the daughter is simply unfocused in class, and the mother has no place telling you how to do your job. Now, get past your first response. Remember to keep an open mind and don't get defensive. Here are the steps to follow when conversing with a parent on this type of issue:

First and always start with a positive comment. Then, indicate what you see occurring in class.
Thanks for coming in Mrs. Thornhill. Cheryl is a good student and, when she focuses her attention, she does well in class. However I'm concerned because she is a slow worker and often doesn't finish her classwork.

State what you feel is the cause of the problem.
What I've been seeing is that Cheryl tries to avoid completing the assignment by using the bathroom and sharpening her pencil.

Validate parental concern (After you've identified the problem, parents will either agree, deny, offer a solution, or ask what you can do about it).
You've said that Cheryl is coming home upset because she's not finishing her work in class, and I know you are concerned about her self-esteem.

Consider whether the solution(s) suggested by parents are an option and if not explain why.
I know you would like me to send unfinished work home, however, (however is better than saying but) I give an ample amount of time for the class to complete classwork. I cannot send the work home to be completed because classroom assignments are one way I make assessments about students' work; if I send work home, it would not be a true assessment of what Cheryl is capable of doing. I cannot assess work that is done outside the class because I'm not sure what guidance she may get at home. It would also not be fair to the other students because they did not have this opportunity. This year is a good year for Cheryl to start to understand that she needs to work a bit faster and use her time more effectively in order to complete her work and to learn to work within the structure of the classroom.

Give a plan of action.
What I will do is tell Cheryl she has a set time to gather her supplies and sharpen her pencil. She can use the bathroom once, and get water once. It may help her focus more if she knows she can't keep leaving her seat until her work is finished. Also, I will continually check to see how much she has completed and give her positive reinforcement as she works through the assignment.

Follow through with updates to parents.
I'll phone you in two weeks and give you an update about Cheryl's progress, but if I see these strategies aren't working, I'll try something else. I'm glad you came in today and I really think that us working together will help Cheryl understand this is a serious matter, we're willing to help her, and she needs to get serious about helping herself first.

Will it always be this easy?

Okay, now every meeting won't always be as cut and dry as that and it's unlikely you'll be speaking in such a formal matter. Also, based on what parents say during the meeting, it may not be possible to follow these steps in order. In addition there are parents that, no matter what you say, may continue to argue their point. But generally, if you are confident in what you're saying, have a viable alternative to their suggestions, and have a well defined plan of action for their child, most parents will listen. If you have a parent who continues to debate the issue, suggest trying your plan for a month and then, if it doesn't work, agree to meet and revisit the issue and try something else.

There will always be the odd set of parents that you cannot make happy, and occasionally you'll have to enlist the help of your principal to solve the problem. In most cases, however, if you follow the basic guidelines discussed, you'll see that most problems can be resolved. Just remember to:

- start with a positive comment
- indicate what you see occurring in class
- state what you feel is the cause of the problem
- validate parental concerns
- consider any suggestions put forth by the parents; if their ideas won't work, explain why
- give a plan of action
- follow through with updates
- don't commit to a plan of action, **or** a follow up method unless you can guarantee parents you'll consistently follow it through

How to Conduct a Term Conference

Term conferences are different than any other meeting you will have with parents. A scheduled meeting usually focuses on one specific academic or social area, whereas a term conference encompasses the student's entire performance in class to date. It is likely that the conversation will ultimately focus on whatever area a student is having difficulty with, but term conferences should cover all academic and social areas.

Schools normally have a set length of time established for conferences. In the past, many schools set aside a whole day for teachers to hold all the parent conferences. Unfortunately today most conferences are done before school, during teacher planning periods, and after school, which greatly limits the amount of time parents have. A typical amount

Send out conference information to parents at least two weeks ahead of time.

Levels of Parent Communication

Sit next to instead of across from parents. It's less confrontational.

of time for a conference is twenty minutes, but it can be as short as ten depending on the school and your class size.

Find out how your school schedules conferences. Some schools simply assign times and expect parents to rearrange their schedules in order to attend the conference, while other schools arrange the conference schedule based on the availability of the parents. Whichever category your school falls into, be sure to send out a conference schedule at least two weeks before conference week. This will give you ample time to arrange your conference schedule.

Because the amount of actual conference time you are able to give each parent is short, it is important that you are prepared for the conference—especially if you are discussing a child who is having difficulties in class.

There are two strategies that you can employ to ensure an efficient and productive conference.

- A few weeks prior to conferences, send home a short form requesting parents to list any areas they would like to discuss. The form should be completed and returned to you *before* their conference. This request is important for two reasons: it gets the parents to focus on two or three specific areas (instead of coming to the conference and wanting to talk about everything from math tests to recess) and, most importantly, it gives you a heads-up on what the parents will be asking you. It's not unusual for a teacher to be prepared to discuss one area only to have the parents bring up something else entirely. You don't want to be unprepared or taken off guard during a conference.

- The second strategy is for *you* to fill in a form that you will use as a guideline **before** the conference. While not an in-depth analysis of the child, the form may take a few minutes to prepare, but in the long run it will keep the conversation on track and help you remember everything you want to say. You'll also have a permanent record of what was discussed, in case the conference is ever called into question. Many schools will provide you with a form to fill out that the parents sign at the end of the conference. If not, you can use the sample form included. On the following page are strategies for handling a typical term conference (using the form as a guideline).

Starting the meeting:

- Begin the conference by asking the parents what areas they would like to discuss. Nine out of ten times they are concerned about the same areas as you. (If you've sent out the parent form, then you already have a starting point.)

- Next, ask what their child is saying about school at home. Many times students will comment on social concerns or problem areas while they're at home that you might not have noticed in the classroom.

- When the parent speaks, LISTEN. The biggest piece of advice we can give you is to **listen to what the parents have to say.** Parents have insights about their child that you don't, and you can gain a lot of information about the child from the very first parent conference. Also, when you actively listen, you are showing that what parents say is important to you.

- Some parents won't want to initiate the discussion, so you can begin by using your form and discussing the topics you've already listed. Remember, this is a conversation, so as you raise a point, ask parents for feedback. You're not just meant to read the form aloud and have the parents sign it.

When discussing student strengths:

- No matter how many difficulties the student has, always find something positive to say. Discuss as many positive attributes of the child as possible, including social and other non-academic strengths.

- Phrases such as *is helpful; is well liked in the class; has a good sense of humor; shows interest in non-content areas such as art, music, and sports* helps demonstrate traits in their children that parents may not get the privilege to see for themselves at home.

When discussing areas of concern:

- Parents don't like to hear the word *weakness*, so instead refer to *areas needing improvement, challenges for the child,* or *targets for next trimester.*

- Don't list every single problem the child has. Focus on your major concerns such as ongoing difficulty with a concept, poor time management skills, lack of interest or ability to pay attention during instructional time, or regular or intermittent refusal to complete homework assignments.

- Don't be accusatory, even if in your heart you feel the parents are not doing enough to help solve the problem.

Start and end conferences on a positive note.

Levels of Parent Communication

- Don't discuss past teachers. Parents will often want to discuss what happened in previous years. Turn the conversation to what is going on this year and how to fix the problem.

- Don't compare the student with other classmates (or, for that matter, even discuss other classmates, unless the problem directly involves them). Many schools have a policy that when another student is under discussion, she must remain anonymous. Be sure you're aware of and adhere to your school's policy regarding this matter.

When creating a plan of action:

- List the strategies you have and explain or demonstrate how they will help the child with her problem area.

- The plan of action doesn't have to apply only to a child having problems—action plans can be created for a student who is doing well academically and need a challenge.

- Remember, the best strategies are ones created by you and the parents. You implement them in school and the parents reinforce them at home, thus creating continuity for the student. When you involve parents they become more pro-active solving their child's problem.

- Also document any commitments parents make regarding reinforcing the action plan at home.

When deciding on the follow-up:

- Decide if there needs to be a second meeting, a phone call, a weekly email or some type of formal follow-up to the plan of action (if any).

- Make sure if you commit to the follow-up meeting or phone call that you actually do it. Put it on your calendar.

When ending the meeting:

- Try to end on a positive note with something simple like, "Don't worry, we're going to work together to solve this problem", even if the meeting was very stressful. Make sure the parents know that you're on their team and will do what you can to help their child.

Don't use "teacher lingo" during conferences—it will alienate parents.

To have an effective parent-teacher communication, you **must** be open minded. You do not know everything there is to know about teaching (no matter how many years you've been doing it) and you don't know everything about every child. Be willing to listen to and take advice when offered, especially when it comes from parents. This is not to say that you should take every piece of parental advice and incorporate it into your classroom—you do not need parents telling you how to run your class, nor should you allow it. But if you think something a parent has suggested will work, simply say, "Thanks. I think I'll see if I can incorporate that strategy for Robert. I'll let you know how it goes." It will not make you look like a weak teacher. On the contrary, you will look like a teacher who has an open mind, is willing to listen, and considers parents partners not intruders. So listen carefully, put the children first, and don't be so regimented in your beliefs that you aren't willing to be flexible when the situation warrants it.

Put all follow-up meetings on your personal calendar.

Communicating with Uninvolved Parents

As we mentioned in the homework section, in the same way that you can have over involved parents, you will undoubtedly meet parents who show little or no interest in their child's educational experience.

There are a variety of reasons why they may not be involved. Past negative experiences with schools or teachers may make parents reluctant to become involved with their child's education. Other parents are simply fearful of talking with teachers. Sometimes parents feel that they are not as educated as the teacher and are therefore intimidated by the idea of meeting to discuss problems their child is having. Or, there could be home problems or personal situations that the parents are going through. Regardless of their reason, however, you'll still need to deal with these parents. Below are some suggestions for communicating with the uninvolved parent:

- Gently try to find out what the situation at home is. We say gently because there might be a private family matter which the parents and/or child are sensitive about. Start by looking in the student's past records, talking to previous teachers, or consulting with the principal if you see a noticeable change in behavior or drop in academic performance. Perhaps there is an illness, a recent unemployment situation, or another major concern the family is grappling with.

- If you find out that the student *is* dealing with a problem at home, you may need to give some extra attention to that child. Try not to change the classroom or homework routine too much though. Children going through crisis at home often find the daily routine, structure, and expectations of the classroom a comfort.

- If there is an issue at home, send a note to the parents offering your assistance with school based matters involving their child. This is

Learn about the home situation to get a better understanding of the student.

Levels of Parent Communication

239

Children experiencing problems at home often find comfort and security in the routines of school.

always tricky because some people don't want outsiders to be involved in private matters. On the other hand, parents are often relieved to know that you are keeping an eye out for their child during the day and giving them a little extra attention during a difficult situation at home. If you're not sure what to do, ask a seasoned teacher or your principal for advice.

- If there is no unusual or tumultuous situation occurring in the child's home but the parents are unresponsive to your calls, emails or notes there is not much else you can do. Continue to send home notes, make phone calls (even if they go unanswered), document all your attempts to contact the parents, and let the principal know about the situation. This way you've done everything that you can do on your end.

- Make sure you document (and keep) every communication attempt and the outcome. You never know when and how you may need it.

Get It in Writing

Perhaps one of the most important tips we can give you is that no matter what type of communication you have with a parent, whether it's a quick email or a term conference, you should get in the habit of documenting what was discussed. Jot down the gist of the conversation in a notebook. Keeping a notebook of parent meetings is a tip you will get from all veteran teachers.

"You don't mind if I document our meeting, do you?"

You don't need to do this for term conferences as you have the conference form, but document informal meetings, drop bys, or telephone calls. Keep a three ring binder (with a page for each student), an index card clipboard, or a running list (by date) in a notebook. It doesn't need to be a completely detailed description of everything said, just quick notes that you can refer back to if a conversation or meeting is ever called into question. A typical entry may read: December 13th—*Spoke with Mrs. Green about chapter three math test. Parent very concerned. Will review concepts with Johnny. Suggested outside tutoring. February 12th—Phone message from Mrs. Jones about Rachel losing 5 minutes of recess. Returned phone call to explain what happened. Mrs. Jones was satisfied with the outcome.*

Document all parent conversations, even the casual ones.

Once you have a year or two of teaching under your belt, you'll learn which conversations need to be written down and which don't. Just be careful. Sometimes what seems like a casual conversation to you can be something totally different to a parent. If you are ever unsure, write it down. It's better to be safe than sorry.

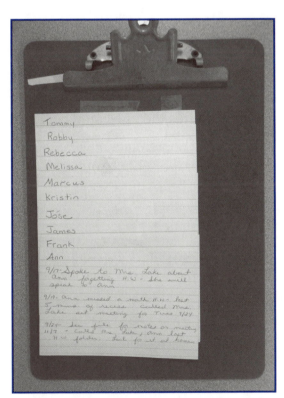

This flip chart, made of index cards taped to a clipboard, is a great recording tool.

Levels of Parent Communication

Final Tips for Effective Parent-Teacher Communication

- Find out at the beginning of the year whether or not parents will require a translator for meetings.

- When sitting down to talk with parents try not to sit across from them. Sitting next to a parent will convey that you're on the same team, while across can seem more formal and even adversarial.

- If you feel that the parents are asking for *too* many accommodations for their child or if they want you to do more than you are prepared to do, be polite but firm. Always back up what you are saying with reasons.

- If parents argue with each other in front of you, stay neutral. Any decisions that they need to make at home—such as what time homework gets done—should be made at home. If asked you can provide *suggestions*, but it's not your place to provide *solutions*. It would be helpful if you could gently remind parents that whatever decision they make, they should present to their child as a unified decision.

- If at any time a parent becomes irate, you become uncomfortable, or you feel the meeting will escalate, always call for back up. Ask another teacher to step in, or call the office for administrative support, but do not stay alone with a parent if they become verbally abusive or you feel uneasy.

- Never conference with a parent in a closed room. Always leave your class door open, so that if a parent becomes confrontational, you can walk them towards the office and get assistance.

- If you anticipate that the conference may become confrontational, arrange ahead of time for the school counselor or vice principal to sit in on the conference. Let parents know that you will be involving a third party. If this is not possible, arrange for another teacher to be within listening distance.

- Be cautious about sharing your personal life with a parent and vice versa. The parent who loves you today may not be so fond of you tomorrow when it comes to their child.

- Never use technical "teacher lingo" when discussing strategies or methods with parents. You wouldn't appreciate it if your doctor or lawyer explained everything to you in technical jargon. You do not want to make a parent feel belittled, unknowledgeable, or stupid. What you do want to do is explain yourself in clear, concise language.

Chapter 29

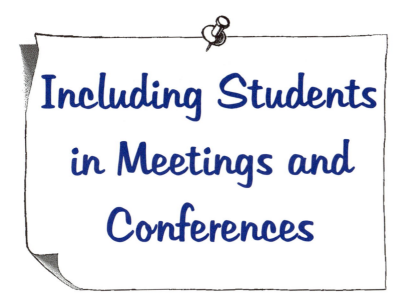

Including Students in Meetings and Conferences

The Pros and Cons

Including students in meetings or conferences is a long running debate amongst teachers. As with any debate, many hold very strong views *for* or *against*, while others fall somewhere in the middle. Check your school's policy—if the decision is in your hands, talk with other teachers and see what they do. Consider both sides of the debate and then make an informed choice. Below are the disadvantages and advantages of including a student when you are meeting with his or her parents.

Why a student should NOT be included in a meeting or conference:

- When you meet with a parent you want to talk openly about the strengths and weaknesses of the child, and this might be hard to do with the student sitting there. Children already know the areas in which they are weak, but their problem may be compounded by having their teacher and their parent sitting in front of them confirming the fact.

- Unless you and the parent have previously discussed matters, parents may become argumentative with you in front of their child. If a child witnesses this, your authority is immediately undermined.

- You never know what a parent's reaction might be to certain matters you discuss. Parents have been known to become verbally and, on occasion, physically abusive towards teachers. The last thing you want is a parent causing a scene with you in front of a student.

- The desired outcome of a parent-teacher meeting or conference is for both the parent and the teacher to put their heads together and form a plan that can be implemented at school and at home. What's important is that the student sees a united front. If the student is present and the parents and teacher cannot agree on how to handle an issue, it gives her the opportunity to "pick sides" or play one off the other.

Why a student SHOULD be included in a meeting or conference:

- The most valid argument for including students is because the meeting or conference is about them. Students may be able to give their parents and teacher insight into what they think the problem is. Sometimes the problem is easier solved than originally thought.

- Many teachers feel that including a student holds the student accountable, especially for behavioral issues. When a teacher and parents show the student a united front, the student realizes she isn't going to get away with the current behavior.

- Including a student gives her ownership of the problem and accountability for the solution. When a student accepts responsibility for the problem, whether it is academic or behavioral, she will be quicker to act on solving it.

- A student normally knows what her strengths and weakness are. By including a student and discussing the areas she is having trouble with you can help her understand her learning style and together come up with a plan that meets her needs.

- Including students in conferences gives them the opportunity to brag! This is an ideal time for them to share with their parents and teacher what they are most proud of and what goals they would like to reach.

When students are involved in solving their problems, it gives them ownership and accountability.

If you choose to include a student when you conference with parents, it's a good idea to have the student fill out a form similar to the parent form sent home before the conference. Often a student is hesitant to complete the form honestly because she's embarrassed to admit the areas that she's struggling with, or afraid she'll get in trouble for what she writes. Remind the student that the form will be used only as a guide to help you and her parents understand her concerns better, and offer to help her fill it out. Let her check the areas that she has concerns with. For example, under social skills she could state: *trouble making friends,* or *getting bullied;* while homework concerns might include *too much homework, boring homework,* or *confusing homework.*

The Best of Both Worlds

If you are on the fence about whether or not to include students in meetings or conferences, it's best to start out with parents only. If there is a situation where you think the child should be included, then you can always schedule a second meeting that includes the student. Doing it this way allows you to first discuss the situation with the parents and form a consensus on what will be said to the student, while still giving the student the opportunity to explain his concerns and have a say in any plan of action.

There was a very quiet girl in my second grade class. She was new to the school and had a slight lisp. She was not outgoing and preferred drawing or reading to playing with the students on the playground. At lunch, she isolated herself by sitting alone at the end of a table. Her parents contacted me and requested a meeting, because they believed their daughter was being intentionally ostracized by the other girls in the class. During the conference they told me their daughter had said other children were teasing her, but I had not seen any indication of this in class. We decided we needed to involve the student in order to get a better idea of what was going on. It wasn't until the parents, the student, and I got together that the problem was solved. The student admitted that she was shy, didn't know what to say, and was afraid people would make fun of her lisp. She also admitted that the other girls hadn't made fun of her. Together we created a plan that she would try to participate more with other children by playing games on the playground instead of drawing, and sit with the other girls during lunch even if she didn't participate in conversations right away. Although the student was never one of the most popular girls in the class, she made several good friends and had an enjoyable school year.

Summary Section Six

- When working with other teachers at your school, always try to solve problems first before enlisting the assistance of your principal.

- Always ask your mentor teacher or other teachers in your grade level for advice. If you need to go to your principal with a problem, have all the facts and any possible solutions.

- Always give your principal the "heads up" if you know a problem with a student or parent is headed her way.

- Get to know the office staff as well as those on the maintenance staff. Meeting everyone who works at the school, not just the other teachers, will be beneficial to you in the long run.

- The goal of the parent-teacher relationship is to work together for the common good of the student. Keep an open mind, be flexible, and work together to solve any problems that might arise during the school year.

- No matter if you are at a private school or a public school you need to make open and effective communication a priority with all your parents.

- Always return parent's messages as soon as possible. Depending on the concern, you can reply with a note, an email, a phone call, or through the agenda.

- Meetings are held to discuss a specific concern that either you or the parent (or both) are having. During meetings, stay as positive as possible, validate the parents' concerns, discuss what you are seeing in class and what you think the cause of the problem is, and identify a possible solution.

- During term conferences, decide whether or not you will include the students. Send out parent conference forms about two weeks before conferences and prepare a conference form for yourself.

- During conferences, remember to stay as positive as possible, discuss the student's strengths and any areas the student is struggling with. Decide on a plan of action with the parents.

Summary Section Six—*cont'd*

- Always be sure to follow-up with phone calls, emails, or notes and don't commit to any plan of action that you cannot carry through.

- If parents are uncommunicative, try to find out why and if possible give assistance. If parents simply do not want to be involved, continue to send home any necessary notes, make any required phone calls, and send home conference forms anyway. Document your communication attempts as you go

- Document everything you can when speaking with parents. Having everything in writing provides you with back up if necessary.

- Including students in meetings and conferences has both pros and cons. Consider all the options and do what works best for you.

Notes

Conference Form for Parents

Please complete and return this form at least **three days before** your conference.

Check the areas that most concern you regarding your child:

Test Grades _____   Classwork Grades _____

Classroom Behavior (i.e. staying on task) _____

Overall Behavior _____

Completing Homework _____   Homework Grades _____

Study Skills _____   Social Skills _____

Other _____

Briefly explain your concerns:

_____
_____
_____
_____
_____
_____
_____
_____
_____
_____
_____
_____

TIPS, Inc.

Parent-Teacher Conference Form For Teachers

Participants: _____ **Date:** _____

Parental Concerns: _____

_____

_____

_____

_____

Items Discussed:

Student strengths: _____

_____

Areas of concern: _____

_____

_____

_____

Plan of Action:

_____

_____

_____

Follow up:

_____

_____

Parent Signature: _____ **Teacher Signature:** _____

TIPS, Inc.

Student Conference Form

Check the areas that are the biggest concern to you:

Test Grades _____   Classwork Grades _____

Classroom Behavior (i.e. staying on task) _____

Overall Behavior _____

Completing Homework _____   Homework Grades _____

Study Skills _____   Social Skills _____

Other _____

Explain why you're concerned:

_____
_____
_____
_____
_____

Do you have any suggestions to help solve the problem(s) you are having in class?

_____
_____
_____
_____
_____
_____
_____

TIPS, Inc.

SECTION SEVEN

Working in the Classroom—Surviving Groups

- ◆ Grouping students
- ◆ Benefits and concerns with grouping
- ◆ Working together through mini-lessons

IN THIS SECTION

Chapter 30

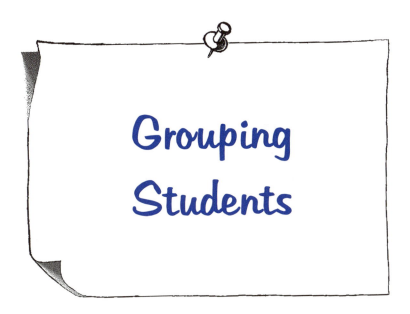

Grouping Students

The General Benefits of Grouping Students

There are benefits for teachers and students when the class is split into small groups. Deciding how and when to group students can be tricky, but consider the positives and negatives for both yourself and your students.

Benefits for the Teacher

- **Meeting various ability levels**
  Small groups allow a teacher to modify the lesson for each group depending on ability or interest. These modifications give students in each group motivation to achieve maximum benefits from the lesson.

- **One-on-one time**
  Working in small groups gives teachers a chance to gain a more in-depth understanding of students' work habits, capabilities, and learning styles.

  One-on-one time also allows teachers to re-teach lessons utilizing different techniques to students who are struggling with specific skills or concepts.

- **Pre-teaching**
  Teachers can use groups to pre-teach and expose students to upcoming concepts. This is especially useful for those students who might otherwise struggle with the new skill.

- **Enrichment**
  Using small groups allows teachers to provide students with work that is more challenging than what is being taught in the whole class setting.

Benefits for the Students:

- **One-on-one teacher attention**
  No matter how many students are in the classroom, it is rare for students to get daily one-on-one attention from their teacher. When students work in small groups, they are given the opportunity to get sustained attention and help from the teacher. This can motivate lower achieving students to gain trust between themselves and others and gain confidence that they too can achieve.

- **Students are more likely to ask questions in smaller groups**
  When teaching a full class lesson, some students are often embarrassed or intimidated to ask questions—especially if they feel everyone else understands the concept. If students are working in a small

> As a veteran teacher, I've seen education go through many different trends regarding whether to teach the class as a whole, or to teach using small groups. The teaching style that works best for me is to have several different types of groups in my classroom at all times—small group instruction for some times along with whole group instruction for other times. I always have mixed groups when students are working on group projects, and I group by interest when students are choosing novels to read or an area to research for a paper. Finally, I tend to be traditional and group by ability for math and reading, although I pay close attention and move students from level to level whenever possible. I've found that by interchanging the way I group students, they rarely feel labeled or singled out.

group, particularly a group that has been assembled based on ability, they are more willing to open up and ask questions.

- **Contact with a variety of classmates**
  Often students will interact with only a small group of friends in the class, especially in a large class setting. Small group settings allow students to work with classmates they might not otherwise interact or associate with.

- **Enrichment groups**
  Small groups provide enrichment for students who need to be challenged. Students will gain motivation due to the challenges set for them.

Concerns with Grouping Students

Concerns for the Teacher

- **Requires more classroom management structure**
  When working with small groups, teachers must make sure that the rest of the class is engaged in meaningful work in order to minimize interruptions.

- **Requires more curriculum planning and differentiating lessons**
  In order to teach small groups you will need to plan more lessons. This will take more time and involves modifying the curriculum to meet the different needs or interests of the students.

- **Requires more actual class time to complete lessons**
  When working with small groups, you will need more class time and planning time to teach a new concept than you would need to teach one large group lesson.

Concerns for the Students

Grouping students, especially by ability, can cause students to feel singled out, labeled, or self-conscious about where they rank compared to other classmates.

Chapter 31

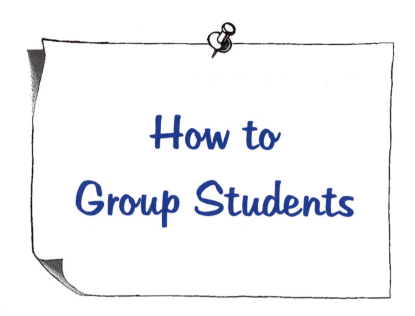

How to Group Students

Reassess students often to see if they can be moved into different ability groups.

There are a variety of ways to group students. The three most common are ability (homogenous) based, interest based, and mixed (heterogeneous) grouping. When grouping students you must decide which of the above methods to use, how many students to have in each group, and how to manage all the groups in your classroom.

Try to limit your groups to six students or fewer. If you are teaching with a class of 30 or more students you may have to have seven or eight students per group to avoid having too many groups. Any more than four or five groups running simultaneously can be tricky to manage. It is usually easier if the groups with higher academic ability assume the larger number of students, while the groups with lower academic ability remain small.

Ability Grouping

In the past, entire classes were grouped by ability level, also know as streaming. Over time, however, the pendulum swung completely in the opposite direction with teachers not grouping students at all. Today the pendulum seems to have landed somewhere in the middle. While the issue of grouping remains a constant debate in the education field, most schools no longer stream the classes. Today's teacher will find students with many different learning levels making up her class.

It is common for teachers to use smaller ability-based groups in math and reading.

Ability grouping is predominately used in these subjects for two reasons. First, in both math and reading a difference in student ability is easily noticeable. Also, the curriculum for both subjects is often geared to accommodate the three basic levels of ability: below average, average and above average.

Determining Ability Groups

INFORMAL EVALUATIONS

During the first few weeks of school you should find out where the students fall academically in your class just in case you'll want to group them by ability for math and or reading. A beginning of the year skills inventory test can be a helpful tool when determining ability groups. Your school may provide you with these tests or you can make them up yourself. The test should be quick and easy for you to give and grade, and should be made up of the following:

- questions containing skills taught the previous year
- questions students may be able to figure out based on skills previously learned
- questions that students have never been exposed to before in previous grades

These tests can help you determine those students who are below grade level, on grade level, or above grade level. Your goal is not to pigeon hole students at a certain level. It is simply beneficial to know approximately where your students fall with their reading and math skills. It's not unusual for students to excel in one area but find the other challenging. Therefore, be careful not to make assumptions about a student's overall academic abilities based on one subject area or test.

ADDITIONAL STRATEGIES

Along with beginning of the year skills inventories, you can use the following strategies to help assign ability groups throughout the year.

- **Pretest**

  A pretest can be made up of a few questions, math equations, or definitions and given **before** you've taught the concept/skill in order to see which children already have an understanding of the subject. Pretests can be used throughout the year to indicate which students already have a foundation for the upcoming concept and therefore can be grouped together—chances are they'll grasp the concept quicker and can move on. But be careful: pretests won't

How to Group Students

guarantee how well any group of students will grasp a concept, so make sure you're prepared to move students up and down through groups if you use this method.

- **Writing**

  A writing assignment can be used as a pretest, and is often quicker and easier for you to assess. Ask the students to write everything they know about an upcoming topic. Read the responses and assign ability groups accordingly. Complete the same writing assignment at the end of the chapter. Keep both answers to show the progress the students have made.

- **Oral assessment**

  Oral assessments often help you identify students who are better at explaining information orally instead of via the more traditional written format. Plan on sitting quietly with each student for a few minutes while he reads to you, explains a math concept, or answers a multi-part question (such as, *"What do you think is easier: adding or subtracting? Can you tell me why?"*)

Trust your teaching instincts when you make decisions regarding moving students between groups.

- **Classwork**

  Classwork reflects a student's ability to complete work independently. Completed classwork gives you a good idea who is grasping new skills quickly. If students are having trouble completing their classwork they may need more time to learn and apply the new skill.

- **Test grades**

  Although tests grades should not be the only, or the predominant, way of deciding groups, test grades do indicate where students are falling academically within the class. By including a writing component on all tests, you can get a further indication about the level to which students understand the given concepts. **If students can't explain it in writing, then they truly don't understand the concept.**

- **Teacher intuition**

  Once the school year begins, you will get a feel for those students who can handle a harder curriculum and those who may need a more gentle hand. If you have a student you know to be a confident hardworking child who enjoys a challenge, you may choose to bump him up a group and feel confident that he will do fine. Alternatively, there maybe another student you believe can be placed in a higher level group but because he is so anxious about his ability you feel that placing him with a lower level group is better for his confidence. Both decisions are right. Use your instincts to help you in all your teaching decisions.

Benefits of Ability Groups

- **Teaching to the same academic levels**
  The biggest benefit to ability grouping is that you can teach at the appropriate pace for each group to ensure that all students fully comprehend the topic being taught. Without grouping, some students get left behind while others get bored.

- **Moving students from group to group allows for enrichment and remediation**
  With ability grouping, you can move a lower level student into a higher level for enrichment, or a higher level student into a lower group if remediation is needed. Shuffling students in this way can help reduce or eliminate the labeling that can accompany ability grouping, because children know the members of the group are constantly changing.

- **Boosting student confidence**
  When students are working with other children of the same level they feel more comfortable and confident when asking questions and participating.

Grouping makes differentiating the curriculum easier.

Concerns with Ability Groups

- **Students can become stuck in one group**
  The biggest drawback to grouping students by ability is the possibility that a child might not move out of the group. A teacher might incorrectly assume that once a child is in a group, she has to stay there. To prevent this, teachers must be sure to pay close attention to each child's progress in the groups, and change her when necessary. For example, a child's ability in math can change throughout the year or even throughout the chapter. As a result, the child may need to switch groups. A quick pretest before each chapter can let you know which students are weak or strong with a particular skill.

- **Students may feel stigmatized, labeled, or singled out, especially if friends are in a higher group.**
  If ability groups are formed and never changed, or no other grouping is done within the class, students will begin to feel labeled and may feel stigmatized or singled out by their peers. This may inhibit motivation among some students.

How to Group Students

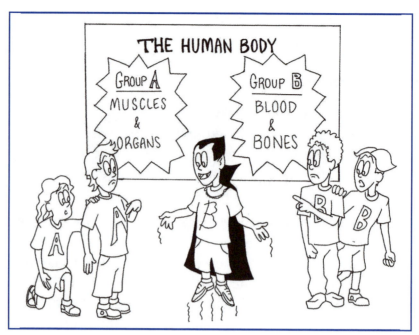

"Hmm, I don't remember you signing up for this group last time . . ."

Interest grouping motivates students.

Interest Grouping

Grouping by interest allows students who share common interests to work together and eliminates the concerns associated with ability grouping.

Determining Interest Groups

Interest grouping is an effective grouping strategy for many subjects, especially for reading and math.

If you use novels in conjunction with your reading curriculum, consider offering a choice between several books and letting the students choose which one they want to read. The various novels can be linked by theme, author, character, era, et cetera. Even though some students may choose a book that seems to be above their reading level, most students will gravitate towards books that are on their reading level.

In math, grouping students by interest can be achieved by having several groups running concurrently, each focusing on a different concept—think multiplication, geometry, or place value. These groups work well for shorter periods and can even be used as a fun one-day math activity.

In the beginning of the year try giving the students a survey that lists all the possible subjects, novels, or themes that you are considering covering, to find where their interests lie. When students gravitate towards what interests and motivates them, they change from being passive learners into active ones.

Benefits of Interest Groups

- **Peer teaching**
  When students are grouped by interest, there will be many academic levels included within the groups. This situation gives students the opportunity to peer teach, a valuable experience for both the student who is teaching and the student who is being taught. Peer teaching works well because the students speak each others language and are able to form strong bonds with one another.

- **Sharing common interests**
  Students who are grouped by interest will often form new friendships based on what they have in common. Students will have the opportunity to interact with others in the classroom with whom they never expected shared their same interests.

- **Motivation**
  Students are rarely given choices in school. When working in ability groups, students are not given a choice to be in the higher math or reading group. With interest based groups, students get to choose their work group. This is very exciting for students and adds to their motivation and confidence when completing the required group work.

Concerns with Interest Groups

- **Curriculum requires more planning**
  Interest based groups usually generate the most work for teachers because, in addition to varying the ability of a lesson, you're working with completely different books or concepts to capture the specific interest of each small group.

  This can be alleviated by working with common curriculum strands to link the groups together. For instance, when working with books, choose one topic, such as characterization or setting, for all the groups to work on—of course, the depth to which the topics get covered will probably differ from group to group.

- **Students not sufficiently challenged**
  When working in interest based groups, some students may not be challenged to the best of their ability if the group is at a lower academic level. In this case, if the group material doesn't challenge the students academically, the assignments you set to accompany the material should be designed to do so.

> When teaching my third grade class about the Holocaust, I allowed them to choose a novel based on interest. One of the books, The Hundred Dresses by Eleanor Estes was chosen by several girls and one boy. Many of the other boys made fun of him for selecting a "girly" book. When the books were completed and the students were discussing their books, this boy told the class he was glad he read the book because it was a great story. He pointed out that the other boys had missed out on a super book simply because of the title. On the second go around, many of the boys chose that book.

- **Groups chosen on social grounds**
  Often students will choose to be in a group simply just because their friends are there. One way to avoid this is to have students write their first two choices on a piece of paper without allowing them to discuss it with friends. Then you can collect the papers and decide on the groups. Or you can have students close their eyes and raise their hands when a novel title or math topic is called. This way they cannot see who else is interested in the particular book or topic.

Mixed Grouping

With ability grouping, you are placing students with others on their same academic level. With interest grouping, students are choosing where to go with little input from you. Mixed grouping allows you to have control over grouping students, without concern for academic abilities or interests.

Determining Mixed Groups

Mixed groups are the quickest and easiest way of grouping students. They do not rely on interest or ability but are created randomly. These groups can be created by:

- Assigning numbers. If you want five groups, have children count off from one to five until all children have received a number. All the number ones work in a group, all the twos in another group, and so on.

- Splitting students up with an even number of boys and girls in each group.

- Creating same sex groups (which can sometimes spark some fun competition).

- Letting students select their own groups. (This may be the most time consuming and problematic method.)

- Getting creative. Groups can be made based on date of birth, first letter of names, number of siblings—the options are endless.

Mixed grouping encourages socialization and keeps "cliques" from forming in the classroom.

Mixed groups can be used for any activity, from field trips to class projects and everything in between. When creating mixed groups the way you determine the groups usually doesn't matter—the trick is to create different groups every time and not to put students together who have a history of conflict.

Benefits of Mixed Groups

- **Opportunity to interact with various classmates**
  By mixing students children are given a chance to work with others in the class that they might not typically work with.

- **Ideal for class projects**
  Mixed grouping works best whenever ability grouping is unnecessary. For example, if you want the students to work in groups on a social studies map making project, mixed grouping could be used. In addition to class projects, this kind of grouping works well if you are reading quietly to small groups of students, working on arts and crafts, or spending time in learning centers.

- **Variety of styles and levels within groups**
  Having a mix of learning styles and academic levels within groups allows for peer teaching opportunities. Don't be fooled into thinking that it is only the children with higher academic standing who can teach or help others. Remember, all students excel in something and, when working in a mixed group, each student will contribute something unique to the group.

- **Grouping requires little set up time for the teacher**
  It takes very little effort on your part to establish the groups. By the time you're ready to assign a group project, you'll know which

students can work together and which ones can't. Creating the groups is quick and easy since no assessment of ability or interest is needed.

- **Small lessons not dependent upon academic ability can be taught**
  Mixed groups can work well not only for student group work but also for teacher-led lessons. If the activity, such as introducing a new game in a learning center, doesn't require ability grouping, a mixed group is an easy, effective, and fun way to deliver the lesson.

Concerns with Mixed Groups

- **You can't teach to ability levels**
  When the mixed group method, teachers should not try to teach concepts where academic levels might play a significant part. Students who are higher academically will become frustrated in this group because they have grasped the skill and want to move on. As well, students who are lower academically will become frustrated and maybe even self-conscious that they are not catching on fast enough and require more time to "get" a particular skill or concept.

A well-maintained classroom combines the three types of groupings with a teacher who changes the grouping style depending on the lessons, and moves students in and out of groups as needed. This keeps the class dynamics fresh and prevents children from being labeled by their peers.

> *I believe that mixed grouping should be utilized as much as possible. I have these groups set up and ready to go on the first day of school. I put all of my second graders in groups and name the groups by color. I continue the grouping throughout the year, changing groups every couple of weeks. When students are asked to put away supplies or get books, I do it by group. I often use this strategy for centers too. This keeps the students mixed together and involved with everyone in the class.*

Chapter 32

Getting Students to Work Cooperatively

When Students Don't Get Along

When students work in groups you will always have students that disagree. Most likely, you'll find your students fall into one of three categories:

- students who want to do everything their way
- students who will do whatever they're told or do nothing at all
- students who try to be the mediator

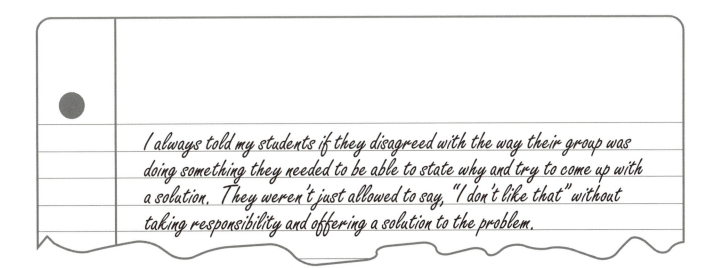

I always told my students if they disagreed with the way their group was doing something they needed to be able to state why and try to come up with a solution. They weren't just allowed to say, "I don't like that" without taking responsibility and offering a solution to the problem.

"But I can't work cooperatively. He refuses to color inside the lines!"

Children don't naturally know how to negotiate; this is a skill that needs to be taught and refined regardless of the grade you teach. Mini-lessons on group work skills can help students learn how to work more cooperatively in groups.

Often students don't know the best way to get their point across. As well, students need to understand that their way might not be the best way of doing something and it's okay to use someone else's suggestions. If you really want to focus on having students work cooperatively, try a mini-lesson on group work.

Mini-lesson on Group Work

In this mini-lesson the overall goal is to try and teach the students work in groups cooperatively. To do this they must understand how to state their point, how to disagree with another person's idea, and how to compromise and come up with reasonable solutions.

First, spend about five to ten minutes brainstorming with the students on what it should **sound** like if a group is working cooperatively. Write all their answers on the board. You're looking for answers such as:

"You should only hear one voice at a time."

"Voices should be soft not loud."

"We should hear phrases such as: *I agree with that, That's a good idea,* or *What about doing it this way?*"

- Try to avoid negative ideas. If, during the brainstorming, students want to include a negative comment, turn it around into a positive one. Therefore, a comment like "*You shouldn't hear yelling*" becomes, *"You should hear classroom voices."*

You've Got the Job—Now Keep It

- After the list is complete, split the students up for a quick group activity relating to something being taught that day. The activity doesn't need to be any longer than 15 minutes. The point of this activity is to have the students practice what you've just discussed.
- While the students are working in groups on the activity, walk around and take notes on conversations the students are having, noting what is working well and what isn't. You can use this information as a spring board for the group discussion that will follow this activity.
- After the group activity, bring the students back together and:
  - begin a discussion on how the students thought the group work went. Be careful not to let them start arguing or trading insults, and, unless they are paying the person a compliment, they should not use names when recounting the events. They might try to use this time to blame group members or vent about problems, but that is not the goal of the discussion. Allow students to discuss what went wrong, but don't let that become the focus—the goal of the activity is finding solutions, not focusing on the problem.

    OR

  - have students independently evaluate how they thought the group worked. It can be quick and easy and students don't need to include their name. Here's how to do it:

    - have students rate the group work on a scale of one to five. For younger children, let them draw the face that best expresses their level of satisfaction with the group activity: happy, sad or so-so.
    - have students list one positive comment they heard and one problem situation they saw during their group experience.
    - have students color in a pie section to rate how much work each group member did.

    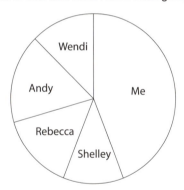

    Use the information from the evaluations to jump start the whole class discussion.

- After students have shared their comments or evaluations, start the group discussion with specific comments you heard, *"The blue group was working well. I heard Rachel tell Robert that she liked his idea on how to label the oceans on the map."* If you need to discuss negative issues, remember to avoid using specific names and bring the point around in a positive light: *"One group had difficulty deciding on what color to use on the background for their project. They were all arguing. Can we come up with any ways to solve this problem if it happens again?"*
- After your discussion, ask the class if there's anything that can be added or changed on the list that was brainstormed earlier.
- Once you have your final list of group work strategies, copy it onto chart paper and put it on the wall. It can be left there all year. The entire mini-lesson, including the group activity, should take no longer than 30–40 minutes.

The next time you can do a similar mini-lesson on what it should look like when people work in a group, followed later with a mini-lesson on how to solve problems when people in your group disagree. You should continue to listen and monitor groups sporadically throughout the year when students are working on group activities.

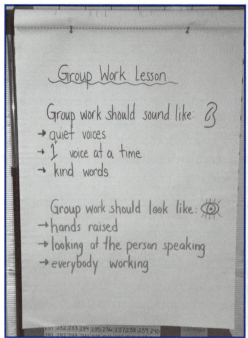

Display suggestions for proper group work skills in your class. Combine an inexpensive clothes rack with hangers to make chart papers easily accessible.

 Teach your students about group work using mini-lessons throughout the year.

In addition to providing students with mini-lessons on group work, you can also try assigning jobs within groups. Depending on the activity, make each student in the group responsible for one of the following:

- gathering and returning all supplies
- recording all information related to the activity
- making sure the directions are followed correctly by the group
- taking any group questions to the teacher
- being responsible for making final decisions
- creating all drawings related to the activity

The number of jobs that you create depends on the number of students you have in each group, as well as the activity. You can let each student in the group decide which job he would like, or you can assign specific jobs to individual students. Giving each student in the group a job creates a team approach to the activity as well as individual accountability within the group.

Now, all this sounds lovely and perhaps even a bit unrealistic, but believe it or not it works! You'll even hear kids mimic what was discussed in your brainstorming sessions—expect to hear lots of, *"Great idea"* or even *"That's a good idea, but I disagree. Could we try to do it this way?"* It's all a bit corny and sounds kind of funny, but as long as it works, that's all that matters.

Finally, no matter what you do to encourage cooperative group work, there will be times that you will need to intervene and help the group make a decision. While it's ideal if you can guide them towards some alternatives, sometimes you'll just have to provide the solution for them. That's okay also. Remember—adults often have trouble working cooperatively in groups and children are no different.

"Looks like they could use a lesson in group skills to me . . ."

Summary Section Seven

- There are three main ways of grouping students: ability, interest, or mixed. All three ways have benefits as well as drawbacks that need to be considered when planning your groups.

- Ability grouping places students in groups based on their ability in a certain subject area. Ability grouping works well for teachers as it allows them to teach directly to a specific academic level. Students must constantly be monitored and you need to make evaluations as to whether or not a student should move to another group. The biggest detriment to ability grouping is the chance that students get pigeon-holed or labeled.

- Grouping by interest allows students to be grouped based on their common interests. This type of grouping works best for reading but can be used for all subject areas. Make sure interest groups don't turn into "friendship" groups, where children choose their groups based which groups their friends are choosing.

- Grouping students in a mixed group means you assign students to work within a group that is not based on ability or interest. Use mixed groups as often as possible.

- When students work together on group projects, monitor the groups carefully. Children do not automatically know how to handle group work on their own. Plan on doing some small mini-lessons to model how to work cooperatively and effectively in groups.

- Assign jobs within groups to keep students on task and accountable.

- Use group work mini lessons often with your students to teach them the most effective way to work in groups.

Notes

Group Work Rating Charts

Names of students in group: _____

Use a smiley face to show how you think your group did working together.

☺   😐   ☹

_____ listening

_____ sharing

_____ finishing the work

- -

Names of students in group: _____

Rate how you well you think your group worked together. Use a scale of one to five, with one being the worst and five being the best.

_____ Making group decisions.

_____ Listening to each others suggestions.

_____ Including everyone's suggestions in the project.

_____ Finishing on time.

_____ Staying on task.

- -

Names of students in group: _____

Write one positive comment you heard while working in your group. _____

_____

Explain one problem situation your group encountered while working together.

_____

_____

TIPS, Inc.

Name: _____   Date: _____

Group Reflection

Easy as Pie!!!!

Your group activity is finished. Below is a circle that you must divide into sections, depending on the amount of work that you feel you and your group members did. If you feel you did a great deal of work, then give yourself a large part of the pie. If you did only a little, give yourself a small part of the pie. Make sure you do a pie slice for each member of your group, and label names on each piece.

What did you do well in this group? _____

_____

_____

What do you need to work on to improve your group work skills?

_____

_____

TIPS, Inc.

Reproducibles

SECTION EIGHT

Livening Things Up—
Learning Centers in the Classroom

IN THIS SECTION

- ✦ The basics of learning centers
- ✦ Different styles of learning centers
- ✦ Learning centers that appeal to students
- ✦ Scheduling time for centers
- ✦ Ideas for center activities

Chapter 33

Starting out with Centers

Centers from Kindergarten to Grade Five

Ask ten different teachers how to utilize learning centers and you'll most likely get ten different answers. The way a center is used depends largely on the grade level in which the center is found. Unfortunately, many teachers stop using centers just at the age when children can benefit most from them. Centers allow children to experience working both independently and in groups. They can self-select activities that not only appeal to their ability, but also to their interest. Center work can help children improve their time management, as they have a limited amount of time for working during centers.

Centers can be an integral part of any grade level classroom, provided they are set up and managed properly, and the students are aware of how they are required to work during center time.

Our surveys found that center time depended largely on the time schedule of the classroom. Teachers in the lower grades (kindergarten and first) tended to use centers more often than teachers in higher ones because the curriculum lends itself towards activities that can blend social and motor (both fine and gross) skills with the basics in content areas. In the higher grades, center time was less frequent and the activities were more academically based. However, many teachers in these grades can still utilize centers (usually a math and writing center) to enrich the curriculum. The actual time in the center could be as short as twenty minutes or as long as forty-five.

Centers, when developed appropriately, are a great way to diversify your teaching.

No matter what grade you teach, if you've decided to enliven your teaching by including centers as part of your curriculum, you'll need to consider:

- the time you have to create centers
- how much class time you plan to allocate for center use
- the purpose of your centers—will you use them to:
  - provide enrichment/remediation for students in certain subjects?
  - introduce new activities that relate to current topics your class is learning about?
  - cover content for the curriculum that you don't think you will have time to teach?

This section will provide only a basic overview of using centers. If you are truly interested in including detailed centers as an integral part of your classroom, check on the internet for ideas or pick up a book specifically designated for learning centers.

What Centers Should Be

If learning centers are not used at your school, if you never saw them growing up, and you've never come across centers in a classroom during your time at university, you might not have any idea what we are talking about!! Here is some background information on centers:

- Learning centers are specific physical areas of the classroom that are devoted to a particular theme or subject.

- Centers usually contain anywhere from six to twelve activities that reinforce, remediate and enrich content being studied in class. Good centers provide all three.

- Centers should be created so students can work independently on the activities, then self-correct or check their performance with a partner.

- It is helpful if the center activities are portable so that students can remove activities to their desks or other parts of the classroom.

- Depending on grade level, students should rotate through centers and spend anywhere from twenty minutes to an hour per a center.

What Centers Shouldn't Be

It is not uncommon to see centers that are poorly set up and dismally run. Neither students nor teachers will look forward to using these kinds of centers. Poorly created centers will often contain:

- **Worksheets**
  Filling a center with worksheets defeats its purpose. Worksheets (when used in moderation) have their place, but most students see them as boring and would rarely choose to do them as a center activity. If you want students to use the centers, be sure to fill them with interesting games and activities.

- **Unfocused students**
  Always set expectations by telling children what the outcome of the center time will be. While there may be times when you tell students they can work in a center of their choice, make sure you include clear directions about what they are expected to accomplish. Try saying, "You may choose to work in the center of your choice this afternoon, but you must complete a checklist for at least three activities." Center time should be structured and organized and should serve an academic purpose connected to the curriculum in your classroom. Center time should not be a "free for all."

- **Mundane activities**
  Learning centers should contain a variety of games and activities which address different learning styles and academic levels.

Types of Centers

There are different types of learning centers. To help you better form a foundation for working with learning centers, we've broken them into two groups: subject and theme centers.

Subject Centers

Subject centers are based on activities that relate to subject areas. Topics for basic subject centers for any grade might include math, science, writing, grammar, and art.

When creating subject based centers, first decide on the subject, then decide on the skills to include and finally choose several games or activities that demonstrate each skill.

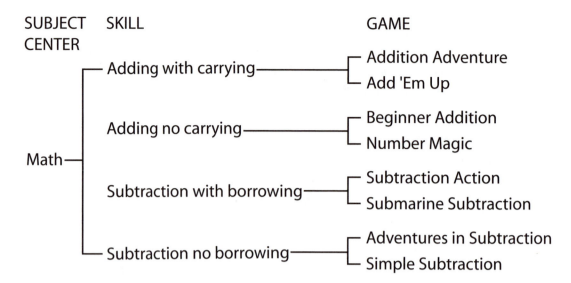

Thematic Centers

Thematic centers are based on a specific theme or unit being studied in class, such as Inventors, Wars of the 20th Century, or Animals of the Past. If a center is theme based, it should contain activities from across the curriculum (math, reading, writing, science, music and social studies) that are linked by the topic being studied. Thematic centers based on various holidays can also be fun.

When creating thematic based centers first decide on the theme, then the subjects, then the skills and, finally decide the activities or games to deliver all the information.

Rob was a little wary of his teacher's new "hands-on" learning center approach.

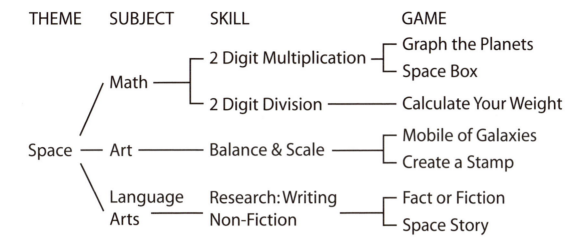

Creating and Organizing Centers

When creating your centers, you'll want exciting activities that can be changed at least once a month, especially for classes that use centers on a daily basis. That means during your first year of teaching, you're going to spend **a lot** of time creating center activities. Don't let that discourage you—what you create now should last for many years. Don't do it all on your own either; enlist some parents to help you, or consider planning centers with other teachers so you to get a variety of activities without too much work.

If you don't have time (or help) to make several centers immediately, at least create a math and a writing center.

To make centers, use items you can easily find around the classroom like construction paper, dominoes, and plastic cups. Ask parents to donate old board games. You can take the pieces from the board games, as well as paper money, dice, timers, or spinners and use them in your centers. You can even cover the old game board with construction paper to make a nice new game.

Once you create your activities, you will need a way to store them. A messy, unorganized center with missing directions, games pieces, or other parts is a center that won't get used. Below are some quick, easy, and catchy ways you can choose from to store activities for your centers.

- Use an upright wire holder to store files or folders.

- Laminate colorful file or pocket folders to hold both the games and the directions. Staple the directions inside, or staple the sides of the folder together to ensure that the activity does not fall out. Be sure to put the game title on the outside of the folder.

Starting out with Centers

"Hello Mrs. Ramirez? Yes, I got him, thanks, but, umm, that wasn't exactly what I had in mind when I requested that you send in old things from home..."

Make multiple copies of games and activities so that more than one student can use them at a time.

- Use plastic baggies with a seal to store game pieces and other loose items inside a folder.

- Use chip clips or paper clamps to attach small baggies to game boards. Place the board with baggies inside a laminated folder.

- Use a large baggie to put the game board and the smaller baggies inside.

- Keep larger games inside plastic tubs or decorated shoeboxes.

- Hang a clothesline across the wall and use clothespins to clip the plastic baggies on it.

- Make a supply box labeled "General Use." Keep baggies with decks of cards, dice, game pieces or other items taken from old board games inside so the students can use them on an as-needed basis. A small hour-glass is a fun addition to games involving timed activities.

Making Centers Appealing to the Students

In order to get the children enthusiastic about using classroom centers on a regular basis you've got to make sure they're interesting. If you put a lot of worksheets in your centers, your students will quickly become bored and less eager to participate in center time. To create interesting centers, take the following suggestions into consideration:

- Make your games and containers as colorful and attractive as possible.

- Teach a small group of students several games in the center, and let them teach their friends. This is a sure-fire way of getting the students actively involved in using the centers.

- Use centers instead of worksheets as reinforcement and remediation. Students are bored of worksheets—it's just as easy and much more educational to have them play a quick multiplication math game with a friend.

- Appeal to their senses and learning styles. Rather than filling your center with boring pencil to paper activities, try having activities that involve chance, logic, and skill. Introduce games that students can physically involve themselves in through touching, listening, or explaining.

- Appeal to the children's interests with current materials and trends. Create some games and activities based on the newest book, latest movie or most popular game you hear the students talking about in class.

Reusing games year after year will save you time and money.

Harry Potter was the hottest book in my fourth grade classroom. I was given a Harry Potter desk calendar as a Christmas gift one year and used the questions from it as part of my writing center. I glued the calendar pages and the questions onto pieces of heavy paper and laminated them. The students could choose any card and answer the question on it. One of the favorites was the card that asked, "If you could create any spell, what would it be?" The students needed to include a list of ingredients, step-by-step instructions, a detailed explanation of the effect and, of course, the antidote. They also made an illustration to accompany the writing activity. I kept that activity in my writing center for the entire year as well as the next.

Starting out with Centers

Chapter 34

Scheduling and Managing Centers

Most teachers would love to use learning centers but it seems there are two problems—fitting centers into their regular day and rotating the students through the centers.

Combining Teaching with Center Activities

In an average day teachers need to teach new skills, revisit old ones, work with groups of students, have students complete work, assess students, the list is endless. Teachers automatically figure with all this to be done, there is no way to integrate centers into today's classroom. If you view center work as something that eats up valuable instructional time then chances are you won't make centers part of your day. But if you are willing to bend a bit on your instructional strategies, it can be done. Instead of viewing center time and teaching time as competitors against each other, integrate them. How? Create small groups and **combine instructional time with your center rotations.** You can do this by:

- **Teaching new skills during centers**
  Instead of teaching one big class lesson, teach the lesson to a smaller group while the other students work at centers. Continue the rotations until you've taught the new skill to all groups.

- **Working on existing skills during centers**
  Set up groups based on subject or ability then meet with them as part of center time. While you work with one group, the others

rotate through the centers, eliminating the dilemma of what to do with the rest of the class while you work with a small group.

- **Using a "non-center" as a center**

    Part of the curriculum in every classroom will require that students complete a certain amount of seatwork. Seatwork is basically any type of work from any content area that a student completes with minimal teacher help. Quite often you will assign seatwork only to find that it can take more time to complete than you had thought.

    A solution to this problem is to integrate seatwork time into your center rotation time. Even though seatwork is not considered traditional center work, combining the two can serve as additional motivation for your students to finish their seatwork quickly. Children are more inclined to finish their social studies questions when they know the art center is waiting for them.

    Here are some other "non-centers" you can include along with your regular centers during center time rotation:

    - **School required activities**

        Every school has requirements that teachers must ensure their students fulfill, such as 15 minutes of computer time or D.E.A.R. (Drop Everything And Read) time. Incorporating these activities into your center rotations gives you an organized structure in which to fit these requirements.

Mr. Hansen's favorite part of the day was always "Drop Everything And Read" time.

Scheduling and Managing Centers

- **Free reading**
    Allow students to free read using the classroom library as the center. Let students read quietly on their own or with a friend in their group.

The Time Factor

The time you allot for center use depends largely on how much time you need for actual teaching, the learning you want to occur, and the grade you teach. Kindergarten teachers often cover all their academics in the morning and set aside time in the afternoon to do centers. In kindergarten the students are given up to half an hour per center as it takes them longer to get involved in, complete, and clean up the activities in preparation to move to the next center. That means in an hour of afternoon center time, each child rotates through two centers. For those that teach half-day kindergarten, center time is even shorter and, in some cases, it's limited to every other day. In the face of such time restrictions, many teachers don't choose to rotate the children through all centers every center time, instead they have the students stay at one center and go to a new center the following day.

"I don't have a clue where we go next, do you?"

Generally, for first and second grades, approximately 15 minutes per center works well; for third, fourth, and fifth grades 20 minutes is adequate. Keep in mind that, depending on the nature of the activities, you may want to increase this time. If you were to teach third grade and had four groups, you would be looking at about 80 minutes of center work in a day. It's very unlikely that you would have that much uninterrupted time—and what would you do if you had more than four groups?

To combat the time issue you could:

- Schedule half the rotations in the morning and the other half in the afternoon.
- Spread the centers over two days.
- Give shorter amounts of time to each center.
- Have larger groups with fewer centers so there are fewer rotations (and less time) required.
- Use centers only once a week, blocking off the appropriate amount of time required to get through a rotation.
- Adjust your center work to reflect the time constraints: you can do four fifteen minute activities, but if you only have three activities, make three groups and give them twenty minutes at each center.

What to do While the Students are at Centers

During center time, teachers often pull children out of their centers for individual work. If you plan on doing this, let the class know ahead of time that, even though but it might not be during *that* day, everyone will get a chance to sit with the teacher.

Using centers also allows you to work with a small group of students while the rest of the class is busy working. You can meet with students

 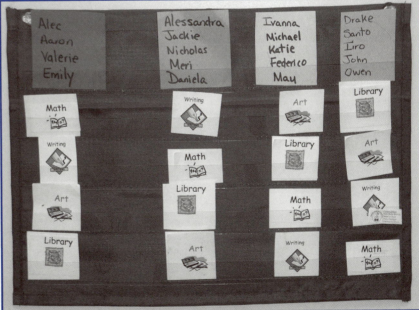

Charts for managing center rotation can be made once at the beginning of the year. Change group and center names as needed.

Scheduling and Managing Centers

who need help in math and reading, or even create a small group that you know needs assistance with a new skill that's been introduced.

In addition to working with students, center time provides you with the opportunity to informally observe students without drawing attention to what you are doing. Watching children work in groups gives you a chance to see some behavior or personality traits that might not emerge during general classroom work: some kids take over, others get bossed around, some don't work unless you are standing over them, while others use center time wisely and do what they need to do.

I used center time to pull students out individually for evaluations. I found center time worked well because the other children were involved in their activity so they were not focusing on who was with me and why. If anything, the other students were usually jealous and wanted a turn!

Plastic cups are a cheap and innovative way to track which students are working in each learning center.

> My co-teacher and I used centers on Friday mornings. Seatwork was always one of the centers, allowing students to catch up on work not completed during the week. Some students missed going to the other centers if their seatwork was not completed. We also used this time to pull students for remediation, special projects, or even enrichment activities. Occasionally, if we weren't pulling students for individual work, we would work with some of the students in one or two centers playing the games or completing the activities. This was a special treat for us and our students.

Samples of Centers in Real Classrooms

The following are two examples of how one third-grade teacher set up an afternoon rotation of centers. The first example mixes center work with teacher-led reading groups. The second example does not include reading groups but allows for students to be pulled out for individual work. The examples are based on her real classroom situations.

MONDAY

Goal: To meet with each group during center rotation

Number of rotations: Four
I used four rotations because I had four reading groups.

Type of groups: Ability groups (High, Medium, Low) and English for Speakers of Other Languages (ESOL). I assigned each group a color: high (green), medium (red), low (yellow) and ESOL (blue).

Types of centers: seatwork, writing, math, and teacher-led reading group

On this day, I chose seatwork as a "non traditional center" because there were social studies questions that some students needed to complete. I also chose the writing center

Scheduling and Managing Centers

because there were students still working on a writing project, and they could work independently without any teacher help, or, if they finished, they could continue working in the writing center on creative writing activities. Finally, I chose the math center and selected specific games relating to multiplication. The teacher-led reading group were the students working with me.

Grouping and rotation

Center work/teacher-led reading groups

The students stayed in their reading groups while rotating through the centers. As the center activities are designed for individual use, it never makes a difference if the students are in reading, math, interest, ability, or mixed groups.

I wrote a chart like the one below on my black board.

Time	Math Center	Writing Center/ Writing Project	Seatwork— Social Studies Questions/ Free Reading	Reading Groups (With Teacher)
12:30–12:50	Red	Yellow	Green	Blue
12:50–1:10	Yellow	Green	Blue	Red
1:10–1:30	Green	Blue	Red	Yellow
1:30–1:50	Blue	Red	Yellow	Green

Each group was assigned a center. To rotate the colors I moved them counter clockwise from right to left. Red started out first on math and then was moved to the end on the second line. Each group then moved one to the left.

I also manipulated the rotations so that I could begin working with the lower or middle groups and end with the higher level groups.

WEDNESDAY

Goal: To work with select students during center rotation

Number of rotations: Four

Type of groups: Mixed Ability (Blue, Green, Yellow, Red)

I used four rotations again, but none of the rotations included working with a reading or math group. In an earlier math lesson I had introduced subtraction with borrowing and I knew there were students from different math groups who needed individual help. I met and worked with two or three students at a time during this rotation.

Types of centers: writing, science, seatwork/math, and quiet reading

For centers I chose the writing and science centers as well as the non-traditional centers of seatwork and quiet reading. I chose seatwork because some of the students did not finish a math page from earlier. If time remained once the seatwork was complete they were to go ahead and work in the math center. I chose quiet reading because children can be pulled from this center without interrupting their work.

Grouping and rotation
Center work/pull out students

Because I was not grouping according to reading or math levels, I created mixed ability groups. I made sure the students I really needed to see were spread out at different centers, that way I'd avoid pulling all the students that I needed at the same time.

Below is a different example of how I grouped and rotated students through the centers. For this chart, I moved the groups clockwise from left to right. Notice the blue group started at the writing center starts, and then moved clockwise to the right at the next line, and finally is the last group to visit the seatwork center. The other colors followed the same pattern.

Time	Writing Center	Science Center	Quiet Reading	Seatwork—Math Page 53/ Math Center
1:00–1:20	Blue	Green	Yellow	Red
1:20–1:40	Red	Blue	Green	Yellow
1:40–2:00	Yellow	Red	Blue	Green
2:00–2:20	Green	Yellow	Red	Blue

Try not to have center groups divided up the same way all the time as this can create cliques. Also, no matter how you name the groups children always seem to know how they rank next to one another in terms of low, middle, or high. By using mixed groups as much as possible it creates less of a stigma for the students, and provides them with the opportunity to work with as many of the other children as possible.

Monitoring Center Use and Activity Completion

True learning centers include mostly self-correcting activities that span remediation to enrichment. Although the activities will be independently completed, you need to have a system for tracking how students spend their center time. Use checklists in the centers to assess and evaluate the students' work and to keep track of the activities completed. Checklists can be kept inside folders stored in or near the learning centers. Collect and initial the checklists several times a week to let the children know that you are keeping an eye on what they are doing. Checklists are helpful for teachers because they indicate where students are spending their time and whether the time is well spent. If you have a gifted student who plays an easy game repeatedly, redirection is needed.

For some activities you might not require that your students complete a checklist. If you've been working with a group of students in math and send them to play a multiplication game for the last five minutes of group time, a checklist isn't necessary.

Here are two options for using checklists:

A General Checklist

A general checklist can be used for most learning centers and can be easily adapted to include whichever aspects of the center are important to you. A general checklist should include the name of the center and the dates the children completed the activities on, as well as an evaluation section where students can rate the activity and make comments.

Sample Checklists

General checklists for centers in kindergarten and grade one

Color the square the right color for the center you used:
Kitchen: Red **Reading Center:** Yellow **Writing Center:** Orange
Math Center: Blue **Theme Center:** Brown

October	Monday	Tuesday	Wednesday	Thursday	Friday	My Favorite Center
Week One	Red	Brown	Yellow	Orange		Red
Week Two	Brown	Yellow	Orange	Blue	Red	Brown
Week Three	Yellow	Orange	Blue	Red		Red
Week Four	Orange	Blue	Red	Brown	Yellow	Yellow

For each center you use, draw a face to match how well you liked the activity.

Use:

	Kitchen	Math Center	Reading Center	Theme Center	Writing Center
Monday	☺				😐
Tuesday		☺		☹	
Wednesday			☺		
Thursday				☺	
Friday				😐	

General checklists for centers in grade two and higher

Checklist to Track by Center

Fill in the chart as you complete the center activities

Center	Activity Name	Date Started	Date Finished	What I Liked	What I Didn't Like
1. Math	Checker Multiplication	12/5	12/5	It was fun and good practice	
2. Writing	Shape poems	12/6	12/7	Making a poem about my dog	I like doing activities with a partner
3. Science	Weighing objects	12/6	12/6	I liked using the little weights and the balance scale	Need more things to weigh

Scheduling and Managing Centers

Checklist to Track by Day

Fill in the chart as you complete the center activities

Dec. 5–9	Center	Activity	Date finished	What I thought
Monday	Math	Checker Multiplication	12/5	Fun way to practice
Tuesday	Writing	Shape poems	12/7	Wrote funny poem about my dog—but I like doing centers with a partner
Wednesday	Science	Weighing objects	12/9	Fun using balance scale needed more things to weigh
Thursday				
Friday				

Checklist to Track by Activity

Fill in the chart as you complete the center activities

Activity Name & Center	Date Out	Date In	Comments	Student Signature
Math Checker Multiplication	12/5	12/6	Fun way to practice	
Writing Shape poems	12/6	12/7	I like writing poems but I like working with other kids in the centers and not by myself	

A Thematic Checklist

If you were to do a center based on a theme, as in the Space example to follow, you may want to have a checklist for the activities in this center only. Below is a sample checklist for a thematic center based on Space.

Checklist to track by theme

Space Log Check List

Fill in the chart as you complete the center activities

Name: _____

	Date Completed	Rate The Activity 0–5 (5 is the best)
Math—You must do at least three of the five activities listed.		
#1 Graph the Planets		
#2 Space Box		
#3 Calculate Your Weight		
#4 Rotations and Revolutions		
#5 Gravity, Gravity and More Gravity		
Language Arts—You must do activity #6 and any other three activities.		
#1 Space Poetry		
#2 What's The Weather?		
#3 Planet Scavenger Hunt		
#4 Name That Planet		
#5 Fact or Fiction?		
#6 Space Story		
Art—You must complete at least three activities.		
#1 Create a Stamp		
#2 Postcard From Outer Space		
#3 Mobile of Galaxies		
#4 Glow in the Dark Solar System		
#5 Space Sale Poster		

Which activity did you like the most and why? _____
_____
_____

Which activity did you like the least and why? _____
_____
_____

Scheduling and Managing Centers

Chapter 35

Do-it-Yourself Math Center Activities

Your math center should include an assortment of bought and self-made games. You're going to be pressed for time in the beginning of the year, so spending days and days preparing center games might not be an option. But don't panic: your store bought and reproducible games from math activity books, along with the card games included in this chapter—and some creative uses of egg cartons and dice—are sure to get your math center stocked with fun (but easy-to-make) math activities.

Exploration Games

Your math center should contain hands-on games that appeal to and challenge all ability levels. Some games, such as dominoes, tanagrams, multi-links or geoboards, can be included without directions—a simple demonstration at the start of the year should suffice, depending on the grade level—and placed in the center for students to simply experiment with. These, along with an assortment of boxed games, can be purchased at most big retail stores. Teacher supply stores are another option for pre-made games, but these stores tend to be more expensive.

Write out simple step by step rules and directions for easy card, dice, and domino games on index

"It says it's supposed to be an "easy" math center idea . . ."

298 You've Got the Job—Now Keep It

cards. Laminate the cards, place on a ring, and hang in the center or place inside the "General Use" box.

Reproducible Games

There are many good reproducible math game books available online, at local bookstores or from teacher supply stores. Most of these games come with game pieces, playing boards, and clear directions. A little cutting out and laminating is all it takes to have a few math games ready to go. Before you go out and buy a bunch of game books, check in the library at your school and with other teachers, as many school libraries have resource books for their teachers.

When you make your reproducible games, you should photocopy everything onto heavy paper or glue it to construction paper. Whichever method you choose, you should laminate your games. (The importance of laminating can't be underestimated—laminate whatever you can including directions, cards, and game spinners—it will save you time and money in the long run.) If you don't laminate you'll find that the games you've taken so much time to create will be ruined within a month.

Place direction cards on a binder ring and hang in centers.

"My name is Barbara, and I have a problem . . ."

Laminate even if you have to pay for it yourself.

Hand-Made Math Games

The following games are designed to be quick and easy so you can implement them in your math center as soon as it's ready. Most of the games have been borrowed from other teachers or are based on old favorites the children will probably already know how to play. While some games use laminated cards and dry erase markers, some may require a little score keeping, adding, or other scratch work so keep a supply of scrap paper nearby.

To create these games you will need the following materials:
old board games and playing pieces

- dice
- decks of cards
- paper
- pencils
- markers
- dominoes
- calculators
- hundred squares (included)

You'll also need to familiarize yourself and your students with the following terminology:

- factor and product:

  $$6 \quad \times \quad 8 \quad = \quad 48$$
  $$\downarrow \qquad \downarrow \qquad \quad \downarrow$$
  factor   factor   product

- facts: 6 times facts (6x1, 6x2, 6x3, 6x4, 6x5, 6x6, et cetera)

- digits: the individual part of the number. 32 is made up of the digits 3 and 2

- reverse digits: 81 and 18 are reverse digit numbers

- repeating digit numbers: 22, 33, and 44 are repeating digit numbers

- non-repeating numbers: 28, 36, and 45 are non repeating digit numbers

Laminate game directions and place on a binder ring for quick and easy access.

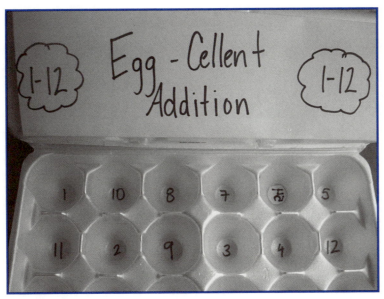

Egg carton games are quick to make and store away easily.

Egg Carton Games

You can use egg cartons for addition, subtraction, multiplication, and division activities. If the games become damaged, it's no big deal—they are cheap to replace and quick to make. Egg carton games also store easily—just open them up and stack one inside the other.

Game One: *Egg-Cellent Addition*
Game Two: *Egg-Cellent Subtraction*
Game Three: *Egg-Cellent Multiplication*

Skills: addition, subtraction and multiplication

Object of the game:
- Children use random numbers to practice adding, subtracting, and multiplying.

Materials:
- Egg cartons
- Markers
- Place markers—marbles work best
- Paper and pencil

Make the game:
- Open the egg carton.
- Number the bottom of each crate from 1 to 12.
- Copy and laminate instruction cards for students.

Do-it-Yourself Math Center Activities

Instruction cards for students. Copy and laminate onto heavy paper.

Game One

Egg-Cellent Addition Directions

Players: 2 or more

How to play: Place 2 place markers in the carton. Close lid, shake carton. Whatever numbers the markers land on get added together. Write the answer down as your score. Each round, add your score to the last.

Example: Round one $2 + 6 = 8$
Round two $12 + 4 = 16$
Your total so far: $8 + 16 = 24$ points

Number of rounds: 10

Winner: The player with the most points at the end of the game wins.

Game Two

Egg-Cellent Subtraction Directions

Players: 2 or more

How to play: Place 2 place markers in the carton. Close lid, shake carton. Whatever numbers the markers land on get subtracted from one another (subtract smaller from the bigger). Write the answer down as your score. Each round add your score to the last.

Example: Round one $12 - 6 = 6$
Round two $10 - 4 = 6$
Your total so far: $6 + 6 = 12$ points

Number of rounds: 10

Winner: The player with the most points at the end of the game wins.

Game Three

Egg-Cellent Multiplication Directions

Players: 2 or more

How to play: Place 2 place markers in the carton. Close lid, shake carton. Whatever numbers the markers land on get multiplied together. Write the answer down as your score. Each round add your score to the last.

Example: Round one 3 x 6 = 18
　　　　　Round two 4 x 2 = 8
　　　　　Your total so far: 18 + 8 = 26 points

Number of rounds: 10

Winner: The player with the most points at the end of the game wins.

Game Four: *Egg-Cellent Fact Fun*

Skill: multiplication

Object of the game:
- Children use cartons to practice specific multiplication facts.

Materials:
- Egg cartons
- Markers
- Place markers—marbles work best
- Paper and pencil

Make the game:
- Label the cover of each carton with the appropriate fact you wish to teach.
- In each carton, number the bottom of each crate from 1 to12.

Do-it-Yourself Math Center Activities

Instruction cards for students. Copy and laminate onto heavy paper.

Game Four

Egg-Cellent Fact Fun Directions

Players: 2 or more

How to play: Place 1 place marker in the carton. Close lid, shake carton. Whatever number the marker lands on gets multiplied by the number on the carton lid. If your answer is correct you get 1 point. If your answer is incorrect you get 0 points. Each round add your score to the last.

Example: Round one 2 x 4 = 8 (1 point)
Round two 4 x 4 = 12 (0 points, incorrect answer)
Your total so far: 1 point

Number of rounds: 10

Winner: The player with the most points at the end of the game wins.

Game Five: *Egg-Cellent Division*

Skill: division

Object of the game:
- Children use cartons to practice specific division equations.

Materials:
- Egg cartons
- Markers
- Place markers—marbles work best
- Paper and pencil

Using a timer with many of the math games improves speed of recall.

Make the game:
- Label the cover of each carton with the appropriate factor you want to teach. (i.e. 6 times facts)
- Number the bottom of each crate with the products belonging to the factor on the cover.

Instruction cards for students. Copy and laminate onto heavy paper.

Game Five

Egg-Cellent Division Directions

Players: 2 or more

How to play: Place one place marker in the carton. Close lid, shake carton. Whatever number the marker lands on gets divided by the number on the carton lid. If your answer is correct you get 1 point. If your answer is incorrect you get 0 points. Each round add your score to the last.

Example: Round one 36 ÷ 6 = 6 (1 point)
Round two 24 ÷ 6 = 3 (0 points, incorrect answer)
Total points so far: 1 point

Number of rounds: 10

Winner: The player with the most points at the end of the game wins.

 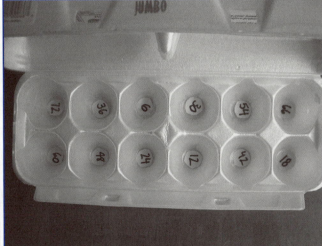

Write the factor outside and the products inside.

Do-it-Yourself Math Center Activities

305

Play games together as a class first to model how they are played.

Dice Games

Dice games are easy activities to include in your math center. Have one big baggie of different colored dice for the students to use for any of the following games. In toy stores and teacher supply stores, it is possible to find dice that have larger numbers, more than six sides, or blank sides so that you can write your own numbers on them.

Game Six: Bin It

Skills: place value, reading large numbers

Object of the game:
- Children create and read large numbers

Materials:
- 2 dice
- Dry erase markers
- Laminated game cards

Make the game:
Copy and laminate the following instruction and game cards.

Student Instruction Card. Copy and laminate onto heavy paper

Bin It Directions

Players: 2 or more

Decide: Will the bigger or smaller number win? What place value number are you playing for? (tens, hundreds, et cetera.)

How to play: Draw place value lines on scrap paper or use the laminated playing card included. Referee rolls dice and calls one of the numbers. Players write number in any empty place value spot or in the bin—once you place a number you cannot move it. Each player must place one number in the bin on bottom of playing card.

Number of rounds: Referee rolls one round more than the place value (see student playing card).

Winner: Player who makes the largest/smallest number.

Student Playing Card. Copy and laminate onto heavy paper.

Bin It Game Card

Place Value/Rounds	Number Created
Tens (roll dice 3 times)	_ _ _
Hundreds (roll dice 4 times)	_ _ _ _
Thousands (roll dice 5 times)	_ , _ _ _
Ten Thousands (roll dice 6 times)	_ _ , _ _ _
Hundred Thousands (roll dice 7 times)	_ _ _ , _ _ _
Millions (roll dice 8 times)	_ , _ _ _ , _ _ _

Do-it-Yourself Math Center Activities

Sample game: Students need to create the largest thousands (4 digit number), so the referee calls 5 numbers over 5 rounds.

Round One: Number called = 2

| Player One (keeps 2) | ___ , ___ ___ <u>2</u> |

| Player Two (bins 2) | ___ , ___ ___ ___ |

| Player Three (keeps 2) | ___ , ___ ___ <u>2</u> |

Round Two: Number called = 8

| Player One (keeps 8) | <u>8</u> , ___ ___ <u>2</u> |

| Player Two (keeps 8) | 8, ___ ___ ___ |

| Player Three (keeps 8) | ___ , <u>8</u> ___ <u>2</u> |

Round Three: Number called = 3

| Player One (bin 3) | <u>8</u> , ___ ___ <u>2</u> |

| Player Two (keeps 3) | <u>8</u> , ___ ___ <u>3</u> |

| Player Three (bins 3) | ___ , <u>8</u> ___ <u>2</u> |

Round Four: Number called = 5

Player One (keeps 5)	<u>8</u> , <u>5</u> ___ 2

Player Two (keeps 5)	8, ___ <u>5</u> <u>3</u>

Player Three (keeps 5)	___ , <u>8</u> <u>5</u> <u>2</u>

Round Five: Number called = 7

Player One (keeps 7)	<u>8</u> , <u>5</u> <u>7</u> 2

Player Two (keeps 7)	<u>8</u> , <u>7</u> <u>5</u> <u>3</u>

Player Three (keeps 7)	<u>7</u>, <u>8</u> <u>5</u> <u>2</u>

Player Two wins because 8,753 was the largest number made.

Do-it-Yourself Math Center Activities

Game Seven: *Number Magic*

Skills: addition, subtraction, multiplication

Object of the game:
- Players perform math operation on spell cards to earn points.

Materials:
- 2 dice
- Spell cards
- Hole punch

Make the game:
- Collect different shaped dice with variety of numbers, or cover regular dice with masking tape and make your own numbers.
- Copy and laminate the spell cards, punch a hole in top corner and put them on a ring.

Instruction cards for students. Copy and laminate onto heavy paper.

Number Magic Directions

Players: 2 or more

Decide: Will the largest or smallest number win? How many dice will you use to play?

How to play: Shuffle spell cards and lay them face down. First player rolls dice and writes down all numbers. First player picks a spell card and performs the operation. The resulting number is the player's score. If any player can't perform the operation, he loses his turn.

Number of rounds: 5

Winner: The player with the largest/smallest number at the end of each round wins.

Playing cards for students. Copy and laminate onto heavy paper.

Number Spell One

A number wizard? Hmm, let's see . . .

Each of your numbers multiply by 3.

Add the answers carefully,

And the number wizard now you'll be!!!

Number Spell Two

As a number wizard you would be wise,

To multiply each of your numbers by 5.

Add the answers carefully,

And the number wizard now you'll be!!!

Number Spell Three

We have wizards but we need more,

So add your numbers together and then subtract 4.

Your number now smaller gets,

So maybe you won't be a wizard yet!!!

Number Spell Four

Number wizards should never be late,

So pick one number and multiply by 8.

If you think that you still need time,

Increase your answer by adding 9.

Number Spell Five

Take the numbers and add 6 to each,

To see what large number you can reach.

Now subtract the numbers from each other,

And after this card, you can take another!!!

Number Spell Six

Take each number and multiply by 2,

Add the answers and when you're through,

Divide your newest number in half,

Now that's what I call hard wizard math!!!

Number Spell Seven

Select one number and to it add 7,

Now turn around and subtract 11.

Check your answer carefully,

And the number wizard now you'll be!!!

Number Spell Eight

Nothing makes a spell as fine,

As increasing each number by adding 9.

Add your answers together and when you're done,

From your final answer take away 1!!!

Number Spell Nine

For an extra bit of subtraction time,

Add up your numbers and take away 9.

If the directions here you cannot do,

Then this turn no longer belongs to you!

Number Spell Ten

For the largest number you've ever seen,

Add your dice numbers to the number 15.

If it's a bigger number than you had last score,

Go ahead and add 10 more!!!

Card Games

Card games are another easy way to add fun to your centers. Either remove the face cards from the decks, or reassign them a value: Jack = 11, Queen = 12, King = 13, and Ace = 14.

"I'll give you an even, and raise you a prime number."

Game Eight: *Name the Number*

Skills: reading large numbers, place value, logical thinking

Object of the game:
- Children create and read large numbers.

Materials:
- Scissors
- Deck of cards (no face cards)
- Colored disposable cups (12 oz. cups work best)
- Permanent marker

Make the game:
- Slit bottom of 7 cups with scissors to make 7 card holders.
- Use marker to label seven cups with place values from ones to millions.
- Create 3–4 different colored sets of cups.

Instruction cards for students. Copy and laminate onto heavy paper.

Name That Number Directions

Players: 2 or more

Decide: Will the smaller or larger number win? How large a number are you trying to make? You will need that many cups.

How to play: Each player chooses a set of cups Sort through deck of cards, keep only cards from 1 to 9. Deal the cards out equally to all players. You will need at least as many cards as cups. (i.e. if you are playing for a 5-digit number, each player needs at least 5 cards).

All players lay their cards face down. Each player selects a card from the player on her right and places it in place holder cup. Once card is placed it cannot be removed. Continue playing rounds until each player has filled his or her own cups.

Winner: Player who created the largest/smallest number.

Game Nine: *Addition Grab-It*

Skill: adding numbers, mental math

Object of the game:
- Children add numbers quickly to win cards.

Materials:
- Deck of cards

Make the game:
- Copy and laminate the direction cards.

Instruction cards for students. Copy and laminate onto heavy paper.

Addition Grab-It Directions

Players: 2 plus referee

How to play: Shuffle deck keeping only cards from 1 to 9. Place deck between the two players, face down.

Player 1: draws card and places it face up.

Player 2: draws card and places it face up on top of first card.

First player to add the numbers, call out answer, and place hand on top of deck calling out "Mine!" wins pile.

Number of rounds: Play until the deck is gone.

Winner: Player with most cards at end of deck wins the game.

Do-it-Yourself Math Center Activities

Variations:
This game can be played by subtracting the numbers or multiplying them.

Subtraction Grab-It Directions

Players: 2 plus referee

How to play: Shuffle deck and keep only cards from 1 to 9. Place deck between the two players, face down.

Player 1: draws card and places it face up.

Player 2: draws card and places it face up on top of first card.

First player to subtract the numbers, call out answer, and place hand on top of deck calling out "Mine!" wins pile.

Number of rounds: Play until the deck is gone.

Winner: Player with most cards at end of deck wins the game.

Multiplication Grab-It Directions

Players: 2 plus referee

How to play: Shuffle deck and keep only cards from 1 to 9. Place deck between the two players, face down.

Player 1: draws card and places it face up.

Player 2: draws card and places it face up on top of first card.

First player to multiply the numbers, call out answer, and place hand on top of deck calling out "Mine!" wins pile.

Number of rounds: Play until the deck is gone.

Winner: Player with most cards at end of deck wins the game.

Hundred Squares Games

Hundred squares games are logic based and are easily created from your computer by copying and laminating a large square made up of 10 rows and 10 columns and numbering each square from 1 to 100 (we've included one at the end of the chapter). Or you can purchase larger more durable hundred squares at a teacher supply store. A pack of 20 squares will cost about five dollars. In either case, allow children to use dry erase markers on the squares so they can be wiped clean once the game is finished. Overhead transparency markers also work on laminated games and come off with a little bit of water or nail polish remover.

For each game below, the starting square should be crossed off or colored in. For example, if a game says start with the number five, then count up and cross out every third number, the student should start by crossing out the number five and then the eight, then eleven, and so on. In some games, children may find themselves needing to put an X through a number that has already been crossed out. This is fine.

Before they begin, students should fold over the bottom part of any game card that contains an answer.

Game Ten: *Guess the Number*

Skills: listening, whole number knowledge

Object of the game:
- Children listen to clues to determine the target number

Materials:
- Laminated hundred squares
- Dry erase markers
- Guess the Number cards

Make the game:
- Copy and laminate the "Guess the Number" cards.
- Attach to binder ring and hang in math center.

Do-it-Yourself Math Center Activities   319

Instruction cards for students. Copy and laminate onto heavy paper.

Guess the Number Directions

Players: 2 or more and referee

How to play: Referee calls out the number clues and players put an X through all the numbers that fit the clue. In some games the same number may need to be crossed out twice.

Winners are the players who finish with the target number.

Number of rounds: Players with the right answer advance to the next round. Play for 6 rounds.

Winner: The player who gets the correct answers for all 6 rounds, or the player who wins the most rounds.

Guess the Number

Skill Level: Easy

Referee calls these clues:

Put an X through

- All numbers that have the digit 8 in them
- All numbers that have the digit 4 in them
- All odd numbers
- All numbers with two digits that are the same (including 100)
- All numbers ending in 0 or 5
- All numbers ending in 2
- All two digit numbers

Guess the Number?

Answer: 6

Guess the Number

Skill Level: Medium

Referee calls these clues:

Put an X through
- All even numbers
- All numbers greater than 30 but less than 67
- All digits with a 3, 5, or 7
- All numbers whose last digit can be divided by 3
- Any one digit numbers
- Numbers with digits that do not repeat

Guess the Number?

Answer: 11

Guess the Number

Skill Level: Challenging

Referee calls these clues:

Put an X through
- All numbers ending with 0 or 5
- All square numbers (2 x 2 = 4 so eliminate 4)
- All numbers that have reverse digits (12 and 21, 14 and 41)
- Any single digit number
- Any number with non-repeating digits
- Odd numbers
- Add the digits of remaining numbers together (22 = 2 + 2 = 4)
- The mystery number is the one whose digits makes the largest number.

Guess the Number?

Answer: 88

Do-it-Yourself Math Center Activities

Guess the Number

Skill Level: Easy

Referee calls these clues:

Put an X through

- Any number with the digit 2, 3, 7, or 8
- Any number with the digit 1
- Any number that has a 0 or 6
- Any number that has a 9
- All repeat digit numbers (88, 44)
- Any number that is 5 or greater

Guess the Number?

Answer: 4

Guess the Number

Skill Level: Challenging

Referee calls these clues:

Starting with 3, count and cross out every third number (3, 6, 9, 12)

Then put an X through

- Any number with 6
- Any number greater than 20 and less than 70
- All odd numbers
- Add the digits in the remaining numbers together. Cross out any sum that is odd (14 because 1 + 4 = 5)
- Any single digits
- Any number that has an 8 in it
- Any number less than 20

Guess the Number?

Answer: 20

Game Eleven: *What's the Pattern?*

Skills: listening, whole number knowledge, recognizing and following number patterns

Object of the game:
- Children listen to clues to determine the pattern that will create the design.

Materials:
- Laminated hundred squares
- Dry erase markers
- What's the Pattern cards

Make the game:
- Copy and laminate the "What's the Pattern?" cards.
- Attach to binder ring and hang in math center.

Instruction cards for students. Copy and laminate onto heavy paper.

What's the Pattern Directions

Players: one player, or 2 or more with a referee

How to play:

One player: read card and put an X through all the numbers that fit the clues.

Two or more players: Refree calls out the number clues and players put an X through all the numbers that fit the clues. In some games the same number may need to be crossed out twice.

Winners are the players who land on the last number as indicated on the pattern card.

Do-it-Yourself Math Center Activities

What's the Pattern?

Skill Level: Medium

Color in the numbers 1, 2, 4, 5, 8, 9, 13, 14, 19, and 20. Follow the pattern and keep going until you run out of squares to color.

What number did you color last?

The pattern is color in two numbers (1 and 2) skip one, color in two numbers, skip two, color in two numbers, skip three and continue. The last number colored is 90.

What's the Pattern?

Skill Level: Easy

Start at 3. Color numbers 7, 11, and 15. Follow the pattern and keep going until you run out of squares to color.

What number did you color last?

The pattern is count on and color every fourth number. The last number you colored is 99.

What's the Pattern?

Skill Level: Challenging

Color the numbers 1, 2, 3, 5, 8 13, 21. Follow the pattern and keep going until you reach the end of the square.

What number did you color last?

The pattern is color the first two numbers and add them together (1 + 2 = 3) Color in the sum, 3 and add that to the last number colored (3 + 2 = 5) Color the sum, 5 and add that to the last number colored, 3. Add those together (5 + 3 = 8) and color the 8. The last number colored is 89.

Game Twelve: *What's the Design?*

Skills: listening, whole number knowledge, recognizing and following number patterns

Object of the game:
- Children listen to clues to create a design.

Materials:
- Laminated hundred squares
- Dry erase markers
- What's the Design cards

Make the game:
- Copy and laminate the "What's the Design?" cards.
- Attach to binder ring and hang in math center.

What's the Design Directions

Players: one player, or 2 or more with a referee

How to play:

One player: read card and put an X through all the numbers that fit the clues.

Two or more players: Refree calls out the number clues and players put an X through all the numbers that fit the clues. In some games the same number may need to be crossed out twice.

Winners are the players who create the proper design as indicated on the pattern card.

What's the Design?

Skill Level: Challenge

Start at number 5. Go forward 10 and count back 1. Color that number. Continue: Move forward 9, back 2, color forward 8, back 3, color forward 7, back 4, color forward 6, back 5 color forward 5, back 6 color forward 4, back 7 color forward 3, back 8, color forward 2, back 9, color forward 1, back 10, color

What number did you color last?

Answer: You should have ended on the same number you started. Try another number with the same pattern and see what happens.

What's the Design?

Skill Level: Easy

Start at 1. Count down one box and to the right one box, color. From here count down one and to the right one, color. Continue to the end.

Start at 10. Count down one box and to the left one box, color. Count down one and to the right one, color. Continue to the end.

What number did you color last?

Answer: The design you should have made is two diagonal lines. The lines end on the numbers 91 and 100.

What's the Design?

Skill Level: Medium

Solve the following equations. Color the answers on the square.

6 x 4 =	8 x 7 =	43 + 43 =
11 x 3 =	9 x 7 =	56 + 32 =
7 x 5 =	36 + 33 =	4 x 11 =
12 + 25 =	75 – 1 =	8 x 6 =
7 x 4 =	68 + 10 =	20 + 18 =
40 – 1 =	100 – 15 =	17 + 17 =

What's the design?

Answer: The design is you should have made is a face with two eyes, a nose, and a smiling mouth.

Do-it-Yourself Math Center Activities

Check the internet for fun game ideas.

Checker Games

Convert checkers into a math game by assigning numbers to each playing piece. Use a sticker and place numbers directly on the pieces. Play the game according to its regular rules, but use the numbered pieces to keep score.

Game Thirteen: *Number Checkers*

Skill: adding numbers, strategy

Object of the game:
- Children play checkers trying to capture the pieces with the highest points.

Materials:
- Old checker game

Make the game:
- On each checker write a number from 1 to 12.
- Copy directions and laminate, place onto rings and hang in math center.

Instruction cards for students. Copy and laminate onto heavy paper.

Checker Math Directions

Players: 2

Players set up checkers on the board. Each round players arrange the pieces differently to see how it changes the game.

How to play: Players play the game following regular checker rules, except that kings **cannot** be captured. The game is over when only kings remain on the board.

Winner: Players determine points by adding up the numbers on each king piece (making sure to count both checkers). The player with the highest points wins.

Setting up a Writing Center

Components of a Writing Center

Every classroom should have a writing center. A good writing center reflects the belief that writing is an important part of the classroom and the curriculum you will be teaching. Although writing should be done across the curriculum, the writing center itself will be geared more towards *creative* writing. To promote creativity when putting together a writing center consider:

- **Location**
  There should be a place where several students can sit to share their writing ideas.

- **Time**
  A scheduled block of time each day for writing should be set aside. Try to include the writing center into your center rotations as often as possible.

- **Supplies**
  Supply different kinds of paper, trays, and folders for holding or storing work. Include a dictionary, an atlas, a thesaurus, a phonebook and even a few maps in your center. For supplies have markers, crayons, and color pencils easily available, as well as staplers, hole punches, tape, and glue. You can stimulate the children's imagination by including different sizes, shapes and textures of papers such as paper bags, sentence strips, chart paper, sand paper or doilies. You may also want to include a full length mirror that the

students can use for reading aloud, tape recorders and blank tapes for recording, and small table lamps, flashlights, and battery powered candles.

Make sure each child has a writing notebook and folder. Spiral notebooks work best as they can be folded back and pages can be removed easily. Folders can be used to keep track of papers that have been torn out or any that are in various editing stages.

- **Wall displays**

    Create a space for finished projects, as well as for a separate word wall. Word walls are easy to make and can be used year round as one of your bulletin boards—many teachers use word walls to post frequently misspelled words. If you have the space, create a word choice section on your wall and provide students with alternatives to overused words such as "said" and "nice."

- **Classroom library**

    A classroom library is important for writing centers. Many good writing ideas come from books. The larger the variety of writing styles your students are exposed to, the better they will write.

Use a word wall to help students discover alternatives to overused words. Add to or change the wall throughout the year

Generating Writing Ideas

If you are unsure about how to get your students writing, here are some simple items to include in your center to help them start.

Story starters

Story starters are exactly what they sound like—they give the start of a story and the student must finish it. Write and laminate five or six story starters and put them in your center. Stick them onto colorful construction paper or florescent copying paper. Put them in strips, cut them out in different shapes, or put them on index cards. You can keep them in a folder, box, or pin them up on a bulletin board.

Below are five story starters:

> *It was the first slumber party of the summer. The five girls were fast asleep after a long night of eating popcorn and watching their favorite scary movie. Suddenly one of the girls got up and began walking towards the window. Slowly the other girls woke up, not believing what they were seeing. . . .*

> *I think my aunt is going crazy. This morning she came to pick me up from baseball practice on a motorcycle. She was dressed head to toe in black, and across her leather motorcycle jacket, written in silver studs, was "Born to Ride." "There's no time to waste," she cried, "Hop on!!!"*

> *Today was the craziest school day ever!! It all started when . . .*

> *I know you're not going to believe this, but as I am sitting here writing this I want you to know one thing: I'm not me. Sounds crazy, I know, but when I woke up this morning I was not in my own body—I had switched places with_____*

> *It's not every day that you wake up and see what I saw this morning. Let me tell you, it's lucky that I'm still able to talk about it . . .*

If you want students to be motivated to use your writing center, be creative in your presentation of activities.

Setting up a Writing Center

When using story starters, remember to tell the students that they are supposed to write a story. You've given them a simple beginning. They need to complete the story, not just add a sentence or two.

Questions

You can make up questions similar to the way you created your story starters. Develop general or even specific questions the class can use to jump start their thinking about a story they've just read. These questions are not so much creative writing as they are a comprehension tool that links reading and writing. You can let the student choose whatever questions they want to answer, or you can choose for them.

Some questions you might include are:

What has the author done to build suspense in the book?

Describe the relationship between two of the characters in the book.

If you could be a new character in the book, who would you be and what would you do?

What was the best part of the story and why?

What part of the story did you least like and why?

If a sequel was written to this book, what do you think would be included in it?

Compare one event from the book to something that has happened to you.

Obviously, you would write questions that fit your grade level. Also, you could make up questions for students to answer as they move through a book, such as "What do you think will happen in the next chapter?" or "What do you think will happen if Jeanie doesn't return her mother's bracelet?"

Writing Prompts

Write different writing ideas on various shapes of construction paper. Laminate them and glue them onto craft sticks. Put the sticks in foam (the type used for floral displays works best). Ideas for writing prompts could be:

Write a letter to your principal about an idea you have for the school, or a rule you'd like to have changed.

Write one word describing something red for each letter of the alphabet.

Describe the color blue without using the word blue. Try telling what blue feels like, smells like, looks like, sounds like and tastes like.

How would your school day be different if you were blind?

Mystery Writing

Take a big shoebox and tape it closed. Cut a hole in the side so students can put their hands through. Place an object inside and tell the students they can only touch it, not take it out of the box. Have the students write a short story about the object. Some ideas for the mystery box are: a piece of fur, or something squishy feeling. Introduce new objects as often as necessary.

Place an odd item (like an old teapot or something strange from a garage sale) on a table in the writing center. Stick a paper note on it that asks "How did I get here? And where did I come from?" Have children write a story about how the object came to be in your classroom.

Poetry Samples

Give students guidelines for poetry writing and encourage them to try writing different kinds of poems. You might shy away from teaching poetry, but the following poems are so easy they practically teach themselves!

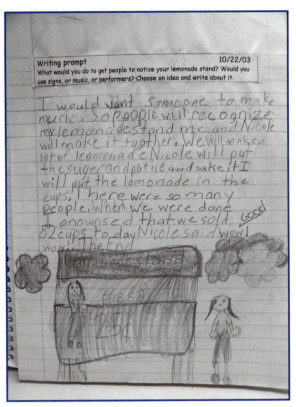

Glue writing prompts into a notebook to keep them from becoming lost.

"Go ahead Randy, just put your hand inside."

Setting up a Writing Center

Include poetry guide books in your writing centers so students can experiment with different types of poetry.

- Form poems follow a predetermined pattern. The body of the poem can be either fill-in-the-blank style where the body already exists but words have been left out for the writer to fill in, or pattern style, where the layout of the poem follows a certain formula. Students work on creating each line separately, then put each line together for the final poem. Examples of pattern poems include cinquain, haiku, and tanke poems.

- Short sentence poems are only a few words long. There are several varieties, including last links, alliteration and list poems.

- Rhyming poems have sentences that usually rhyme with simple end rhyme. Couplets and quatrains are examples of rhyming poems.

- Shape poems take the shape of the item they describe, or a shape related to the subject of the poem. Acrostic and concrete poems are examples of shape poems.

- Free verse poems are the opposite of form poems, shape poems, and rhyming poems. They follow no rhyme scheme or pattern—the poem says whatever the author wants to say.

The following poems are easy enough that the students can write them on their own without teacher directions. **Copy and laminate these poetry guides onto heavy paper to create mini-poem guide books.** Fold along line A then line B, and display them in the writing center. Students can use them as a reference when creating rough drafts of poems in their writing workshop notebook. Here are a few form poems to have them start with.

Form Poems

Form poems follow a set pattern. Follow the directions, plug in the words, and tah-dah! You've created a poem!

2

Cinquain: A five-line poem that takes the shape of a diamond.

Line 1: The subject of the poem
Line 2: Two words that describe the first word
Line 3: Three verbs about the subject
Line 4: A metaphor or simile about the subject (four-five words)
Line 5: A summary word that is different from the first but still related to it

WINTER
*Snow
Cold Crisp
Floating Drifting Dancing
Gentle whispers that fall from the sky
Magic*

Now you try: Copy these blank lines into your writing workshop notebook and try a cinquain poem for yourself!

_____ (title)

_____ _____ (subject)

_____ _____ (two describing words)

_____ _____ _____ (three verbs)

_____ _____ _____ (a metaphor or simile)

_____ (one summary word)

Read you poem aloud. How does it sound?

3

Haiku: A 3-line, 17-syllable poem (originating from Japan) that, in its truest form, is based on something occurring in nature.

Line 1: 5 syllables
Line 2: 7 syllables
Line 3: 5 syllables

AUTUMN
*Branches softly sway
Falling leaves of gold and red
Winter starts to creep*

Now you try: Copy these blank lines into your writing workshop notebook and try a haiku poem for yourself!

_____ (title)

_____ (5 syllables)

_____ (7 syllables)

_____ (5 syllables)

Read you poem aloud. How does it sound?

4

Tanke: Another form of Japanese poetry that doesn't rhyme. The five lines describe one subject and contain 2, 3, 2, 3, and 3 words per line respectively.

The Window Painter
*Winter night
Frost on windows
Means that
Mother Nature is
Hard at work*

Now you try: Copy these blank lines into your writing workshop notebook and try a tanke poem for yourself!

_____ (title)

_____ _____ (two words)

_____ _____ _____ (three words)

_____ _____ (two words)

_____ _____ _____ (three words)

_____ _____ _____ (three words)

Read you poem aloud. How does it sound?

Setting up a Writing Center

Short Sentence Poems

These poems are only a few words long. Short on vocabulary? Then this is the poem for you!

Last link poem: Each word begins with the last letter of the previous word.

Talking gets students "shhshshed"

Now You Try: Copy the blank into your writing workshop notebook and try a last link poem for yourself!

_____

Read you poem aloud. How does it sound?

Alliteration poem: Each word begins with the same letter sound.

Bill's bakery bakes beautiful bagels!!

Now You Try: Copy the blank into your writing workshop notebook and try an alliteration poem for yourself!

_____

Read you poem aloud. How does it sound?

List poems: A list created to match one subject.

> When I am sick . . .
>   ears throb
>   throat hurts
>   head pounds
>   skin sweats
>   body aches

Now You Try: Copy the blanks into your writing workshop notebook and try a list poem for yourself!

> **When I am** _____
>
> _____
>
> _____
>
> _____

Read you poem aloud. How does it sound?

336 — You've Got the Job—Now Keep It

Rhyming Poems

Can you think of pairs of rhyming word? If so, these poems are for you!

Rhyming Couplet: A two sentence poem where the last words of each sentence rhyme with each other.

At recess I will take a walk,
See my friends and have a talk.

Now You Try: Copy the blanks into your writing workshop notebook and try a rhyming couplet poem for yourself! Pick a subject. Now pick a pair of rhyming words about the subject. Build a sentence around each word.

_____

_____

Read you poem aloud. How does it sound?

2

Quatrain: A four-line rhyming poem made up of two rhyming couplets. Very popular in older and modern day poetry. A poem can consist of one or more quatrains.

THE CITY
Below the stars the flashing lights
Brighten up the darkest night
Car horns honking loud and deep
In the city of life that never sleeps

Now You Try: Copy the blanks into your writing workshop notebook and try a quatrain poem for yourself! Pick a subject. Next pick two pairs of rhyming words about the subject. Build a sentence around each word.

_____

_____

_____

_____

Read you poem aloud. How does it sound?

3

Setting up a Writing Center

Shape Poems

Tired of writing the same old way? Try a shape poem and give new dimension to your writing!

Acrostic Poetry: A word is spelled out vertically on the page and the beginning of each sentence starts with each letter.

S ilently falling from the sky
N ight becomes blanketed in white
O n treetops and rooftops
W ill it last until first morning light?

Now You Try: Copy the blanks into your writing workshop notebook and try an acrostic poem for yourself! Pick a word and write each letter on its own line.

_____
_____
_____
_____
_____

Read you poem aloud. How does it sound?

Concrete Poetry: The poem takes the shape of whatever you write about, or something that relates to it.

SNAKE

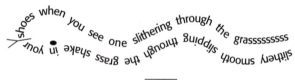

slithery smooth slipping through the grass shake in your shoes when you see one slithering through the grasssssssss

Now You Try: In your Writer's Workshop notebook, lightly outline a shape that relates to the subject of your poem. Write the words along the outside of the shape you've created.

Read you poem aloud. How does it sound?

338   You've Got the Job—Now Keep It

Space Aliens

2 heads and one big eye
Skinny fingers and little mouths
And a ship full of
A
   Billion
     Lights
Zooming from our dark backyard
Into the starry night sky

Now You Try: Copy the blanks into your writing workshop notebook and try free verse poem for yourself!

_____

_____

_____

_____

_____

3

Want to write whatever way you want? About whatever you want? Then this poem is for you!

Setting up a Writing Center

Now you have enough material to get a writing and math center up and running. Don't leave the same activities there all year: introduce new ones, rotate old games and ideas by storing some activities away for a few months then bring them back later during the year. See which games are most popular with your students, and remember to always be on the look-out for activities that will keep the students interested and excited about using the center.

Summary Section Eight

- Teachers use learning centers in various ways depending on the grade they teach and the time they have to create and use them. Before using centers in your room consider also the academic purpose for incorporating centers in your classroom.

- Learning center activities can be used for reinforcement, remediation, or enrichment. They can be based on subjects or themes. They should be created so that they are easy to use, simple to store, and appeal to the students.

- Scheduling centers and planning rotations is often the most difficult part of using learning centers. All teachers will schedule their center time differently, so experiment with different rotation schedules. Centers can be used to teach your reading or math group, to cover school mandated activities such as computer or D.E.A.R time, or to work with individual students who need extra help.

- To monitor the use of centers you can use a general checklist, a thematic checklist or alternatively, you can use no checklist at all. A checklist can show you the activities each student has used in the center, however, by assigning specific activities for the students to complete you can eliminate the need for a checklist at all.

- Begin your year with at least a math and writing center. Create some quick math and writing center activities to get students started.

- Laminate all the games and other activities that you create for your centers. It may cost money but will save you time in the long run.

Notes

General checklist for centers in kindergarten and grade one

Color the square the right color for the center you used:

_____ center: Red _____ center: Yellow _____ center: Orange

_____ center: Blue _____ center: Brown

Name: _____

Month _____	Monday	Tuesday	Wednesday	Thursday	Friday	My Favorite Center
Week One						
Week Two						
Week Three						
Week Four						

TIPS, Inc.

General checklist for centers in kindergarten and grade one

For each center you use, draw a face to match the activity.

Use: ☺ 😐 ☹

Name: _____

Monday					
Tuesday					
Wednesday					
Thursday					
Friday					

TIPS, Inc.

Checklist to track by center for grades two and higher

Fill in the chart as you complete the center activities

Name: _____

Center Center	Activity Name	Date Started	Date Finished	What I Liked	What I Didn't Like
1.					
2.					
3.					
4.					
5.					
6.					

TIPS, Inc.

Checklist to track by day for grades two and higher

Fill in the chart as you complete the center activities

Name: _____

Week of:	Center	Activity	Date finished	What I thought
Monday				
Tuesday				
Wednesday				
Thursday				
Friday				

TIPS, Inc.

You've Got the Job—Now Keep It

Checklist to track by activity for grades two and higher

Fill in the chart as you complete the center activities

Name: _____

Activity Name & Center	Date In	Date Out	Comments	Student Signature

TIPS, Inc.

Thematic Checklist

Fill in the chart as you complete the center activities

Name: _____

	Date Completed	Rate The Activity 0–5 (5 is the best)
Subject:		
#1		
#2		
#3		
#4		
#5		
#6		
Subject:		
#1		
#2		
#3		
#4		
#5		
#6		
Subject:		
#1		
#2		
#3		
#4		
#5		
#6		
Subject:		
#1		
#2		
#3		
#4		
#5		
#6		

TIPS, Inc.

(Copy and laminate onto heavy paper.)

1	2	3	4	5	6	7	8	9	10
11	12	13	14	15	16	17	18	19	20
21	22	23	24	25	26	27	28	29	30
31	32	33	34	35	36	37	38	39	40
41	42	43	44	45	46	47	48	49	50
51	52	53	54	55	56	57	58	59	60
61	62	63	64	65	66	67	68	69	70
71	72	73	74	75	76	77	78	79	80
81	82	83	84	85	86	87	88	89	90
91	92	93	94	95	96	97	98	99	100

TIPS, Inc.

Reproducibles

SECTION NINE

Unavoidable Interruptions—Vacations, Celebrations, and Other Distractions

IN THIS SECTION

- ✦ Occasions at school
- ✦ Giving gifts
- ✦ Holiday, parties and other special events
- ✦ Student vacations

Chapter 37

You Give and You Give and You Give . . .

Staff Celebrations

It's a part of the work environment that you might not have ever thought about when you decided to be a teacher: not only the never ending religious and cultural celebrations that occur during the calendar year, but also those special occasions that just seem to pop up—such as weddings and baby showers—that will need to be acknowledged. On the one hand, you're a new teacher and you'll probably want to take part in some of these festivities, because it's a great way to socialize and get to know the other teachers at your school. On the other hand, you're a new teacher and there's a good chance that you're flat broke in the cash department and won't be able to contribute to every party fund or group present.

Whether it's the holidays, birthdays, or the end-of-the-year celebrations, you may want to buy gifts for different people on the staff or for certain parent volunteers in your classroom. Don't feel obligated to spend lots of money—often a card with a simple, handwritten message inside is the best choice. If you do decide to give gifts, there are less expensive items you can buy, make, or give. Below are some economical ideas on what to purchase or make as well as some of the people you may want to remember:

- **Administration**
  Your principal and vice principal should receive cards for the holiday season and for her birthday. Either send a card just from

"Do we really need to celebrate this??!!"

When celebrating students' birthdays during the year, don't forget to celebrate summer birthdays too.

yourself or send one from the class—have a student in your class make a card and have everyone sign it.

- **Office and maintenance staff**
  It's very nice to remember the office and maintenance staff during the holidays, on their birthdays, and at the end of the year. Just a brief note saying thanks for all they do is fine. If, during the year, you find yourself making homemade goodies, bring some in to share with the staff.

- **Other teachers**
  Teachers don't usually buy other teachers gifts unless they are close friends. If your school does a staff gift exchange, don't feel obligated to participate, but if you do, don't feel you have to spend a lot of money on a person you barely know.

- **Teaching assistants**
  If you have a classroom assistant, you should buy her something at the end of the year. How much you want to spend depends on how much time she spends in your classroom helping. If there is only one assistant for the whole grade level, see if the other teachers will chip in so you can buy one gift from everyone. If you have an assistant in your classroom on a regular basis, you may want to consider giving her something for the holidays or for her birthday as well.

- **Students**
  Giving students gifts for birthdays, holidays, or the end of the year can be time consuming and costly. Many teachers don't do it—the

choice is up to you. If you want to do this sort of thing, think cheap: for younger students having a birthday try:

- decorating the birthday child's chair with a balloon
- having a birthday crown, a badge, or something else that is special to show it's her birthday
- providing a special treat at recess (candy bar, cookie) for the birthday girl

If you don't want to spend any money, try using cheap class incentives to double as birthday treats, such as:

Wearing something special, like this birthday hat, is an inexpensive way to help a child celebrate a birthday.

- a birthday homework pass
- a birthday lunch with the teacher
- a special pen to use for all work completed on the birthday

For calendar celebrations such as Valentine's Day, Thanksgiving, Christmas, or an end of the year celebration, you may want to do something special for the entire class. Again, cheap and cheerful is a good way to go. Ideas for class treats are:

- goodie bags (from the dollar or teacher supply store)
- sweet treats (cookies, a class cake)
- Gelatin cups with whip cream (Gelatin comes in every holiday color and spray whip cream adds an extra treat)
- gift certificate for book orders (use your teacher bonus points to secure these)

Due to food allergies, some school only permit store bought baked goods and not homemade ones. Check with your mentor teacher to see what your school does.

- **Parents**

    You don't need to wait until the end of the year to thank room moms and other parent volunteers that have been in your classroom. Something as simple as a thank you note, a quick phone call, or a mention in the class newsletter will go a long way.

    At the end of the year, you should acknowledge your room mom and other parents that have been regular volunteers in the classroom, or those that have helped out from home. Have students create cards, draw portraits and include a written description of the person, or even recite poems of thanks—anything to show that you and the children have appreciated the time and effort the volunteers have given. A small personal gift from you to your room mom is also appropriate.

You Give and You Give and You Give . . .

A written message can be more meaningful than a gift.

Cheap and Cheerful Gift Ideas

Only you know what you can afford to spend on gifts, and keep in mind that homemade gifts are often appreciated more because of the thought and effort that is put into them. Here are some suggestions for gifts from you and your class that will do nicely for some of the special people that you'll work with during the year:

From you:

- Gift certificates to a book store, a nail salon, or any store that might be appealing to the person you are buying for.

- If giving to a teacher or assistant, make a coupon indicating that you will take on her carpool or lunch duty for a set period of time. This costs you nothing, except perhaps a higher stress level!

- Home-made baked goods (or a coupon for them) are a great treat.

- Buy a colleague lunch, or make a home-made lunch and bring it in for her at school.

- Pick up a bunch of flowers at the grocery store and purchase a dollar store vase. You'll have a lovely, inexpensive arrangement, which would likely cost double had it been purchased at a flower shop.

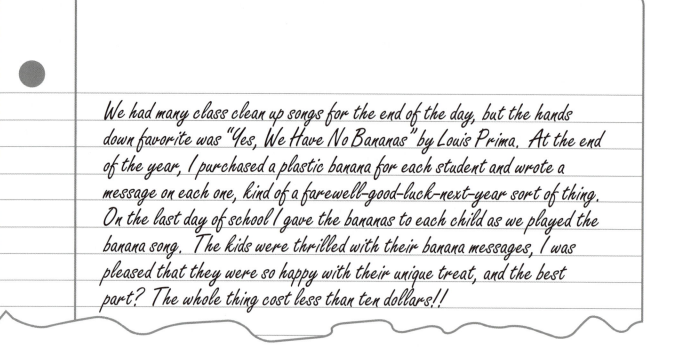

We had many class clean up songs for the end of the day, but the hands down favorite was "Yes, We Have No Bananas" by Louis Prima. At the end of the year, I purchased a plastic banana for each student and wrote a message on each one, kind of a farewell-good-luck-next-year sort of thing. On the last day of school I gave the bananas to each child as we played the banana song. The kids were thrilled with their banana messages, I was pleased that they were so happy with their unique treat, and the best part? The whole thing cost less than ten dollars!!

- Cut and root some of your classroom or house plants. Place them together in a decorative glass bottle, tie a ribbon around the cuttings, and you have a nice-looking, inexpensive arrangement.

From the students:

- Buy a small clay flower pot and have the students paint the pots (school paints work well on terracotta pots). After it dries, have the students sign their names in marker and then plant a pretty flower or plant inside. This idea works well for large groups, especially for parent volunteers, room mothers, or assistants.

A clay pot with your students' name on it is an inexpensive yet eye-catching gift to give.

- Using fabric paints, paint the names of the students on a plain white apron as a gift for room moms and volunteers; or let students create designs on the apron using fabric markers.

- Have the students make a small memory book for a room mother or a teacher assistant. Have each student create a page with a drawing and a sentence or two thanking the room mom or assistant for something nice they did during the year.

- Buy a piece of cheap, pretty fabric. Use pinking shears to cut into a five inch square for each student. Place a spoonful of potpourri mixture in the center. Gather the sides and tie with a pretty ribbon.

- Teach your class a song and invite your room mom and other parent volunteers in for an end-of-the-year get together. It doesn't have to be a big production: 20 minutes right after lunch or at the end of the day is fine. Have your students sing a song as a thank you for all the work the parents did. Reciting poems of thanks, either written by the students or selected from a poetry anthology is a nice touch too. To make the presentation extra special, bake some treats and share them with the volunteers and class.

As the saying goes, "It's the thought that counts." It's important to show people that you appreciate the help that you've been given. No matter how small the gesture has been and no matter how large the thank you is, a little thought goes a long way.

You Give and You Give and You Give . . .

Chapter 38

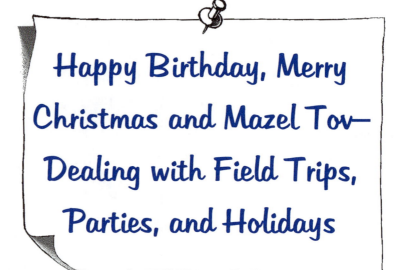

Happy Birthday, Merry Christmas and Mazel Tov— Dealing with Field Trips, Parties, and Holidays

No matter how many volunteers are present, you are the adult in charge of your class.

Field trips, birthday parties, and holiday celebrations are all activities that you'll be involved in that will require extra planning, superb organizational skills, and above all else, patience! Children thrive on routine, and when it changes, there are bound to be some bumps in the road. The following section offers helpful hints to ensure that school trips, class parties, and other celebrations run as smoothly as your day in the classroom does.

Preparing for Field Trips

Students look forward to field trips and most parents view field trips as a wonderful part of their child's learning experience. For many teachers however, field trips are more exhausting than teaching a full day in the classroom. No matter how many parent chaperones are accompanying your class, you are the adult in charge. This means that if anything goes wrong you will be the one held accountable. Therefore, before you head out on your field trip, set the guidelines with the students and parents. Here are some tips for a successful field trip.

A few weeks before:
- Send out a note to the chaperones (try to arrange for as many as the school will allow) with the following information:
    - when to be at the school
    - the duration of the field trip
    - the location of the field trip

> On one field trip I took my first graders to the zoo. We had one student who was highly allergic to bee stings and I was required to have his anaphylactic shot on hand in case he was stung. Being that I was a first year teacher, Murphy's Law (whatever can go wrong will go wrong) prevailed and (of course) the child was stung. I grabbed the needle with one hand and grabbed the child with the other. As I went to administer the shot, he moved and I injected myself!! The next thing I knew I was passed out on the ground. In the end, both the child and I were fine, and I had a great story to tell at parties. But I also have a new rule: any child that requires medication on field trips must be accompanied by a parent or caregiver who is responsible for administering it.

- when you're expected back
- what to wear (sneakers, sweaters, et cetera)
- what to bring (lunch, cushions, paper) and a reminder that cell phones are reserved for emergency use only

- Remind volunteers that they need to be available before and after the trip—some parents like to leave with their child from the site once the field trip is over but before all the students have returned to school. This won't work because, in addition to her own child, the parent volunteer still has a group of students that she is responsible for.

- Let parents know that cell phones are reserved for emergencies during school field trips. Parents are responsible for a group of students and can become side tracked if their cell phone is constantly ringing. Also, in public places students need constant supervision. For safety reasons, politely but firmly request that parents do not use their cell phones while chaperoning students unless there is an emergency.

Happy Birthday, Merry Christmas and Mazel Tov . . .

- Ask the parent of a child with constant behavioral issues to volunteer on the trip. When assigning students to that group, try to keep the group small.

A few days before:
- Decide on student group arrangements **before** the field trip. Don't wait until the last minute and don't let the students pick the groups. Always put a child and her parent chaperone together, and try to have each student be with one friend. You know your students, so split up any students who might create problems if they are together.

- Keep your group small. Students that require extra supervision should be in your group.

- Allow students whose parents are not chaperones to indicate two friends they would like to be placed with. As long as it won't cause problems, try to accommodate the request, especially if it's an extended trip.

- Create a plan of action for what volunteers and students should do if they become separated.

The day of the trip:
- Talk to the class before the trip and discuss acceptable behavior and the consequences for misbehavior. Let students know that if they misbehave on the trip, they will be moved to your group and that you will contact their parents after school.

- Inform both students and volunteers of what they should do in the event they become separated.

- Discuss what volunteer parents do at the end of the trip—do they accompany you back to the classroom, or do they leave students at the school entrance?

- Bring all parent phone numbers and emergency information with you. A binder ring containing students' emergency contact information on index cards is a compact way to carry all this information.

- Ensure you have the correct dosages of any medications required and know when and how they are to be administered. At most schools, a child who requires some type of medication during the day must be accompanied by their parent on the trip to administer the medication.

- Keep a headcount of students throughout the day, especially when you get on or off the bus. You'd be surprised at how quickly children wander off when you change locations during the day—even though they are being supervised by parents.

- Check in with parent volunteers frequently to ensure all is going smoothly.

Remember, field trips are supposed to be fun, but it is imperative that you keep a constant count of the students and a close eye on behavior. The students, the parents, and you are now representing the school. And no matter how many other adults and supervisors are on the trip, ultimately you're responsible for what happens to your students.

Planning for Parties

Part of school fun for students, teachers, and parents alike is having parties. Class parties can be lots of fun or lots of work—it all depends on how you handle them. Check with the other teachers at your school for guidelines regarding parties. Before the year even starts, make a decision about class parties and birthdays, let the parents know what your policy is, and stick with it. Here are some guidelines to follow:

For birthday celebrations:

- Establish procedures at the beginning of the year regarding how you'll celebrate birthdays in the classroom. Parents (especially if their children are in the younger grades) can get quite excited when it comes to birthdays—it's not unheard of for them to show up with cupcakes, balloons, and a clown!! Check with your school and other teachers to see if there is a policy. regarding birthday celebrations. If there isn't one, keep birthdays simple: cupcakes, a cake, or ice cream sent in by the birthday child's parents is enough.

- Set a time limit. Ten to fifteen minutes after lunch or at the end of the day is sufficient for birthday cookies or cupcakes.

For class parties:

- Enlist the help of parents. If you have a room mother that you feel comfortable with, feel free to let her take charge. A few weeks before the party, take some time and plan the party with her. If she wants to create and run the activities, all the better for you. She can get other parents to help also.

- Set a time limit. One to one-and-a-half hours is enough time for activities, food, socializing and clean-up at a class party.

"I'm here to help celebrate Charlie's birthday. Where should I tell the ringmaster to set up?"

Happy Birthday, Merry Christmas and Mazel Tov . . .

- Make sure you have activities for the students during a party. Think about having anywhere from one to three projects for the students (usually arts and craft type activities work best). Consider having three groups rotating through activities for 15 minutes at a time. Letting the children simply eat and hang out will lead to students quickly getting out of control.

- Have everything you need organized and ready. You need to have the materials laid out, the parent volunteers need to know what you've got planned, and the students need to be informed of the order of events for the party. A statement like *First everyone will rotate through each craft center for about 20 minutes. When your group has finished at center two, you can go to the snack table for some party treats. At 2:30 we'll start cleaning up and get ready for dismissal* will help things get off to the right start, let parent volunteers know how the activity will run and sets the parameters early for the children.

- Parents will appreciate it if you don't have too much in the way of sugar and sweets at a party. Have some fruit, a vegetable platter with dip, and one or two sweet treats.

"Oh boy!!! I hope there's hummus and veggies!!!"

- Depending on where you are teaching, you may have parents who cannot afford to send in food. On the other hand, you may have parents who want to bring in sushi. Let parents know ahead of time what types of food you want and keep it simple.

- Be the disciplinarian. It is amazing how some students will act up during parties when their parents are around. Do not be intimidated about taking a student aside and quietly speaking to him or her about inappropriate behavior. Remember, it's your classroom and you need to keep control.

Being Politically Correct about Winter Holidays

It seems that in many schools, celebrating "winter holidays" has become a mine field of controversy. During December teachers are often frustrated and stressed over how to handle the holiday issue in their classrooms. Some schools have adopted the policy of completely ignoring Christmas and Hanukah while others have gone the other direction completely, choosing to celebrate every single holiday that falls in or near December.

To be politically correct, Mr. Chapa decided to celebrate all the December holidays.

The holiday season can be an opportunity to teach tolerance, understanding and acceptance. It is often not the students who have issues with celebrating particular holidays, but rather parents and the administrators instead. **All schools have a holiday policy (often developed due to parental concern) and you need to completely understand the policy used by yours.** Here are some basic guidelines you can follow to keep this time of the year productive and non-controversial:

- If you're going to teach about holidays, teach all the major holidays. Don't limit the scope of holiday celebrations to what's being celebrated within your classroom. Incorporate holidays from different parts of the world even if they're not being celebrated by your students.

- Have students share family traditions pertaining to the holidays they celebrate.

- Take advantage of parents or others who would like to teach a lesson about a holiday they celebrate. Meet with parents before the lesson to make sure its content is appropriate for your class. Involving parents takes some of the work off you and allows the parents to share their personal experiences.

- Devote the same amount of time to each holiday.

- Stress the importance of learning about other people's religions and celebrations by allowing students to celebrate their holidays as freely as you celebrate your own.

- Don't squelch your personal beliefs. If you want to wear jingle bell earrings or a Jewish star to celebrate your holiday do so, unless it is specifically forbidden by your school. By embracing your holiday, you are modeling what you're teaching the students. Enjoy and celebrate your beliefs while appreciating and learning about others.

Try and enjoy this time of the year. It can and will be crazy, but as time gets closer to that coveted winter break, fill your last few days with fun activities.

Chapter 39

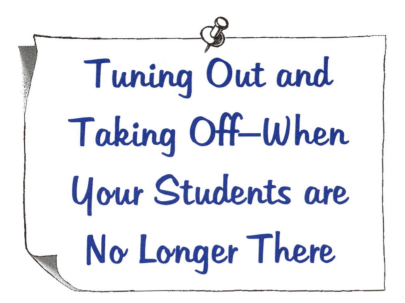

Tuning Out and Taking Off—When Your Students are No Longer There

Brains on Break

It is very hard to keep students attention focused on academics before a vacation—especially the winter break. The week leading up to any break is usually a real mix of exhaustion and exhilaration and, chances are, if you're counting down the days until a break, your students are too. Parents can also be slightly dazed or frazzled as they deal with holiday plans and preparations, and a break from homework would probably be as welcomed by them as by the students. If you're up-to-date on teaching and testing, plan ahead and take advantage of the few days before the break to do fun activities in your classroom.

Don't let your teaching slide during the week leading up to a break.

Before the breaks there are always the typical activities (making gingerbread houses and holiday cards in December, cleaning out the classroom desks in June), but what about doing some of those more inventive things that you might like to do during the year but doubt you'll have the time for?

- **Poetry**
  If you haven't already incorporated poetry into your writing curriculum (or even if you have) the week before a break is a great time to do so. Check out some poetry books or websites and teach the students several different types of poetry during the week. They can spend their time writing holiday or seasonal poetry and sharing it with classmates or incorporating it into holiday cards.

- **Read, read, read**
  Take this opportunity to read wonderful picture books to the class. When teaching in the higher grades you'll have less and less of an opportunity to read books aloud to your class so don't miss this chance.

- **Internet projects**
  If you have internet access in your classroom, computer lab, or at the school library, create an internet search on a topic you're studying in class or have students research something about holidays from around the world.

- **Class game projects**
  If you're really on the ball, plan an in-class book report, but make it fun. Give students a choice of three or four books, and finalize selections a month in advance to allow for reading time. Limiting book selection allows students to work on final projects together. During those days before a vacation, have the students do the book reports in class. Some fun book report ideas are creating puppet shows or plays that re-enact favorite scenes, making dioramas, drawing comic strips, or devising board games.

- **One-on-one work**
  While the class is spending time writing poetry, finishing activities, doing book reports or working on internet searches, take the time to work one-on-one with students who need some extra help. It always seems hard to find the time to work with students independently during the year, so take advantage of the slightly slower pace just before a holiday break.

Bodies on Break

If students are going out of town while school is in session, parents will often ask for work to take with them. While sometimes the parents know well in advance, giving you time to gather important work, many trips can come up at the last minute. The nature of teaching doesn't always make it possible to send work and you should not feel obligated to do this. Explain to parents your policy at the beginning of the year, and that some of the work needs to be taught first before the student can complete the assignments. Absent students will work with you during school time the week they come back to make up important missed work, but may also need to do some work at home.

Some work that you may be able to send is:
- any reading material that you will be covering during the absence

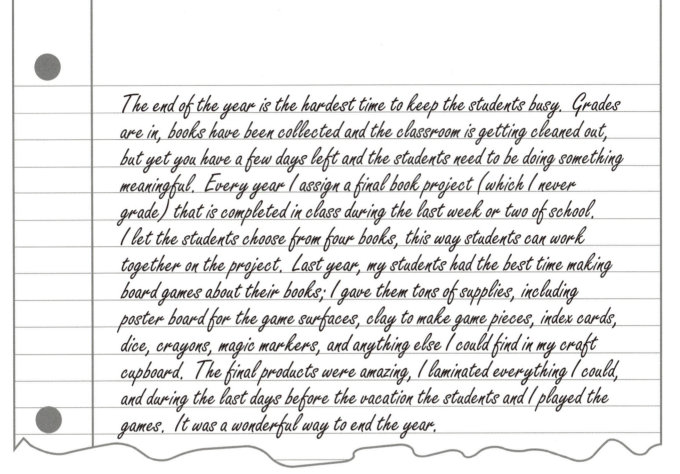

The end of the year is the hardest time to keep the students busy. Grades are in, books have been collected and the classroom is getting cleaned out, but yet you have a few days left and the students need to be doing something meaningful. Every year I assign a final book project (which I never grade) that is completed in class during the last week or two of school. I let the students choose from four books, this way students can work together on the project. Last year, my students had the best time making board games about their books; I gave them tons of supplies, including poster board for the game surfaces, clay to make game pieces, index cards, dice, crayons, magic markers, and anything else I could find in my craft cupboard. The final products were amazing, I laminated everything I could, and during the last days before the vacation the students and I played the games. It was a wonderful way to end the year.

- reinforcement of math concepts previously taught
- social studies, science, or spelling pages scheduled to be covered while the child is away

Vacations can be a crazy time for the family. While parents will likely lend a hand when it comes to doing homework on a trip, any work you do not want parents helping their children with or even completing for their children should not be sent along.

Tracking the Trip: Vacation Math, Reading and Writing

Parents are concerned that when their child goes on vacation, she will miss a lot of school work. And this is true—she will. But there is education to be had in the trip itself. Give parents some guidelines about how to incorporate grade level appropriate math, reading and other activities into their vacation activities.

It will be impossible for a student on vacation to make up all missed work: concentrate on key skills and concepts only.

- **Math**

  Calculating mileage, establishing a budget for the trip, creating and tracking a daily allowance, managing a time schedule, and converting currency are all vacation tasks that involve math.

- **Reading**

  Reading guidebooks, brochures, even dinner menus all count. Pick up a picture book or chapter book written by a local author. Read daily journal entries to family members.

- **Writing**

  Keep a daily journal of activities. Take pictures on the trip to coincide with journal entries; interview other family members about what they did during that day and write what they say; or write a letter to the teacher and class detailing the trip's adventures.

- **Drama**

  Have a student research her trip destination. During the trip the student can use a video camera and "report" on landmarks and other interesting places she visited. Or a vacationing student can use a hand held tape recorder to document funny incidents occurring on the trip, then write it out as a skit, and have classmates help act it out when she returns to school.

Have the vacationing student keep all writings in a journal or notebook so it can be shared with the class when the student returns.

Students seem to enjoy these types of activities and parents feel better knowing their child is still managing to further her education despite the fact that she is not in the classroom.

Once a student returns, you will need to work individually with her during class time on missed lessons, or place her with a small group you're working with that is reviewing concepts that she missed. It should not take longer that one week to make up important work that has been missed.

Summary Section Nine

- Set a budget and decide how much you'll be contributing to school occasions such as birthdays, school parties, weddings, and other staff events.

- Presents don't have to be elaborate or expensive—get creative with gift giving instead.

- Field trips will run more smoothly if you prepare ahead of time, and make sure students and parents understand what is expected of them during the trip.

- Let parents know how you will be handling in-class parties, class celebrations, and birthdays.

- Plan to mix crafts and other activities along with special munchies to keep kids busy during a class party.

- Plan to celebrate all holidays equally during the year and educate your students on the importance of learning about other people's celebrations.

- Interesting activities that aren't typically done during the year will help keep students focused in the week leading up to a break.

- Math, reading and other subjects can all be integrated into a trip if a student is leaving school. Instead of loading students up with school work, have students utilize different means of documenting their trip so that they can share when they return to school.

Notes

SECTION TEN

A View from the Top—Tips for New Teachers from the Principal

- ◆ Areas of weakness
- ◆ Strengths for success
- ◆ Identifying stressful situations
- ◆ When credibility crumbles
- ◆ Final words of wisdom

IN THIS SECTION

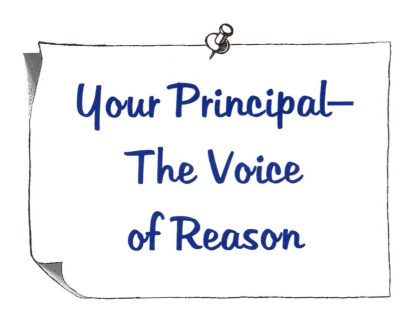

Your Principal—The Voice of Reason

There is a steep learning curve for new teachers. You need to understand school policies and procedures, acquaint yourself with the curriculum, and decide on classroom rules, procedures, behavior management and much more—all of which needs to be done before the students arrive. We hope that this book has taken some of the mystery out of what to expect your first year, as well as given you strategies to manage the variety of demands you will be faced with. However, no book for first year teachers would be complete without some advice from the people who are in charge, the ones ultimately responsible for the overall running of schools—principals.

Teachers often make the assumption that principals have been out of the classroom too long and have forgotten the challenges and problems that teachers need to handle in the classroom. You will see from the answers they provided that principals are well aware of what's going on in the classroom and in which areas teachers struggle the most. Overall, principals are quite attuned to the daily stresses that teachers face.

For this section principals from all parts of the world were surveyed. Whether they worked in the United States, Canada or India their concerns, tips, and advice for new teachers were very similar, indicating that issues new teachers face are similar too, regardless of where they teach. (Of course different countries, cities, and schools all have challenges unique to their area, but don't assume one setting is *easier* than the other, the situations are merely *different*.) So no matter where you find yourself teaching, you'll still have to deal with behavior management, teaching strategies, parent communication, and administrative demands—there's no denying it, they're all part of the job.

The Good News Is . . .

When principals identify strengths first year teachers should possess before they step into a classroom, enthusiasm, motivation, and the ability to accept advice and new ideas are frequently mentioned. (Hang on to the enthusiasm for teaching; it's what gets you through the most challenging parts of the year.)

We asked principals "What are some of the unique qualities that you see in first year teachers?" Here are some of their replies . . .

> *They love their students.*
>
> *Even though they've been told it's not true, they still believe they can change the world.*
>
> *New teachers are eager to learn new things and incorporate everything into their classrooms.*
>
> *They usually have the newest methodologies and research under their belts.*
>
> *They accept change in curriculum and school policies.*
>
> *They are usually willing to accept and implement advice and recommended practices easily.*
>
> *New teachers spend more time planning and grading than veteran teachers.*
>
> *They're eager to prove themselves.*
>
> *They take their first year and all its responsibilities very seriously.*

Be Prepared

New teachers often think that their college degree or teacher certification makes them prepared for teaching. Unfortunately, there are many areas that new teachers are not ready for simply due to their lack of experience. Although you may not be able to prepare for them right now, simply being aware of some common areas of difficulty can help you when those situations arise.

Classroom management and parent interaction were the two areas most often mentioned for which principals felt new teachers were unprepared. Classroom management included having an effective reality based behavior plan. Some plans—though they might look good on paper or sound great in a college class—don't work well in a classroom in real life. Other keys to success, most principals felt, included straight-forward rules, routines and procedures that are explained, practiced and reviewed with the children during the first few days of school. Parent communication and interaction were other areas of concern for principals when it came to new teachers on their staff. Teachers—new and old alike—should remain professional at all times, should never develop close personal friendships with parents of children in their class, and should accept the fact that they will, occasionally, have to deal with difficult parents. Principals also listed being prepared for parent conferences as very important, especially when having to explain difficulties a student is having in class. Explanations to parents need to include what the problem is, how you arrived at your conclusion, and the solution you plan to implement—all of which need to be educationally sound and well documented.

We asked principals "For which situations do you think first year teachers are most unprepared?" In their responses, principals felt new teachers should be better prepared for . . .

> *Knowing what to grade and why.*
>
> *Identifying the difference between the child who is encountering temporary difficulties and the child who might need a referral.*
>
> *Integrating into the culture of the school by getting to know veteran teachers without putting them off.*
>
> *Balancing all the paperwork as well as the curriculum demands.*
>
> *Getting the big picture by reviewing the entire year's curriculum and planning topics and lesson plans in advance, instead of one lesson at a time.*
>
> *Being able to effectively communicate ideas to children.*
>
> *Clarifying the doubts of children and developing their confidence.*
>
> *Handling time schedules within the school working environment.*
>
> *The "instantness" of primary school teaching.*
>
> *Establishing order and consistency in everyday classwork.*

Stressful Situations

During the first year it's easy to let stress get to you. Make sure that you're making time for yourself. Take a few minutes during the day and take a deep breath, especially when you feel the stress escalating. Don't let work consume you and be sure that you're making time for friends and family. Knowing what areas most new teachers find stressful is a way to avoid falling into those traps yourself.

In response to the question "What situations or areas do you think first year teachers find the most stressful?" principals replied . . .

Meeting deadlines.

Grading and assessing work.

Preparing report cards.

Learning the curriculum and being prepared to implement lessons every day.

Dealing with the variety of learning levels in the classroom.

Being comfortable enough to ask for help.

Being observed and evaluated by supervisors.

Gaining a supervisor's approval.

Handling parent conferences.

Learning how to deal with emotionally needy children.

Finding a behavior management system that works.

Doing the Right Thing

During the first year, most new teachers are concerned about just making it to June. Obviously though, you'll want to be hired back the following year. If you work hard, do your best, and ask for help when necessary, you'll do just fine. Principals were asked to identify what actions a teacher could take to lead them to question a teacher's credibility. A principal will come to doubt a teacher's ability or commitment if she sees him . . .

> *Give up on a child.*
>
> *Demonstrate a lack of care towards children.*
>
> *Demoralize students.*
>
> *Become friends with students instead of an authoritative figure in the classroom.*
>
> *Harbor personal vendettas against other teachers.*
>
> *Not being a team player.*
>
> *Display a lack of commitment.*
>
> *Demonstrate insincerity.*
>
> *Be dishonest or avoid responsibility for a mistake.*
>
> *Not communicate their problems or concerns with the administration.*
>
> *Avoid solving their problems independently.*
>
> *Use extraordinary measures of discipline in the classroom.*
>
> *Demonstrate a lack of effort with grading, preparing lessons, or other teaching tasks.*
>
> *Approach teaching as if there is nothing new to learn.*
>
> *Display a lack of planning (it connotates a disorganized mind).*
>
> *Refuse to take and act on advice.*
>
> *Be unable to evaluate own ability (teachers need to evaluate not only students, but also themselves).*

Finally, the number one piece of advice from principals to first year teachers—find a mentor teacher. If you don't know who to approach, or your school does not assign mentors, ask your principal for some suggestions, or put up "Mentor Wanted" signs in the staff lunch room. Chat with several teachers before asking anyone though, because you want a mentor who is helpful with a positive attitude towards the school and towards teaching.

Words of Wisdom

Teaching is a tough job, there's no doubt about it. It's also a job that's not suited to everyone. If you don't enjoy teaching then you shouldn't stay in the profession—but don't make that decision after only one year. Becoming a teacher takes time, and it will take a few years for you to learn your strengths and weaknesses as an educator.

No matter what, you are the supreme ruler of your class.

When principals were asked for the most important piece of advice they could offer a new teacher, they replied . . .

Believe in yourself.

Find joy in what you do and smile often.

Work hard.

Look after yourself physically and mentally.

Establish a long-term savings plan.

Treat yourself well during the year.

Eat, sleep, exercise and make sure you enjoy quality time with family and friends.

Be a well rounded person—it is extremely important.

Navigate your way around negativity diplomatically.

Develop strategies to stay calm in stressful situations.

Have a lot of patience but be sure to command the respect of your students.

Never stop learning.

Be creative in your teaching.

Spend time at the beginning of the year establishing routines and procedures.

Organize your first week of school carefully. Set the tone and the atmosphere that you want in the very first hour.

Be consistent with rules and procedures.

Get to know each student and model good values.

Demonstrate daily to your students that you respect them as individuals.

Be fair and consistent—it will earn your students respect.

Make students feel welcome and at home in the classroom.

Master teachers are not developed immediately; don't pressure yourself into doing everything perfectly.

Be consistent and firm but also be caring—a formidable task.

Don't come across as a "know-it-all."

Learn the school or district teaching strategies.

Treat everyone in the school community with respect.

Your Principal—The Voice of Reason

Examine your teaching performance on an on-going basis.

Be confident but not arrogant.

Meet with grade level team members whenever possible.

Go to the staffroom and unwind. Talk to other teachers, but don't get hooked into negative conversations.

Be aware of what's going on around you, not only in your classroom but in your school. Little things, like being late for an assembly, can ruin your day.

Know who to turn to in the school hierarchy so you can get help when you need it.

Don't take yourself too seriously: have a sense of humor about things.

Things are not always your fault.

Remember, you are not alone but an integral member of your team.

Have a sense of humor—we all need to laugh once in a while.

One final tip—when you're having a bad day, take a deep breath and keep in mind that no matter what time of year it is, summer vacation is right around the corner!

Index

A

Ability grouping, 258–261
   benefits, 261
   concerns, 261
   determining placement, 259–261
Activities, for first week, 156–159
Afternoon routine, 145–147
Agendas
   for students, 70–73
   in afternoon routine, 145–146
Arrival times, 3
Assessment
   cumulative, 198
   grading, 198–199
   informal observation, 198, 199
   quizzes, 199
   tests, 199
   verbal, 198
Assignments
   missed
      folder for, 63–64
      form for, 100
Assistant, 84–85
   gifts for, 354
Attendance, 4

B

Back-to-school night, 171–174. *See also* Open house
Behavior management, 103–134
   behaviors to permit, 110–112
   class code, 108
   classroom environment, 105–106
   consistency, 131
   definition, 105
   determining system, 108–110
   disruptive student, 125–126
   expectations, 110
   from first day of school, 108–112
   guiding behavior, 114–116
   negative, 124–128
   positive praise, 106
   rewards based system
      balance, 114–115
      incentives for students, 120–122
      individual and class, 119–120
      positive vs negative, 116
      public vs private, 116–118
      school based, 122–123
   schedule changes, 127–128
   special situations, 129–131
Bin It directions, 306–309
Binders
   organizing, 57
   setting up, 66–67
Birthday celebrations, 361
Board(s)
   bulletin, 23–26
   setup, 18
   teacher, 54–55
Book(s). *See also* Library
   availability, 27–28
   collecting, 28–30
   lending
      from classroom library, 35–37
      for special books, 37–38
   reading area, 39–41
   storage, 33–35
   student storage, 75–76
Book clubs, 30
Book fairs, 29
Book order folder, 62–63
Book reports, grading, 205–206
Bookcases, 35
Bookstores, 29
Bulletin boards, designing, 23–26

C

Calendars
   classroom, 54, 55

Calendars—cont.
   teacher, 54
Card games, for math learning center, 314–318
Celebrations, staff, 353–355
Centers, thematic, 282–283
Checker games, for math learning center, 328
Checklists for learning centers, 294–297
   in grade one, 343–344
   in grade two and higher, 345–347
   in kindergarten, 343–344
   thematic, 348
Child study team meetings, 233
Class behavior management systems, 119–120
Class chart, as public behavior system, 116–117
Class collage, 157
Class communication folder, 64
Class game projects, before holidays, 366
Class rules, 140–141
Class schedule
   form, 188
   sending to parents, 161–162
Classroom
   atmosphere, 21–22
   calendars, 54, 55
   classroom mom, 168, 171
   environment, 105–106
   jobs, 149–151
   library, 27–38. *See also* Library
   procedures, first days, 141–154. *See also* Procedures
   reading area, 39–41
   setting up, 13–20
      board, 18
      remaining space, 18–19
      sample layouts, 19–20
      student seating, 16–18
      teacher area, 14–15
      teacher work area, 16
   students leaving, 151–152
   volunteers. *See* Volunteers, parent
Classwork
   assessment, 198
   determining ability groups, 260
   grading, 201–202
   how long to keep, 209, 211
   organization of, 73–74
Communication, 219–251
   faculty, 221–225
   with other teachers, 221–223
   parent-teacher, 226–242
      child study team meetings, 233
      documentation, 240–241
      effective, 242
      levels of, 231–242
      meetings, 233, 234–235
      notes/email, 232
      private vs public school, 230
      term conferences, 233, 235–239
      unscheduled visit or phone call, 232–233
   with principal, 223–224
   with staff, 224
   with uninvolved parents, 239–240
Concrete poetry, 156–157
Conferences, parent-teacher
   including students, 243–245
   parent form, 249
   steps, 236–238
   student form, 251
   teacher form, 250
   term, 233, 235–239
Consistency, in behavior management, 131
Cooperative work, 267–271
Crates
   book storage, 33
   non-teaching, 61–64
   outside class, 64–65
   private, 66
   setting up, 59–67
   student work, 65–66
   teacher, 59–61
Cumulative assessment, 198
Curriculum
   grade level cooperation, 82
   planning ahead, 85–88

D

Daily folders, 53
Daily routines, 147–148
Daily schedule, 144
Desk(s)
   student, 16–18
   teacher, 14–15
      organizing, 51–53
Detention, 125
Dice games, for math learning center, 306–314
Dismissal, 5
Disruptive student, 125–126

Documentation, of parent-teacher communication, 240–241

E

Egg carton games, for math learning center, 301–305
    Egg-Cellent Addition, 302
    Egg-Cellent Division, 305
    Egg-Cellent Fact Fun, 304
    Egg-Cellent Multiplication, 303
    Egg-Cellent Subtraction, 302
Emergency, 5
Emergency contact and medication form, 165, 189
    sending to parents, 162
Evaluations, teacher, 7–8
Events
    behavior management, 127
    future, folder, 63
    school, classroom mom, 171
Exploration games, for math learning center, 298–299

F

Faculty communication, 221–225
Field trips
    classroom mom, 171
    folder, 64
    preparing, 358–361
Files, hanging 56–57. *See also* Folder(s)
Fire drills
    policies and procedures, 6
    procedures for, 152–153
First day(s), 135–193
    activities, 156–159
    breaking ice, 155–159
    creating structure, 137–139
    establishing class rules, 140–141
    establishing procedures, 141–154. *See also* Procedures, classroom, establishing
    establishing yourself as teacher, 137
    games, 155–156
    homework help, 175–185. *See also* Homework
    parent relations, 160–174
Folders
    book order, 62–63
    class communication, 64
    completed photocopies, 61
    daily, 53
    to do, 61
    field trip, 64
    Friday, 78–79
        insert for, 98
    future events, 63
    future tests, 61
    grade level, 65
    grading sheets and subject grade, 60
    information for parents, 65
    items for others, 65
    items-to-be-filed, 61
    lesson plan, 60
    missed assignments, 63–64
    new student, 63
    non-teaching crate, 61–64
    to the office, 65
    outside class crate, 64–65
    parent information, 66
    pocket, in student organization, 76–80
        daily, 77–78
        Friday, 78–79
        other, 79–80
        work-in progress, 77
    private crate, 66
    September-June, 59
    skill-specific, 59–60
    specialty area, 64
    student file, 66
    student work crate, 65–66
    subject, 59–60
    substitute, 60, 90
    teaching crate, 59–61
    theme, 60
    things to be copied, 60–61
    workshop, 65

G

Games
    first week, 155–156
    math learning center
        card, 314–318
        checker, 328
        dice, 306–314
        egg carton, 301–305
        exploration, 298–299
        hand-made, 300–328
        hundred squares, 319–327

Games—cont.
    reproducible, 299
Gifts
    administration, 353–354
    cheap and cheerful ideas, 356–357
    fellow teachers, 354
    maintenance staff, 354
    office staff, 354
    parent volunteers, 355
    students, 354–355
    teaching assistants, 354
Grab-It directions, 317–318
Grade level cooperation, 82
Grade level folder, 65
Graded work, 66, 77
Grades, 208–211. *See also* Grading; Report cards
Grading, 195–217. *See also* Grades; Report cards
    assessing, 198–199
    assignments, 199–206
    classwork, 201–202
    homework, 204–206
    necessity of, 197
    scales, 206–207
    sheet, 217
    tests, 202, 203–204
Grading sheet folders, 60
Graphing, 157
Group(s), 253–275. *See also* Grouping
    working cooperatively, 267–271
Group reflection, 275
Group work rating charts, 274
Grouping, 253–275. *See also* Group(s)
    ability, 258–261
    interest, 262–264
    mixed, 264–266
Guess the Glyph, 157
Guess the Number game, 319–322

H

Hallway travel, 5
Hand-made games, for math learning center, 300–328
Hanging files, 56–57. *See also* Folder(s)
Holidays
    days before, activities, 365–366
Homework, 175–185
    contract, 193
    extra, 125
    folders, for students, 77
    grading, 204–206
    how long to keep, 209, 211
    keeping track, 72–73
    lack of parental involvement, 185
    long-term, 205–206
    making hassle free, 182–185
    policy, 175–181
        sending to parents, 162, 191–192
Honor system, for classroom library, 37
Hundred squares games, for math learning center, 319–327

I

Incentives for students, 120–122
Index cards
    in classroom library management, 36
    in private behavior system, 118
    in public behavior system, 117
Individual behavior management systems, 119–120
Informal evaluation, 259
Informal observation, 198, 199
Interest grouping, 262–264
Internet projects, 366

L

Learning centers, 277–349
    combining teaching with, 286–288
    creating and organizing, 283–284
    good, attributes of, 280
    making appealing to students, 284–285
    math
        activities for, do-it-yourself, 298–328
        card games, 314–318
        checker games, 328
        dice games, 306–314
        egg carton games, 301–305
        exploration games, 298–299
        hand-made games, 300–328
        hundred squares games, 319–327
        reproducible games, 299
    monitoring use of and activity completion in, 294–297
    plastic tubs, 68
    poor, attributes of, 281
    rotation examples, 291–293
    starting with, 279–285

subject, 281–282
time factor, 288–289
types, 281–283
using "non-center", 287
writing
   components of, 329–330
   generating writing ideas, 331–340
      mystery writing, 333
      poetry samples, 333–339
      questions, 332
      story starters, 331–332
      writing prompts, 332–333
   setting up, 329–340
Leave, long-term, planning, 91–92
Lesson, sections of, 87–88
Lesson plan folders, 60
Lesson planning, 87–88
Letter trays, 56, 57–59
Letters
   requesting parent volunteers, 169–170
   welcome
      on first days, 163–164
      before school starts, 10–12
Librarian, student, 36–37
Library. *See also* Book(s)
   classroom, 27–38
Line order, 148
Lock downs, 6
Long-term homework, 205–206
Lunch period, 4

M

Maintenance staff, gifts, 354
Math
   activities for vacation, 368
   learning centers, 298–328. *See also* Learning centers, math
Medical emergency, 5
Medication, dispensing, 5
Meetings
   child study team, 233
   parent-teacher communication, 233, 234–235
      including students, 243–245
Mentor teacher, 83–84
   principals on, 378
Milk crates. *See* Crates
Missed assignments
   folder, 63–64

form, 100
Mixed grouping, 264–266
Mom, classroom, 168, 171
Money, lunch, 4
Monthly folders, 59
Morning routine, 141–144
Morning work, 143–144
Mystery Students, 159, 190
Mystery Writing, 333

N

Name the Number game, 315–316
New student folder, 63
New teacher program, 7–8
Notes, in parent-teacher communication, 232
Number Magic directions, 310–314

O

Observation, 198, 199
Office staff, gifts, 354
Open house, hosting, 171–174. *See also* Back to School Night
Oral assessment, 260
Organization
   importance, 47–48
   of learning centers, 283–284
   of paper trail, 56–69
   of personal space, 50–55
   of students, 70–80. *See also* Student(s), organization of
   for substitute, 89–92
   of time, 81–88. *See also* Time, organization of
Organizational checklist, 96–97

P

Paper trail, organization of, 56–69
   binders, 57
   hanging files, 56–57
   letter trays, 56
   milk crates, 56–57
   plastic tubs, 57
Parent(s)
   conference form, 249
   establishing relationship, 160–174
   expectations of, 227–228
   on first day, 139

Parent(s)—*cont.*
  folder of information for, 65, 66
  note to, 125
  sending important stuff, 160–165
  and teachers, 226–242. *See also* Communication, parent-teacher
uninvolved, 239–240
as volunteers
    gifts, 355
    incorporating into schedule, 166–168
    scheduling of room mom, 171
    sending information, 162
    student behavior, 127–128
Parties, classroom
  classroom mom, 168
  planning, 361–363
Peer teaching, 263
Personal file folder, 66
Personal space, organizing, 50–55
Phone calls, in parent-teacher communication, 232–233
Photocopy folders, 60–61
Plastic tubs
  book storage, 35
  paper organization, 57
  setting up, 67–69
Playtime, missed, in behavior management, 125
Poetry, 156–175, 335–339, 365
Policies
  disagreeing with, 8–9
  school and district, 3–6
Praise, positive, 106
Preparation, for teaching, 375
Pretest, 259–260
Principal(s)
  being prepared, 375
  communicating with, 223–224
  doing the right thing, 377
  strengths of new teachers, 374
  stressful situations, 376
  tips for new teachers, 371–380
  words of wisdom, 378–380
Private school, public school, 230
Private system, public system vs, 116–118
Procedures
  classroom, establishing
    afternoon routine, 145–147
    classroom jobs, 149–151
    daily routines, 147–148
    daily schedule, 144
    fire drill, 152–153
    giving directions, 141
    morning routine, 141–144
    students leaving classroom, 151–152
  school and district, 3–6
    disagreeing with, 8–9
Projects, long-term
  grading, 205–206
  weighting, 206
Public school, private school, 230
Public system, private system vs, 116–118

Q

Questions, for writing learning center, 332
Quizzes, in assessment, 199

R

Reading
  activities, for vacation, 368
  area, 39–41
  before holidays, 366
Recess, 4, 125
Reimbursements, 6
Relationship, parent-teacher, 226–242
  different perspectives, 228–229
  private vs public school, 230
Report cards, 212–214. *See also* Grades; Grading
Rewards based behavior management system, 114–123. *See also* Behavior management, rewards based system for
Rules, class, 140–141

S

Schedule
  changes, 127–128
  class
    form for, 188
    sending to parents, 161–162
  school, sending to parents, 161
School, private vs public, 230
School based behavior system, 122–123
School events, classroom mom and, 171
School supplies, 6
Shoe organizer, for book storage, 34
Shoeboxes, for book storage, 34
Sign-out sheets, for classroom library, 35–36

Skill-specific folders, 59–60
Special projects, grade level cooperation on, 82
Specialty area folder, 64
Staff
　celebrations among, 353–355. *See also* Gifts
　communicating with, 224
　gifts for, 354
Story starters, for writing learning center, 331–332
Stressful situations, 376
Structure, in first week, 137–139
Student(s)
　benefits of grouping, 256–257
　books, 75–76
　concerns of grouping, 257
　conference form, 251
　disruptive, 125–126
　gift ideas from, 357
　gifts for, 354–355
　grouping of, 253–275. *See also* Grouping; Group(s)
　incentives, 120–122
　including in meetings and conferences, 243–245
　leaving classroom, 151–152
　making learning centers appealing to, 284–285
　organization of, 70–80
　　agendas, 70–73
　　following classwork, 73–74
　　pocket folders, 76–80
　　submitting homework, 72–73
　permissible behaviors, 110–111
　personality changes in, home/school, 227
　seating, 16–18
　special situations, 129–131
　supplies
　　plastic tubs, 68
　　storing, 74–75
　work, 209, 211
Student file folders, 66
Subject centers, 281–282
Subject folders, 59–60
Subject grade folders, 60
Substitute
　activities, 90–91
　folders, 60, 90
　information sheet, 99
　organization, 89–92
Supplies
　list, 162

for writing center, 329–330

T

Teacher(s)
　area, 14–15
　conference form, 250
　credibility, 377
　desk
　　in classroom, 14–15
　　organizing, 50–51
　establishing yourself, 137
　fellow, gifts for, 354
　gift ideas, 356–357
　information, 6
　intuition, 260–261
　long-term leave, 91–92
　mentor, 83–84
　principals on, 378
　as model of behavior, 106–107
　new
　　programs, 7–8
　　strengths, 374
　other
　　communicating, 221–223
　　problem, 223, 225
　parent expectations, 227–228
　and parents, 226–242. *See also* Communication, parent-teacher
　substitute. *See* Substitute
　time organization, 81–88. *See also* Time, organization of
　work area
　　classroom setup, 16
　　organizing, 51–53
Teacher aide, 84
Teacher assistant, 84–85
Teacher bucks, 118
Teaching assistants, gifts for, 354
Term conferences, 233, 235–239
Term planning, 86
Tests
　administering, 203
　assessment, 199
　grades, 260
　grading, 202, 203–204
　how long to keep, 211
Thematic centers, 282–283
Theme folders, 60

Theme units, 68–69
Tickets, 118
Time
   learning centers, 288–289
   organization, 81–88
   while children at centers, use of, 289–291
   wise use of, 81–85
      in first days, 139
   in writing center, 329
Time out, 124
To do folder, 61
Tokens, 118
Travel, hallway, 5

U

Unions, 6

V

Vacations, while school in session
   arranging work for, 366–367
   educational activities for trip, 367–368
Verbal assessment, 198
Visits, unscheduled, 232–233
Volunteers, parent
   gifts, 355
   incorporating into schedule, 166–168
   letters requesting, 169–170
   scheduling of, room mom, 171
   sending information to parents, 162
   student behavior, 127–128

W

Wall displays, for writing center, 330
Welcome letter
   on first days, 163–164
   before school starts, 10–12
What's in a name? (game), 155–156
What's the Design? (game), 325–327
What's the Pattern? (game), 323–325
Who's missing? (game), 155
Winter holidays, 363–364
Working cooperatively, 267–271
Workshop folder, 65
Writing
   activities, for vacation, 368
   learning center, 329–340. *See also* Learning centers, writing
Writing assignment, 260
Writing prompts, 332–333